MEXICAN GOVERNANCE

Significant Issues Series
Timely books presenting current CSIS research and analysis of interest to the academic, business, government, and policy communities.
Managing Editor: Roberta L. Howard

The Center for Strategic and International Studies (CSIS) is a nonprofit, bipartisan public policy organization established in 1962 to provide strategic insights and practical policy solutions to decisionmakers concerned with global security. Over the years, it has grown to be one of the largest organizations of its kind, with a staff of some 200 employees, including more than 120 analysts working to address the changing dynamics of international security across the globe.

CSIS is organized around three broad program areas, which together enable it to offer truly integrated insights and solutions to the challenges of global security. First, CSIS addresses the new drivers of global security, with programs on the international financial and economic system, foreign assistance, energy security, technology, biotechnology, demographic change, the HIV/AIDS pandemic, and governance. Second, CSIS also possesses one of America's most comprehensive programs on U.S. and international security, proposing reforms to U.S. defense organization, policy, force structure, and its industrial and technology base and offering solutions to the challenges of proliferation, transnational terrorism, homeland security, and post-conflict reconstruction. Third, CSIS is the only institution of its kind with resident experts on all the world's major populated geographic regions.

CSIS was founded four decades ago by David M. Abshire and Admiral Arleigh Burke. Former U.S. senator Sam Nunn became chairman of the CSIS Board of Trustees in 1999, and since April 2000, John J. Hamre has led CSIS as president and chief executive officer.

Headquartered in downtown Washington, D.C., CSIS is a private, tax-exempt, 501(c) 3 institution.

The CSIS Press
Center for Strategic and International Studies
1800 K Street, N.W., Washington, D.C. 20006
Tel: (202) 887-0200 Fax: (202) 775-3199
E-mail: books@csis.org Web: www.csis.org

MEXICAN GOVERNANCE

From Single-Party Rule to Divided Government

EDITED BY ARMAND B. PESCHARD-SVERDRUP AND SARA R. RIOFF

THE CSIS PRESS

Center for Strategic
and International Studies
Washington, D.C.

Significant Issues Series, Volume 27, Number 2
Cover design by Robert L. Wiser, Silver Spring, Md.
Cover photograph: Palacio Nacional, Mexico City © Photodisc/Getty Images.

09 08 07 06 05   5 4 3 2 1

ISSN 0736-7136
ISBN 0-89206-457-9

Library of Congress Cataloging-in-Publication Data
Mexican governance : from single-party rule to divided government / edited by
Armand B. Peschard-Sverdrup and Sara R. Rioff.
    p. cm. — (Significant issues series ; v. 27, no. 2)
  Includes index.
  ISBN 0-89206-457-9
  1. Mexico—Politics and government—1988– 2. Divided government—Mexico. I.
Peschard-Sverdrup, Armand B. II. Rioff, Sara. III. Title. IV. Series.
  JL1231.M415 2005
  320.972—dc22

                              2005003673

CONTENTS

PREFACE

Armand B. Peschard-Sverdrup

"Don't forget us people, who believe in you and need you."

The above words were spoken to president-elect Vicente Fox as he visited Tepito, a destitute and crime-ridden barrio in Mexico City on the morning he was sworn into office. It was a simple plea by a hope-filled woman—a plea that presumed that the once-limitless powers of the Mexican president would persist and that failed to realize that the days of *presidencialismo* had come to an end and divided government had emerged.

The 71-year reign of single-party rule in Mexico not only shaped the country's political culture. It also had an intense effect on the institutions of government and how they evolved over time. Some of the institutions or areas in which the transition from single-party rule had the greatest impact were the relationship between the executive and legislative branches, the structure and role of the government as a whole, the powers of the judiciary, the economic sector, the Mexican military and its relationship with civil society, the relationship between church and state, and the role of the media.

In an effort to deepen understanding of the political transition that Mexico is undergoing, the Mexico Project of the Center for Strategic and International Studies (CSIS) commissioned seven of Mexico's most renowned experts to contribute a chapter on a particular facet of Mexico's transition from single-party rule to divided government. The task of these experts was threefold: (1) to analyze the evolution of their respective fields under single-party rule; (2) to evaluate the positive (and negative) changes that have occurred under divided government; and (3) to propose areas in which democratic governance can be advanced.

Benito Nacif, a research professor in the Department of Political Studies at Mexico's Center for Research and Economic Policy (CIDE), analyzes the evolving relationship between the executive and legislative branches in Mexico in his chapter, "Congress Proposes and the President Disposes: The New Relationship between the Executive and Legislative Branches in Mexico." Nacif examines the shift in the traditional balance of power from the executive branch to the legislative branch and the difficulties this development has posed for post-transition governance.

Specifically, Nacif analyzes Mexico's transition from a system of government that was based on a "fusion of powers" to one based on true "separation of powers"—from a nation with a dominant presidency to one with a limited presidency. Noting that the Mexican Constitution bestows more powers on the Congress than on the presidency, Nacif asserts that it was the system of single-party rule, and not the Constitution, from which the long line of presidents belonging to the Institutional Revolutionary Party drew their power. This assertion informs his analysis of the evolution of relations between the executive and legislative branches under divided government—that is, governance in the absence of an entirely subordinate, rubber-stamp legislature. Nacif closes with an analysis of the dichotomy between legislative action and inaction (gridlock) under the current framework of divided government, and he proposes some recommendations as to how Mexico can ensure that gridlock and paralysis do not become synonymous with divided government.

It is apparent from Nacif's chapter that many of the mechanisms and instruments of governance were inherited from the era of single-party rule. In many instances, these features are relics of Mexico's political past and are inadequate for advancing the democratic principles of separation of powers, transparency, accountability, and representative government. With this in mind, Jeffrey Weldon, a professor in the Department of Political Science at the Mexico City-based Autonomous Technological Institute of Mexico (ITAM) and an adjunct fellow of the CSIS Mexico Project, examines in more detail the various components of state reform in his chapter, "State Reform in Mexico: Progress and Prospects." Weldon's chapter describes the status quo, provides a diagnosis, examines proposals for reform, and discusses the prospects for change in each of the major areas in which state reform is currently being debated: electoral reforms, relations between the executive and legislative branches of government, strengthening of the legislative branch, and the budget process.

The chapter examines what steps, if any, the 57th and 58th Legislatures (1997–2000 and 2000–2003, respectively) have taken to address the various components of state reform. Weldon also describes what has transpired thus far in the 59th Legislature (2003–2006). In addition to his qualitative analysis of the status quo and prospects for reform of the state, Weldon offers an in-depth quantitative analysis of specific reform proposals that have been introduced, leaving the reader with an appropriate sense of the magnitude of the challenge facing Mexico in the area of state reform.

To examine Mexico's judiciary, CSIS commissioned José Ramón Cossío, one of Mexico's most acclaimed legal scholars, who was appointed justice of the Mexican Supreme Court in November 2003. In his chapter, "The Judicial Branch of the Mexican Federation," Cossío analyzes the judicial reforms passed in 1988, 1994, and 1999, paying special attention to those he considers incomplete as of 2005. His analysis pertains exclusively to reforms related to the Supreme Court, collegiate and single-judge courts, and the Council of the Federal Judiciary—that is, he discusses judicial reform in the strictest sense of the word.

Cossío observes that, as Mexico became more pluralistic, it also became a more complex society in which social and political conflicts could no longer be resolved by simply appealing to the Constitution. This assessment was fueled by a perception that the Constitution was outdated and in need of major modification—an assessment many still consider apt today. Nevertheless, consensus existed on the need to elevate the role of the Supreme Court to guarantee its supremacy vis-à-vis all other national actors and phenomena. Cossío believes that each of the three judicial reforms served to further deepen or strengthen the Supreme Court as a constitutional court, thereby, at least in theory, making the Court a guarantor of the democratic process in Mexico. Cossío concludes by reiterating that Mexican society's transition to greater plurality and complexity will make it progressively more litigious. Hence, resolution of societal conflicts will increasingly be left to the nation's federal judiciary, a development that underscores the importance of advancing the judicial reforms that are pending.

Cossío asserts that a national debate on judicial reform not only is overdue but also is likely to trigger a further round of reforms, which, Cossío insists, must be ongoing if they are to meet the needs of a constantly evolving democratic society.

In his chapter, "The Mexican Economy: Are Further Reforms Necessary?" economist Jonathan Heath, head of research for HSBC Mexico and an adjunct fellow of the CSIS Mexico Project, examines the evolution of the Mexican economy and the need for further reform. Heath's starting point is the notion that the implementation of certain policies can lead to long-term structural weaknesses in the economy and ultimately increase the urgency and criticality of reform. Heath examines the structural weaknesses induced by the pursuit of an import-substitution policy in the 1960s and describes how the fiscal imprudence and expansionist monetary policies of the populist presidencies of Luis Echeverría (1970–1976) and José López Portillo (1976–1982) exacerbated these deficiencies. The author then analyzes the efforts of former president Carlos Salinas (1988–1994) to implement a series of structural reforms that broadly followed the so-called Washington Consensus.

Heath examines the fiscal discipline of the Zedillo administration (1994–2000) as well as the setback to reform caused by the 1995 peso crisis and the subsequent bailout of Mexico's banks; the discussion notes that Zedillo was constrained by a divided government upon the loss of his party's majority in the Chamber of Deputies in 1997. Heath then analyzes President Fox's structural reform agenda and its rationale as laid out in the 2000–2006 National Development Plan and in the National Program for Financing Development (Pronafide). Of the long list of reforms, Heath focuses on those that he considers the backbone of Fox's strategy: (1) financial reform, (2) electricity reform, (3) fiscal reform, and (4) labor reform. The chapter concludes with an analysis of the prospects for economic reform during the remainder of the Fox administration. Heath's portrayal of a future Mexico absent these reforms is discouraging at best.

In the chapter by Oscar Rocha, "Civil-Military Relations and Security Policy in Mexico," the volume shifts to one of the least talked-about but no less important institutions in Mexico: the military. The author of the chapter is president of the Joaquin Amaro Foundation and an experienced observer of the Mexican military who was responsible for overseeing cooperation between the U.S. military and Mexican military while at the Mexican embassy in Washington, D.C.

Rocha begins by examining the domestic and international events and phenomena in the twentieth century that shaped the character and mission of the Mexican military and its interaction with society. He traces the evolution of civil-military relations from the days of unconditional loyalty to the president—an allegiance that was facilitated by single-party rule and the existence of a rubber-stamp Congress—to the more nebulous chain of command that exists today under divided government. Rocha considers the events of the early twenty-first century—the September 11, 2001, terrorist attacks on the United States, the wars in Afghanistan and Iraq, and the global war on terrorism—and the implication of these events for the Mexican military, given both the changing international environment and Mexico's geographic proximity to the United States. Rocha stresses that these external events, combined with the pressures arising from Mexico's political transition (pressure to become more professional and more accountable, for example) have led to an identity crisis of sorts for the Mexican military. He points out that the civil-military relationship is complicated by the fact that, until recently, Mexico did not have a national security doctrine. Civil society had no formal mechanism for working with the military on security matters, and there were no thematic or administrative parameters for such collaboration. Rocha's chapter sheds light on the historical barriers to increased cooperation between the civil sector and the military, on the tools both civil society and the military have at their disposal to strengthen cooperation, and, perhaps most insightfully, on the mind-set of the Mexican military apparatus, all of which represent a key dimension of Mexico's transition to democracy.

Raúl González Schmal, a professor at the Ibero-American University and a prominent ecclesiastical scholar, has contributed the chapter titled "The Evolving Relationship between Church and State," in which he examines the impact of religion—and, more specifically, the relationship between church and state—on Mexico's history and how it has changed under the new framework of democratic governance. González Schmal looks at the evolution of religion on the basis of Mexico's constitutional history, noting that, from the time that Mexico gained its independence from Spain in 1821 to the passage of the current Constitution in 1917, the constitutional status of the church passed through three stages: (1) recognition of Catholicism as the only religion in the country and prohibition of all other faiths; (2) separation of church and state and the granting of (limited) freedom to worship in the religion of one's choice; and (3) withdrawal of legal status for the Catholic Church and all other religious organizations and bans on public worship, religious associations, and religious instruction in private schools, as well as the granting of authority to the state to determine the number of religious officials eligible to serve in each jurisdiction.

González Schmal then analyzes the package of constitutional reforms presented by President Salinas in December 1991 and passed by Congress in 1992, which provided for a wider range of religious freedom. Despite the significant progress the new legislation made in guaranteeing religious freedom, a number of constraints and ambiguities remained. The author examines these in the context of Vicente Fox's campaign platform. The chapter concludes with the assertion that upholding the human right to religious freedom is a necessary and irreplaceable condition for transcending Mexico's divisive past.

Sergio Sarmiento, one of Mexico's foremost opinion leaders, the host of a political talk show, a nationally syndicated columnist for the Mexican daily newspaper *Reforma*, and a CSIS Mexico Project adjunct fellow, authored "The Role of the Media in Mexico's Political Transition." Sarmiento classifies the media as one of the pillars of Mexico's political system throughout the decades of single-party rule. Through a system of threats and incentives, the Mexican government maintained almost total control of the media. Sarmiento examines this subordinate relationship between television, radio, and print media and the government, pointing out the events and circumstances that paved the way for an independent media. Sarmiento also provides a fascinating account of one of the more recent clashes between the political system and the media—the May 2000 conflict, known as "Black Tuesday," over whether to televise a debate between the presidential candidates, an event that was considered a major turning point in the election. Sarmiento concludes that even though the Mexican media no longer have to struggle for independence, the media must meet the challenge of abandoning the lingering vices fostered by the old system of government threats and incentives and raise the level of professionalism of their members. Sarmiento outlines some of the measures that could help advance this cause.

It is our hope that this volume will deepen the public's understanding of and appreciation for the intricate and multifaceted political transition upon which Mexico has embarked. Although the country's trajectory toward democratic governance is clearly mapped out, the final destination is largely uncertain. We can only hope that, as Mexico's democracy evolves, the country's leaders remain mindful of the symbolic plea of the woman in Tepito: *"Don't forget us people, who believe in you and need you."*

ACKNOWLEDGMENTS

This book would not have been possible without the generous assistance of several individuals. First and foremost, we are indebted to the chapter authors for their insight into the dynamics of Mexico's democratic transition and for so expertly reflecting our vision for this volume. We could not have asked for a more thoughtful group to carry out this endeavor.

We would also like to extend our gratitude to the seven individuals who reviewed and provided comments on early versions of the chapters: Luis Carlos Ugalde, an expert on the Mexican Congress and the current president of Mexico's Federal Electoral Institute, who reviewed Benito Nacif's chapter on executive-legislative relations; Todd Eisenstadt, assistant professor at American University, who conducted a review of Jeffrey Weldon's chapter on state reform; Rafael Estrada Samano, a legal scholar, practicing attorney, and former deputy attorney general of Mexico, who reviewed José Ramón Cossío's chapter on judicial reform; Sidney Weintraub, William E. Simon Chair in International Political Economy at CSIS, who reviewed Jonathan Heath's chapter on economic reform; Guadalupe González, professor at the Center for Research and Economic Policy (CIDE), who reviewed Oscar Rocha's chapter on civil-military relations; Alberto Ortega Venzor, Vicente Fox's liaison with religious groups during the 2000 election and currently senior adviser for international and business affairs at the presidential Office for Public Policy, who reviewed Raul González Schmal's chapter on church-state relations; and José Carreño Carlón, director of professional studies at the Ibero-American University and former communications director for the Salinas administration, who reviewed Sergio Sarmiento's chapter on the media.

Several people at CSIS were instrumental in the production of this volume. First, we would like to thank former CSIS Mexico Project intern-scholar Rocío García, whose assistance in reviewing both the Spanish and English versions of the chapters for consistency and fluidity was invaluable. Two other CSIS intern-scholars, Jennifer Phillips and Catherine Hendrix, provided important support at various phases of the project. Roberta Howard of the CSIS Press tirelessly reviewed the manuscript and skillfully transformed it from a stack of paper into a decipherable volume. We thank Roberta for her patience, good nature, and diligence. Roberta worked under the guidance of Jim Dunton, director of the CSIS Press, without whose support and leadership this book would not have been possible.

We also owe a debt of gratitude to Bita Lanys, who edited and corrected early versions of the chapters. Bita was instrumental in bringing this work to fruition.

ABBREVIATIONS AND TERMS

AFI   Federal Investigation Agency (Agencia Federal de Investigación)

CERE   Commission for the Study of State Reform (Comisión de Estudios para la Reforma del Estado)

CFE   Federal Electricity Commission (Comisión Federal de Electricidad)

CIDE   Center for Research and Economic Policy (Centro de Investigación y Docencia Económica)

CISEN   Center for Investigation and National Security (Centro de Investigación y Seguridad Nacional)

CD   Convergence (formerly Convergence for Democracy) (Convergencia)

DFS   Federal Security Directorate (Dirección Federal de Seguridad)

EMP   Estado Mayor Presidencial (Presidential General Staff [presidential military support unit])

EPR   Popular Revolutionary Army (Ejército Popular Revolucionario)

IFE   Federal Electoral Institute (Instituto Federal Electoral)

INEGI   National Institute of Statistics, Geography, and Informatics (Instituto Nacional de Estadística, Geografía, e Informática)

INEHRM   National Institute for the Historical Study of the Mexican Revolution (Instituto Nacional de Estudios Históricos de la Revolución Mexicana)

ITAM	Autonomous Technological Institute of Mexico (Instituto Tecnológico Autónomo de México)
NAFTA	North American Free Trade Agreement
PAN	National Action Party (Partido Acción Nacional)
PAS	Social Alliance Party (Partido Alianza Social)
Pemex	Petróleos Mexicanos
PFP	Federal Preventive Police (Policía Federal Preventiva)
PGR	Office of the Attorney General (Procuraduría General de la República)
PND	National Development Plan (Plan Nacional de Desarrollo)
PNR	National Revolutionary Party (Partido Nacional Revolucionario)
PR	proportional representation
PRD	Democratic Revolutionary Party (Partido de la Revolución Democrática)
PRI	Institutional Revolutionary Party (Partido Revolucionario Institucional)
priístas	members of the PRI party
Pronafide	National Program for Financing Development (Programa Nacional de Financiamiento del Desarrollo)
PSBR	public-sector borrowing requirements
PT	Labor Party (Partido del Trabajo)
PVEM	Green Party of Mexico (Partido Verde Ecologista de México)
SEGOB	Ministry of Government (Secretaría de Gobernación)
TRIFE	Federal Electoral Tribunal (Tribunal Electoral de la Federación)
VAT	value-added tax

ONE

CONGRESS PROPOSES AND THE PRESIDENT DISPOSES

THE NEW RELATIONSHIP BETWEEN THE EXECUTIVE AND LEGISLATIVE BRANCHES IN MEXICO

Benito Nacif

In his inaugural address on December 1, 2000, Mexican president Vicente Fox spoke of a new era in the relationship between the executive and legislative branches of government—one in which the "president proposes and the Congress disposes." The aim of using this phrase was to recognize the independence that the Mexican Congress had recently achieved and to distinguish the current political regime from the one in place previously, when the Institutional Revolutionary Party (PRI) was in sole charge of both branches of government. In fact, during the decades of the PRI's political hegemony, the power that the Constitution apportioned among the three branches of government was, in practice, concentrated in the presidency of the republic. The chief executive operated as the primary axis of policymaking. Once the president pronounced himself in favor of a change in government policies, there was no authority that could stop him.

In the past, Mexico's presidential regime had an enormous capacity to enact changes in public policies. The scope and speed of these changes were sometimes dramatic, as was the case with the expropriation of the Mexican oil industry in 1938 and the banking system in 1982. The ability to produce such changes was usually manifested in sudden shifts in government policies—changes that were orchestrated by the executive branch.

By the 1990s, the erosion of the PRI's hegemony and the development of a competitive three-party system had given rise to constitutional checks and balances to presidential power in Mexico. This long and complicated process culminated in 1997 with the first electoral contest in which the PRI lost its majority in the Chamber of Deputies.

As a result, during the second half of his presidential term, President Ernesto Zedillo had to govern without a PRI majority in Congress. The balance of power that the 1997 election produced was a mere prelude to what was to come. The PRI's defeat in the 2000 presidential election delivered the office of the chief executive to the candidate of the National Action Party (PAN), Vicente Fox, while none of the parties won a majority in Congress.

Deprived of its party's control of the decisionmaking process in Congress—a situation known as divided government—the presidency of the republic lost the dominant position that it had held for so long. Today, all changes in policy depend on cooperation between opposition parties and the party of the president. This situation poses a problem: If political parties maintain a competitive relationship in the electoral arena, is it logical to expect them to cooperate with one another in an effort to change public policies? Given this new balance of power, another question arises: What is the new role of the executive branch in the policymaking process?

The lack of cooperation among political parties has major implications for Mexico's nascent democracy. If the government cannot respond to the demands of the electorate by making substantive changes in public policies, then frustration about change and the opportunity costs of maintaining existing policies might put the stability of that democratic system at risk. Data relative to the survival of twentieth-century democracies, as evaluated by comparative studies, show that presidential democracies with divided governments face a higher risk of breaking up than any other type of regime does.[1] This risk is generally attributed to the lack of incentives for political parties to cooperate with one another when formulating policies.

Instead of taking for granted the absence of these incentives for cooperation in presidential democracies with divided governments, this chapter analyzes the empirical evidence on legislative productivity in Mexico since 1997. These facts about the legislative process show that the conditions that make policy change possible in divided government have been met in Mexico with sufficient frequency to sustain a volume of legislation that is similar to the amount produced during periods of unified government. What makes cooperation possible are the "gains from exchange" that the president's party and the opposition parties may capture if they modify the status quo.

Today in Mexico, the president's party is no longer the dominating force in Congress. Its place has been taken by the party occupying the center of the ideological spectrum, with the other political parties tending to converge around the centrist party to form lawmaking majorities in Congress. The role of the president has not been reduced to that of a mere spectator, however. His veto power has made him an important actor in the legislative process. Nevertheless, Congress has the power to set the agenda—that is, to make proposals and to force the president into a take-it-or-leave-it situation. This power represents a clear advantage in congressional relations with the executive branch. Consequently, contrary to what President Fox expected at the beginning of his administration, the best way to characterize the new relationship between the executive and the legislative branches is that "Congress proposes and the president disposes."

THE OLD PRESIDENTIAL MODEL

The primary characteristic of the presidential model that prevailed in Mexico in the past was the subordination of other constitutional powers—specifically those of Congress—to presidential initiatives. Instead of separation of powers, as proclaimed in Mexico's Constitution, in practice a "fusion of powers" took place, and this gave rise to a highly hierarchical regime led by the chief executive. According to analyst Jeffrey Weldon, the fusion of powers required three necessary conditions that were met in the 1930s, at the very origin of Mexico's pre-revolutionary regime:[2] (1) "unified government," that is, simultaneous control of the presidency of the republic and the majority of Congress by a single party; (2) party discipline, which meant cohesive and coherent voting by parliamentary groups belonging to the president's party in the Chamber of Deputies and the Senate;[3] and (3) presidential leadership over his party, which required the president to have the authority to define the party's position and the instruments needed to ensure acceptance by the parliamentary factions in Congress.

An analysis of these necessary conditions clearly shows that the power of the Mexican presidency during the long era of PRI hegemony did not spring from the authority conferred to it by the Constitution but from what Jorge Carpizo called the "meta-constitutional" powers of the presidency. More specifically, María Amparo Casar refers to these as "partisan" powers, because they had their source in the president's ability to maintain his party's dominant position and to control access to elected offices and administrative positions throughout the overall political system.[4]

The true constitutional powers of Mexico's presidency are less impressive. In fact, a comparison of Mexico's executive branch with that of other countries that have presidential systems shows that Mexico's chief executive does not appear to be among the most powerful.[5] The Mexican Constitution confers the most powerful role to Congress, by making it the main depository of legislative power. The most powerful instrument the Mexican chief executive can use to influence congressional decisionmaking is veto power. The president has no other constitutional means to deal with Congress, such as the so-called executive decree authority, which Brazil's Constitution refers to as "temporary measures" and Argentina's calls "urgent and necessary measures." The executive decree is an act that, although temporary, has the full force of law. Executive decrees in both Argentina and Brazil retain their temporary authority for 30 days, although the president can reissue them when the initial period expires. In practice, the power to issue and enforce executive decrees means that the chief executive can force Congress to take legislative action on issues where the status quo has already been modified according to the president's wishes.[6]

In Mexico even the president's veto power is fairly limited when compared with Argentina. Argentina's Constitution gives the president the authority to partially veto a congressionally approved initiative, thus permitting him to enact those parts of the legislation with which he agrees and to send back to Congress those to which he objects. In Mexico, the president can only wield a "package" veto, which means that he is not authorized to partially enact bills passed by Congress, even though the Constitution allows him to make observations "in whole or in part."

The constitutional instruments available to the Mexican president for influencing Congress's legislative agenda are fairly innocuous. The president can, in effect, introduce legislative initiatives, although nothing compels either chamber of Congress to act on them by putting them to a vote.[7] In contrast, the president of Chile, for example, has the authority not only to submit initiatives but, if he considers it necessary, also to assign a maximum period of time for the Congress to act on them. Moreover, not only does the president of Chile have the exclusive authority to submit his proposed budget; if Congress does not approve it within the time established in the Constitution, the president's budget automatically goes into effect. In Mexico, the president has the exclusive responsibility to submit his proposed federal budget, but once it reaches Congress, he has few instruments to use to influence the result. In fact, Mexico's Constitution does not even clearly stipulate the president's authority to veto the budgetary expenditures approved by the Chamber of Deputies.[8]

Despite their limited constitutional authority, during the long period of PRI dominance, Mexican presidents were able to exert a high level of control over the legislative process, greater than that of other constitutionally strong presidents in Latin America. The numbers and success rates of legislation submitted to Congress shown in table 1.1 can serve as indicators of the relationship between the executive and the legislative branches during the last two legislative sessions in which the PRI had a majority in both chambers of Congress—the 55th (1991–1994) and the 56th (1994–1997). The numbers in the table refer to legislative initiatives for which the Chamber of Deputies was the "chamber of origin."[9] The numbers take into account only initiatives involving changes in legislation—both constitutional and secondary—and do not include symbolic bills such as permits and official awards.

It should be noted that the figures given in table 1.1 assign the same value (a value of one) to each legislative initiative, even though the initiatives can be quite different from one another in both scope and importance. In addition, the data do not take into account any amendments to the initiatives that may have been introduced in committees or in the plenary session of the Chamber of Deputies. Despite these qualifications, the data in the table reflect general patterns in the legislative process and thereby point to the role of the executive branch in the making of policy during the last two legislatures under PRI control.

The first column in table 1.1 presents the number of bills submitted to the Chamber of Deputies according to the source that presented them. The Mexican Constitution gives the prerogative to submit legislative proposals not only to members of both chambers of Congress but also to the president of the republic and to state legislatures. Bills introduced by members of Congress are classified according to the

Table 1.1
The Legislative Process in the Chamber of Deputies under Unified Government (55th and 56th Legislatures, 1991–1997)

	Bills introduced		Bills approved		Contribution[a]		Success rate[b]	
Source	1991–94	1994–97	1991–94	1994–97	1991–94	1994–97	1991–94	1994–97
Executive	124	84	122	83	81.9	76.9	98.4	98.8
PRI	30	19	11	7	7.4	6.5	36.7	36.8
PAN	26	79	4	8	2.7	7.4	15.4	10.1
PRD	32	45	2	3	1.3	2.8	6.3	6.7
PARM	9	–	1	–	0.7	–	11.1	–
PPS	5	–	0	–	0.0	–	0.0	–
PFCRN	4	–	0	–	0.0	–	0.0	–
PT	–	8	–	3	–	2.8	–	37.5
Independent	1	12	0	2	0.0	1.9	0.0	16.7
State legislatures[c]	2	2	1	1	0.7	0.9	50.0	50.0
Other	10	2	8	1	5.4	0.9	80.0	50.0
Total	243	251	149	108	100.0	100.0	61.3	43.0

Source of data: Sistema Integral de Información y Difusión de la Cámara de Diputados.

Note: The data include legislative bills originating in the Chamber of Deputies. Permits, symbolic legislation, and bills originating in the Senate were excluded.

[a] (Bills approved by source/ Total of bills approved) x 100
[b] (Bills approved / Bills introduced) x 100
[c] Including the Asamblea de Representantes del Distrito Federal.

party to which the legislator belongs. Mexico's legislative process is quite open concerning the initiation of legislation. Congressional procedures do not require garnering support from any majority for a bill to be introduced and referred to committee. In fact, introducing legislation is relatively easy, and for this reason the proportion of bills passed by Congress relative to those that were introduced can be fairly low (between 43 and 61 percent).

The legislative process really begins in committee, which is where the fate of an initiative is decided. The committees actually set the legislative agenda in Congress, for it is their reports that are debated and voted on in the plenary session, not the bills as they were originally introduced. Most initiatives die in committee, because this is the outcome when a proposal is simply ignored. The last column in table 1.1 shows the success rate, that is, the probability that an initiative is reported by committee and approved by the plenary for the 55th and 56th Legislatures. The data clearly show that an initiative submitted by the executive branch had an almost 100 percent probability of being approved. This finding suggests that the president could be certain that any legislative proposal he sent to the Chamber of Deputies would become law. This indicator must be interpreted with caution, however, because a high success rate may also mean that the president submitted only those initiatives that he knew Congress would approve.

Nevertheless, table 1.1 shows interesting variations in the success rate of other sources of legislation, which confirms the prevailing view that the chief executive controlled the Congress in the legislatures examined. Even though the success rate of legislation introduced by the PRI was higher than that of all the other parties, the PRI was still substantially less successful than the chief executive was. The difference seems to confirm the perception that the president exerted leadership over his party. In addition, during the sessions analyzed, legislators from opposition parties knew—with near certainty—that their initiatives would remain stalled in committee. The probability of a PAN initiative becoming law varied between 10 and 15 percent. The probability was even lower for legislators belonging to the Democratic Revolutionary Party (PRD).

The figure that most forcefully reflects the balance of power that prevailed when the PRI held a majority in Congress is the contribution of each source to the total volume of legislation produced during the session. As table 1.1 indicates, the executive branch initiated between 76.9 and 81.9 percent of all the bills that were passed by the 55th and 56th legislatures, greatly exceeding the combined contribution of all the political parties represented in Congress.

Together with the success rate, the contribution of each source to the total volume of legislation indicates that, during the period in which the PRI controlled both branches of government, changes in public policies were drawn up in the chief executive's offices. The Chamber of Deputies spent most of its time revising and passing the president's initiatives. Administrative officials from the executive departments could, with almost complete certainty, count on the president's initiatives being approved with the backing of the PRI majority. In other words, the figures show that when Mexico had unified government, the president of the republic was simultaneously chief executive and chief legislator.

The primary result of the balance of power that existed during the PRI's hegemony was the centralization of the policymaking process. Policy changes were drafted within the executive branch, confining Congress to their review and ratification. The contribution of other actors to policy change was minimal; even the PRI congressional majority had a very limited role in the legislative process. The main task of the PRI's congressional leadership was to shepherd presidential initiatives though the different stages of the lawmaking process and minimize any possible interference from opposition parties and the president's legislative contingent.

THE FALL OF THE DOMINANT PRESIDENCY

The source of change in the balance of powers was the transformation of the party system that took place between 1988 and 1997. During this period, the PRI gradually lost its hegemony, and Mexico's electoral system became increasingly competitive. Parties that competed with the PRI—mainly the PAN and the PRD—experienced remarkable growth, garnering an ever greater share of both the electoral "market" and seats in Congress with each election.[10]

A turning point in this process was the 1997 midterm election in which all 500 seats in the Chamber of Deputies were renewed. In that election, the PRI experienced a drop in voter support of approximately 10 percent. As a result, the ruling party lost its majority in the Chamber of Deputies for the first time since its founding—originally as the National Revolutionary Party—in 1929, falling 13 seats shy of the majority. It did, however, manage to retain its majority in the Senate.

The 1997 elections had a tremendous impact on the balance of constitutional powers. The outcome eliminated the first of Weldon's three conditions for the continuation of Mexico's dominant presidency: unified government.[11] With the emergence of divided government, a lengthy period of presidential dominance over Mexican politics was brought to an end. At the same time, Mexico was no longer an exception among those presidential regimes in Latin American countries in which multiparty systems regularly produce governments without a majority in Congress.

The 2000 election was extremely significant in Mexican political history. After 70 years in power, the PRI lost its first presidential election. Moreover, after 60 years as an opposition party, the PAN won the highest prize in Mexican politics: the presidency. However, the 2000 election did not substantially change the balance of power that had been established three years earlier. In fact, as a result of the 2000 election, the legislative contingent of the president's party lost ground in both chambers of Congress. Unlike the PRI during the second half of Ernesto Zedillo's administration, the PAN did not have a majority in the Senate. Yet even without a Senate majority, President Vicente Fox and his party retained the power to prevent legislative change through the use of the presidential veto backed by at least one-third plus one of the votes in either chamber. In other words, the president could uphold his veto against an opposing majority in Congress.

Beginning with the period of divided government initiated in 1997, the power of the president and his party has been transformed into one that is essentially negative. They have the authority to prevent changes to existing legislation, but they cannot by themselves define the content of new legislation, as they could in the past. In other words, a "minimum winning coalition" cannot be formed without the participation of the president and his party; however, in order to form minimum winning coalitions, the president and his party need the backing of opposition parties.[12]

Mexico's experience with divided government has affected the relationship between the executive and the legislative branches when it comes to formulating public policies. Table 1.2 shows the significance of the impact. First, there has been a substantial increase in the number of bills introduced by opposition parties and a notable reduction in the volume of executive-initiated legislation. All actors made adjustments to their lawmaking behavior as the new balance of power emerged. Opposition legislators anticipated that their influence in the legislative process would increase substantially under divided government. They responded by introducing bills in areas of legislation that were previously reserved for executive-initiated legislation. They began to compete with the administration as a relevant source of policy initiatives.

Table 1.2
The Legislative Process in the Chamber of Deputies under Divided Government (1997–2003)

Source	Bills introduced 1997–00	Bills introduced 2000–03	Bills approved 1997–00	Bills approved 2000–03	Contribution[a] 1997–00	Contribution[a] 2000–03	Success rate[b] 1997–00	Success rate[b] 2000–03
Executive	32	61	28	50	20.4	18.2	87.5	82.0
PRI	86	306	15	54	10.9	19.6	17.4	17.6
PAN	168	265	31	65	22.6	23.6	18.5	24.5
PRD	157	294	20	45	14.6	16.4	12.7	15.3
PT	23	41	7	6	5.1	2.2	30.4	14.6
PVEM	44	74	8	14	5.8	5.1	18.2	18.9
State legislatures[c]	25	86	1	15	0.7	5.5	4	17.4
Independent	10	11	2	1	1.5	0.4	20	9.1
PAS	–	13	–	0	–	0.0	–	0.0
PSN	–	8	–	0	–	0.0	–	0.0
CDPPN	–	6	–	0	–	0.0	–	0.0
Joint	–	42	–	25	–	9.1	–	59.2
Other	61	–	25	–	18.3	–	40.9	–
Total	**606**	**1,207**	**137**	**275**	**100.0**	**100.0**	**22.6**	**22.8**

Source of data: Sistema Integral de Información y Difusión de la Cámara de Diputados for the period 1997 to 2000, and Gaceta Parlamentaria (http://gaceta.cddhcu.org.mx) for the period 2000 to 2003.

Note: The data include legislative bills originating in the Chamber of Deputies. Permits, symbolic legislation, and bills originating in the Senate were excluded.

[a] (Bills approved by source/ Total of bills approved) x 100
[b] (Bills approved / Bills introduced) x 100
[c] Including the Asamblea de Representantes del Distrito Federal.

At the same time, anticipating that the probability of his initiatives being reported by committee and voted on the floor of the Chamber of Deputies had decreased, President Zedillo reduced his legislative agenda. During the second half of his administration, the number of executive-initiated bills dropped from 84 to 32. By reducing his legislative agenda, President Zedillo was able to maintain a success rate in Congress of 87.5 percent.

The legislative agenda of the executive branch increased quite notably when President Fox took office in 2000. The total number of executive-initiated bills rose to 61 during the 58th Legislature (2000–2003), and the president's success rate, despite being the lowest in modern Mexican history, was still high (82.0 percent) considering the strength of the opposition in Congress.

The most important indicator of the impact of divided government on the constitutional balance of power is the contribution of the executive branch to the total volume of legislation produced by the Chamber of Deputies. In the last two legislatures in which the PRI had a majority (the 55th and 56th), the president initiated from 76.9 to 81.9 percent of the volume of legislation. When the PRI lost its majority in 1997, executive-initiated legislation amounted to a mere 20.4 percent of the total number of bills passed by the Chamber of Deputies. During the first half of the Fox administration, executive-initiated legislation represented only 18.2 percent of the total volume of legislation.

Clearly, the president is no longer chief executive and chief legislator at the same time. In fact, the contribution of legislation initiated by opposition parties to the total volume of legislation enacted by the Chamber of Deputies has become quantitatively more significant than that of the president and his party taken together. The main initiators of legislative change from 2000 to 2003 have been the opposition parties in Congress.

Another significant aspect of the legislative process illustrated in table 1.2 is that divided government has not entailed a reduction in total legislative output. The data do not substantiate the correlation between divided government and legislative gridlock predicted by the critics of presidentialism.[13] In fact, as table 1.2 shows, the total volume of legislation measured by the number of bills passed by the Chamber of Deputies has been higher during the period of divided government than during the last two legislatures in which the PRI controlled both the Congress and the executive. The total legislative output rose from 149 and 108 bills in the 55th and 56th legislatures respectively to 137 in the 57th and 275 in the 58th Legislature.

It is possible that part of the explanation for the greater volume of legislation during the period of divided government lies in an increase in comparatively insignificant changes to legislation. The data do not

Figure 1.1
Legislative Coalitions (1998–2000) by Number of Parties

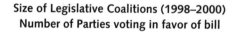

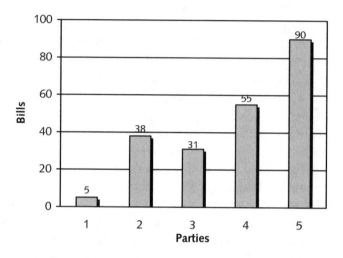

Size of Legislative Coalitions (1998–2000)
Number of Parties voting in favor of bill

Source of data: *Gaceta Parlamentaria* of the Chamber of Deputies (http://gaceta.cddhcu.gob.mx).
Note: standard deviation = 1.21; median = 3.84; N = 220.

distinguish significant from trivial legislative change, however. We do not know if the legislative changes enacted during the period of unified government were of greater significance on average. What the data clearly show is that divided government is associated with less executive-initiated legislation both in relative and absolute terms. The reason why this change did not involve a drop in legislative output is that the contribution of parliamentary factions, notably from the opposition parties, has grown substantially during divided government.

The PAN parliamentary faction became the main single source of legislative change, placing slightly above the executive branch itself. This new pattern developed after 1997 even though the PRI controlled both the presidency and the Senate. Not only did the PAN's contribution to the total volume of legislation grow; the PRI's also increased

Figure 1.2
Legislative Coalitions (1998–2000) by Rice Index

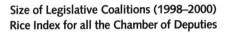

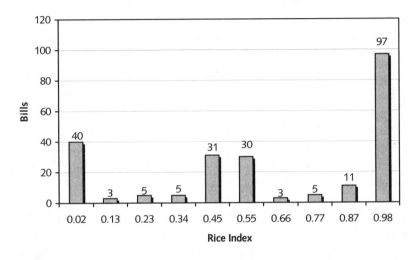

Source of data: *Gaceta Parlamentaria* of the Chamber of Deputies (http://gaceta.cddhcu.gob.mx).
Note: standard deviation = 0.37; median = 0.63; N = 238.

notably after the party lost its majority in the Chamber of Deputies, as did the contribution of the PRD. In sum, the relevant sources of legislative change multiplied with the onset of divided government. One of these new sources, the legislative coalition, is explored below.

What are the characteristics of the legislative coalitions that approved legislative changes in the Chamber of Deputies under divided government? Figure 1.1 shows the size of coalitions as measured by the number of parties and the number of initiatives that the lower house approved between 1998 and 2000.[14] Legislative approval required the support of a maximum number of five parties and a minimum of one; thus, the abstention of a dozen legislators was sufficient for the PRI to get a majority.

The data presented in figure 1.1 show that the size of congressional coalitions varies significantly. Achieving consensus among an average of 3.8 parties seemed to be the way to gain the votes needed for ratification. This pattern implies that, even though a total consensus of all parties voted to approve a substantial proportion of the legislation, on average there was always one party that voted against the proposal. It is important to emphasize that at least 20 percent of the initiatives that were approved were backed by a minimum coalition of only two parties.

Another way of measuring coalitions is by looking at the difference between those members of Congress who voted in favor of the initiative and those who voted against it. Figure 1.2 shows the Rice Index for votes cast by the entire Chamber of Deputies.[15] An index approaching a value of zero indicates that the Chamber is very narrowly divided, with 50 percent voting one way and the remaining 50 percent voting the opposite. An index with a value of 1.00 signifies that all members of Congress voted the same way.

Figure 1.2 also shows a noticeable dispersion in the size of the coalitions, with the trend continuing to be ratification by consensus voting. About 40 percent of the initiatives were approved with the backing of all the members of Congress who voted. However, the average Rice Index of votes was 63 percent, implying that, on average, one-third of the members of Congress voted against the majority. In addition, close to 20 percent of all initiatives were approved with a margin of less than 5 percent.

THE LOGIC OF POLICY CHANGE UNDER DIVIDED GOVERNMENT

The new patterns observed in the legislative process that began with the emergence of divided government are the result of the strategic interaction between the president and a Congress in which no single party holds a majority. Two key factors are involved in this interaction: the preferences of the actors (political parties) and the institutions that set the rules for the policymaking process. In view of the policymaking authority that the Constitution grants to both branches of government, one way to characterize the relationship between the executive and the legislative branches in Mexico is to compare it to a sequential game involving a proponent (in this case, Congress), which has the first move,

Figure 1.3
Representation of Executive-Legislative Relations in the Lawmaking
Process

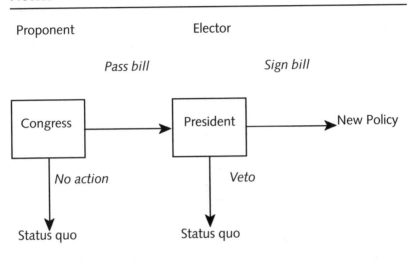

Source: Author.

and an elector (the president), which has the next move.[16] (See the flowchart in figure 1.3.)

The proponent (Congress) has the complete power to set the agenda through (1) being able to open and close the door, which means that the proponent is the only party that can submit proposals to the elector (the president);[17] and (2) denying the elector the opportunity to make amendments to the proponent's proposals.[18] The second feature of this power to set the agenda assumes that the proponent's proposal to the elector takes the form of a "take it or leave it" proposition. Given the authority to set the agenda, majorities in Congress are regularly faced with two options: (1) to propose change by sending a legislative initiative to the president for modification, or (2) to take no action and thus maintain the status quo.

Once the amended proposal is sent to the president, there is no assurance that the legislation will be accepted and that the intended change in policy will be achieved. Because the elector has veto power on initiatives approved by the proponent, each time the proponent submits an initiative the elector may opt to veto it or to sign it into law and thus change the policy involved. In keeping with the Constitution, if the president exercises his veto power, Congress can override the presidential veto if members approve the same initiative with a qualified two-thirds majority in each chamber. When the president's party controls more than one-third of the votes in both chambers, however, it is highly unlikely that Congress will be able to override the presidential veto. For this reason, this analysis has omitted the third stage of the game between the president and Congress. As shown in figure 1.3, once the president decides to veto a bill, the status quo prevails.

Figure 1.3 indicates that the strategic interaction between the president and congressional majorities can result in two possible scenarios: (1) policy change, which is tantamount to enacting a new policy and imposing a new status quo, or (2) gridlock, that is, maintenance of the status quo. In this analysis, "gridlock" means a situation in which the old status quo prevails, despite the fact that a majority in Congress prefers change;[19] in other words, for the purpose of this analysis, congressional support for an alternative to the status quo is a necessary condition for gridlock.

Legislative change is relatively easy to register and account for, even though it is rather complicated to estimate its magnitude. In fact, the data previously shown indicate that the number of changes made to existing legislation was equal to the number of new initiatives that were passed. On the other hand, it is practically impossible to quantify gridlock. Quite frequently, gridlock goes unnoticed because, in anticipation of the president's veto, political parties abstain from introducing and passing new legislation. Thus, the president does not even have to exercise his veto power for gridlock to take effect. The most precise way to measure gridlock is by counting the number of additional initiatives Congress would have approved if the president did not have veto power. The available data have no way of showing this calculation, however.

Congress is in reality a collective actor that makes decisions according to the rule of the majority. Because of the high indexes of party unity and the strong incentives for legislators to adhere to the party line,[20] Congress regularly operates by forming cohesive blocs of legislators belonging to parliamentary groups of the political parties, including the president's party. Although the Chamber of Deputies consists of 500 legislators, and the Senate has 128, both chambers actually operate as if they conformed to the positions held by between three and five legislators with weighted voting power (that is, the relevant political parties).

Each party contributes a portion of the votes needed to pass an initiative. For example, in the 57th Legislature (1997–2000), the PRI had 47 percent of the votes in the Chamber of Deputies. Together with the PAN or the PRD—both with almost 25 percent of the seats—the PRI was able to form the majority needed to have legislation approved in the plenary session. The situation did not change radically after the 2000 election. The PAN gained the presidency, but the number of seats the party had in the Chamber of Deputies and the Senate did not even reach 40 percent. The PRI continues to be the largest parliamentary faction in Congress.

How does the decisionmaking process operate in Congress when none of the parties has 50 percent of the seats plus one? The answer is provided by the "theory of the median voter," which in this case could be renamed the "theory of the median party."[21] The median party is nothing more than the party that occupies the center of the ideological spectrum. The median position has two characteristics that make it very important in processes that involve decisions made by a majority.

- First, to be in a median position signifies that there is no majority among the actors (parties) who are to the left or to the right of center.

- Second, the initiative proposed by the party located in the median position defeats other proposals in binary voting or at least has the assurance of a tie when there is an even number of voters.

The theory of the median party indicates that, if all parties behave strategically, proposals made by the party in the center will prevail in congressional decisionmaking. In fact, if the president did not have veto power, the policymaking process would regularly favor median-party proposals. The only requirement for change would be that the median party's ideal endpoint differed from the status quo. However, as established in the constitutional model, Congress proposes and the president disposes, not vice versa.

How does the presidential veto affect the outcome of the legislative process? To answer this question, it is necessary to identify the conditions under which the president and his party would be willing to accept a proposal submitted by Congress and those under which he would respond by vetoing the proposal. Each time Congress sends legislation to the executive branch, the president must compare the proposal to the status quo. If he concludes that Congress's proposal is better than the policy that is in effect, then the proposal will be accepted and change will take place. On the other hand, the president can also exercise his constitutional authority to prevent any change by vetoing the bill. In fact, President Fox wielded the executive veto on five occasions during the first half of his administration. Although this number seems unimpressive considering that the Chamber of Deputies passed 275 bills in the same period, no other president had used the veto so frequently since the 1930s.

The value of maintaining the status quo is a key variable in determining the outcome of the lawmaking process. If the value is very low, the president will accept almost any proposal Congress submits, and, these initiatives tend to converge around the party of the center. Another influencing factor is the direction in which the median party and the president want to move the status quo. If they want to move it in the same direction, there is room for compromise, with Congress having the upper hand in the negotiations. However, if the president and the median party want to move the status quo in opposite directions, gridlock will ensue and the status quo will prevail.

The model for policy formulation discussed above helps to explain some of the patterns observed in the legislative process in Mexico starting in 1997. The model shows that gridlock is not necessarily the usual result of legislative negotiations that take place under divided governments. Public policies undergo change when the median party in Congress and the president's party confront each other, recognizing that they can both achieve potential victories if they cooperate in an effort to modify the status quo. The fact that the volume of total legislation approved by the Chamber of Deputies has not been substantially reduced as a result of Mexico's divided government confirms that conditions today are propitious for producing changes just as often as under unified governments.

There are, however, substantial differences between divided and unified governments. Under unified governments, the president and his party have the capacity to direct changes in policy; whereas under divided governments, they can affect change only in a limited way. The president and his party can use the presidential veto power to block change in cases where maintaining the status quo is preferable to any other congressional proposals, or when a compromise with Congress is seen as possible. But the president can also opt to let Congress follow its own path, which he is likely to do when any modification to the status quo would move the existing policy closer to his ideal endpoint.

These patterns of strategic behavior explain variations observed in the legislative process after the appearance of divided government. Because the power to propose passes from the chief executive to Congress, the president becomes less active than before when it comes to initiating legislation. At the same time, the center of gravity in Congress moves from the president's party to the party that happens to be located in the center of the ideological spectrum. The identity of the median party may change, however, depending on the matter under discussion. Thus, under divided governments, the sources of initiatives approved by the Chamber of Deputies multiply: the party that contributes more to legislative production is more frequently the party that is found in the median position, as was the case with the PAN in the 57th Legislature (1997–2000).

The model can also explain the variations in the size of coalitions approving legislative changes. Convergence around the median party is the result of the strategic behavior of the actors involved. This outcome signifies that the parties are ready to sacrifice their first options in order to avoid placing the new policy even further from their ideal endpoint. However, when one of the parties sees that its proposal is closer to the status quo than the median party's proposal is, the first party will opt to vote in favor of the status quo. As a result, the closer the status quo is to the median party's proposal, the smaller the size of the coalition will be if the median party votes against the status quo in the plenary session.[22] Moreover, the more extreme the status quo is perceived to be, the greater the convergence among all other parties will be in favor of the median party's proposal.

FINAL CONSIDERATIONS

President Vicente Fox—the first president to come from the ranks of the opposition after 70 years of PRI dominance over Mexico's political landscape—came to power with an ambitious agenda for change. In his inaugural address, Fox proposed a series of reforms designed to transform Mexican society in a number of ways. He spoke of making substantial changes to the Constitution as well as to ordinary legislation in order to carry out indigenous rights reforms, reforms of the energy and petrochemical sectors, and fiscal, labor, and state reforms.

In the first half of his administration, only two of Fox's proposals produced results: the initiative to protect the rights and culture of indigenous peoples, and to a much lesser extent his fiscal reform package. The ratified   initiatives have been substantially different from those the president originally proposed, and a significant segment of society has received these changes with strong criticism and utter disappointment. This reaction has been more pronounced among groups that favor radical and comprehensive change, with these critics calling the changes achieved by President Fox incomplete and insufficient. The four remaining reforms (energy, petrochemical, labor, and state) did not appear prominently on the agenda of the 58th Legislature (2000–2003), and there is little probability that Congress will vote on any legislative changes to enact these reforms in the 59th Legislature (2003–2006).

The difficult relationship between President Fox and Congress has reignited the discussion about governabilty in presidential democracies and ways to address the problem of gridlock in divided governments. The administration itself has promoted the debate by organizing a working group to discuss various aspects of state reform. Participants have brought up proposals and ideas about how other democracies—principally European parliamentary democracies—have solved the problem of policy gridlock in their countries.

Nevertheless, it is not clear—as critics of the Mexican presidential system caution—whether the enormous difficulties President Fox has encountered in his attempts to advance his more important proposals demonstrate gridlock or indicate the existence of a fundamental problem. The lack of legislative success is a problem, of course, for President Fox and his team, but it does not necessarily mean that it is a failure induced by the constitutional regime.

The minimum requirement for change in a democracy is the existence of a congressional majority backing a shift in the status quo. If a minority—regardless of its size—could bring about changes, this not only would violate one of the rules of procedural justice that define democracy but also would produce enormous instability in public policies. This development would make it entirely possible for Congress to pass two contradictory measures at the same time. For these reasons, it is incorrect to speak of gridlock only in cases where Congress does not approve changes proposed by the president or by any other source. The reason for the lack of change whereby the status quo prevails can also be explained by everyone's anticipation that another alternative would face defeat in a vote by Congress.

Mexico's presidential democracy demands more than the minimum requirement for a change to take effect. It is not sufficient to have a majority in Congress; the president's approval is also necessary. If the president does not give his approval, a vote by two-thirds of the Congress is needed to achieve the same change. As a result of the presidential veto, the executive branch and a minority of one-third plus one in either chamber may stop the majority. In this way, the presidential veto represents a type of contribution to—or even a subvention of—the status quo.

The reason for subsidizing the status quo is to achieve greater stability in legislation and public policies. The presidential veto reduces the incidence of change by limiting the power of congressional majorities. In Mexico's constitutional regime, the president is more a guardian of stability than a promoter of change. In fact, the constitutional instruments available to the president to bring about change are rather limited; thus, the president's constitutional powers are characterized as essentially negative. According to the Constitution, the source for change lies in Congress.

While the PRI exercised hegemony, the source for change was transferred to the executive branch. With the arrival of divided government, however, this practice has disappeared, and any attempt to revive it is anachronistic if nothing else. Nevertheless, the disappearance of this practice has not reduced the incidence of change. Gridlock cannot be measured, because it is impossible to know how many initiatives have not been approved by Congress as a result of the expectation that the legislation would not survive the presidential veto. It is possible, however, to count the number of legislative changes, identify the sources of initiatives, and measure changes in the relative size of the coalitions that were formed to pass legislation. These data point to a system that moves the status quo from extreme to more central positions on policies. Moreover, the president and his party are not mere spectators in this process. They mold the content of the change while limiting total convergence toward the median party's position, and they protect the status quo when it is in the president's interest to maintain it.

Mexico's system is not devoid of defects or disadvantages. The country's presidential democracy has all the disadvantages of proportional systems.[23] There is no central coordinator that directs the aggregation of preferences. Therefore, changes do not comform to any comprehensive design; rather, they are the result of complex negotiations. The final outcome of the decisionmaking process is the creation and implementation of policies that fall short of a coherent approach. Policy formulation under divided government can be characterized as a system of mutual adjustments in which changes are not really formulated but adopted (as is the case of prices in a competitive marketplace). Quite frequently, changes are only marginal modifications to the status quo.

An additional problem with the mutual adjustment system is that dispersion of power leads necessarily to dispersion of responsibility for policymaking. Actors involved in decisionmaking blame one another when the outcome is negative and compete for praise when it is positive. In addition, when viewing the results of government policies, the electorate cannot clearly distinguish between who should receive credit and who should receive blame. This uncertainty creates an accountability problem, because voters cannot clearly identify those who may be responsible for the policy.

Nevertheless, pluralist systems also have advantages. Dispersion of power inhibits extremism and promotes moderation among actors. Mexico's system is one with clear centrist tendencies. Moderation is not very popular among those who prefer integral reforms and comprehensive changes in government policies. However, when one takes into account the uncertainty regarding policies that have been implemented and their results, it is obvious why moderation may present an advantage.

Any change in policy is an experiment, and great experiments face the risk of resulting in great failures. Because integral reforms and comprehensive changes carry an enormous potential for unforeseen and irreversible consequences, it is advisable for politicians to refrain from undertaking those great experiments that they proposed in the heat of electoral campaigns or public pressure. Proportional systems have checks and balances to achieve this restraint, but at the same time they leave open the possibility for change. In the equilibrium between stability and change, proportional systems lean heavily toward stability.

Another advantage of proportional systems is that the dispersal of power increases "horizontal accountability." Political actors keep an eye on one another's actions, because they are interested in exploiting their adversaries' failures and exposing them to the public. Competition compels political actors to spread information and make adoption of policies more transparent. The conflict between government branches, which frequently preoccupies those favoring rapid decisions and harmonious relations between the executive and the legislative branches, usually results in strategic decisions by opposing sides to submit the case to the court of public opinion and enlist the people's support in order to win the battle in the polls. In this process, political actors usually have a clear interest in involving the average citizen in government decisions and thereby mobilizing public support. These advantages of proportional systems ought to be borne in mind when trying to solve political problems by means of constitutional reforms, because this approach runs the risk of "throwing out the baby with the bath water."

Notes

The author wishes to express his gratitude for the valuable assistance provided by Mariella García, Javier Rojas, and Ingrid Sada in preparing this work. A preliminary version was presented at a seminar cosponsored by the Iberoamerican School of Government and Public Policy and the Center for Research and Economic Policy (CIDE) entitled "Divided Government in Mexico: Risks and Opportunities," CIDE, Mexico City, May 6–7, 2002.

❖ ❖ ❖ ❖ ❖

[1] See Juan Linz, "The Perils of Presidentialism," *Journal of Democracy*, no. 1 (1990); Juan Linz, "Presidential or Parliamentary Democracy: Does it Make a Difference?" in *The Failure of Presidential Democracy*, ed. Juan Linz and Arturo Valenzuela (Baltimore: John Hopkins University Press, 1994); and Scott Mainwaring, "Presidentialism, Multi-partyism, and Democracy: The Difficult Combination." *Comparative Political Studies*, no. 26 (July 1993): 198–228.

[2] Jeffrey Weldon, "Political Sources of *Presidencialismo* in Mexico," in *Presidentialism and Democracy in Latin America*, ed. Scott Mainwaring and Matthew Soberg Shugart (New York: Cambridge University Press, 1997). See also

María Amparo Casar, "Executive-Legislative Relations: The Case of Mexico," in *Legislative Politics in Latin America*, ed. Scott Morgenstern and Benito Nacif (New York: Cambridge University Press, 2001); and María Amparo Casar, "Las bases politico institucionales del poder presidencial en México," *Política y Gobierno* 2, no. 1 (1996): 61–92.

[3] Actually, the bicameral nature of the Mexican Congress makes party discipline a dual requirement. On the one hand, it is necessary to have unity within the parliamentary groups; on the other hand, coherence is necessary as well—that is, parliamentary groups of the same party must vote the same way in the Chamber of Deputies as they do in the Senate.

[4] See Amparo Casar, "Las bases político institucionales del poder presidencial en México."

[5] See Matthew Soberg Shugart and John M. Carey, *Presidents and Assemblies: Constitutional Design and Electoral Dynamics* (Cambridge: Cambridge University Press, 1992); and Scott Mainwaring and Matthew Soberg Shugart, "Presidentialism and Democracy in Latin America: Rethinking the Terms of the Debate," in *Presidentialism and Democracy in Latin America*, ed. Scott Mainwaring and Matthew Soberg Shugart (New York: Cambridge University Press, 1997); and Matthew Soberg Shugart and Stephan Haggard, "Institutions and Public Policy in Presidential Systems," in *Structure and Policy in Presidential Democracies*, ed. Stephan Haggard and Mathew D. McCubbins (New York: Cambridge University Press), 2000.

[6] In this respect, see John M. Carey and Matthew Soberg Shugart, eds., *Executive Decree Authority: Calling Out the Tanks or Just Filling Out the Forms?* (New York: Cambridge University Press, 1998); and Gabriel Negretto, "Does the President Govern Alone? Legislative Decree Authority and Constitutional Design in Brazil and Argentina" (documento de trabajo, no. 133, División de Estudios Politicos del CIDE, Mexico D.F., 2000).

[7] The Organic Law of Congress provides that committees must report to the floor on all the initiatives submitted to them within five working days. However, there is no enforcement mechanism for this provision and it is therefore seldom observed.

[8] With regard to this controversy, see Felipe Tena Ramírez, *Derecho constitucional mexicano*, 21st ed. (Mexico City: Porrúa, 1993).

[9] Therefore, table 1.1 excludes Senate decrees—those initiatives originating in and approved by the Senate and sent to the Chamber of Deputies. In such cases, the Chamber of Deputies operates as a "revising chamber."

[10] With regard to the Mexican electoral system, see Juan Molinar Horcasitas, *El tiempo de la legitimidad* (Mexico D.F.: Cal y Arena, 1991); Alonso Lujambio y Horacio Vives Siegl, *El poder compartido: un ensayo sobre la democracia mexicana* (Mexico D.F.: Océano, 2000); and Juan Molinar Horca-

sitas and Jeffrey Weldon, "Reforming Electoral Systems in Mexico" in *Mixed-Member Electoral Systems: The Best of Both Worlds?*, ed. Matthew S. Shugart and Martin P. Wattenber (New York: Oxford University Press, 2001).

[11] Weldon, "Political Sources of *Presidencialismo* in Mexico."

[12] It is necessary to have winning minimum coalitions in order to convert an initiative into law. In accordance with the Mexican Constitution, these are one of two types of coalitions: (1) a majority in the Chamber of Deputies and a majority in the Senate plus the president; (2) two-thirds of the members of the Chamber of Deputies plus two-thirds of the members of the Senate.

[13] Mainwaring, "Presidentialism, Muti-partyism, and Democracy"; and Linz, "The Perils of Presidentialism."

[14] The criteria used to calculate the number of parties supporting a given legislative initiative is based on the number of legislators who vote for the initiative: if a majority of legislators from a particular party vote in favor of the initiative, that party is considered to form part of the coalition that approved the initiative.

[15] The Rice Index was calculated in the following manner: votes in favor minus votes against, divided by total votes. Abstentions and absences were not taken into account. Also note that the number of cases (N) is greater than in figure 1.1 because figure 1.2 includes bills that were defeated on the floor of the Chamber of Deputies.

[16] The proponent and elector model is based on the work of Stephen Matthews, "Veto Threat: Rhetoric in a Bargaining Game," *Quarterly Journal of Economics* 104, no. 2 (1989): 347–369, as well as a subsequent application of spatial analysis to the legislative process in the United States, and negotiations related to the U.S. presidential veto, by Keith Krehbiel (see Keith Krehbiel, *Pivotal Politics: A Theory of U.S. Law Making* [Chicago: University of Chicago Press, 1998]; see also Charles Cameron, *Veto Bargaining: Presidents and the Politics of Presidential Power* [New York: Cambridge University Press, 2000]).

[17] This also means the president cannot present proposals to himself; he must wait for Congress to take the initiative.

[18] Kenneth A. Shepsle and Mark S. Bonchek, *Analyzing Politics: Rationality, Behavior, and Institutions* (New York: W. W. Norton, 1997).

[19] This is the best definition of paralysis, and it was formulated by Krehbiel (see Krehbiel, *Pivotal Politics*).

[20] Benito Nacif, "Understanding Party Discipline in the Mexican Chamber of Deputies: The Centralized Party Model" in *Legislative Politics in Latin America*, ed. Morgenstern and Nacif.

[21] The theory of the median voter was developed by Duncan Black, *The Theory of Committees and Elections* (Cambridge: Cambridge University Press,

1958). For an explanation of the theory and its applications, see Melvin J. Y. Hinich and Michael C. Munger, *Analytical Politics* (New York: Cambridge University Press, 1997).

[22] It must be kept in mind that in the plenary session, the vote is for or against the committee report. If one assumes that the report is equivalent to the median party's proposal, the plenary session of both chambers decides between two options: the proposal and the status quo.

[23] For an exhaustive comparison of pluralist and majority systems, see Binghan G. Powell, Jr., *Elections as Instruments of Democracy: Majoritarian and Proportional Visions* (New Haven: Yale University Press, 2000).

TWO

STATE REFORM IN MEXICO: PROGRESS AND PROSPECTS

Jeffrey A. Weldon

As a candidate in 2000, Vicente Fox committed to a comprehensive political reform if he were elected president of Mexico. While president-elect, he inaugurated a major study of Mexico's current Constitution, asking for recommendations for state reform. Within two months of taking office, Fox began convening formal forums within the Interior Ministry to study the different recommendations. At the time, it seemed that this political reform initiative—called State Reform (*Reforma del Estado*) in Mexico—would become part of the major legislative accomplishments of Fox's presidency. Indeed, once Fox was elected, there were calls for a brand new Constitution. Considering this move to be too bold, the Fox administration opted to undertake a comprehensive reform of the 1917 Constitution, amending as many articles as necessary without replacing it completely. In addition, instead of introducing a single omnibus reform bill to Congress, the executive and legislative branches scrapped the idea in favor of piecemeal reform measures.

Electoral reforms have a long history in Mexican politics. Since 1964, there have been frequent amendments to the Constitution, generally making the electoral formulas more proportional over time. Political actors have usually classified these modifications as political reforms (*reformas políticas*). State reforms, however, would involve measures affecting not only the electoral system but also other areas:

- the three branches of government and the relationships among them;
- the structure of federalism, including the basic structure of local

governments and the relationships among federal, state, and municipal governments;

- guarantees of civil and human rights; and

- enhancement of citizen participation in government, including such measures as popular initiatives, referendums, and recall motions.

Several important reforms have been enacted in some of these areas, such as the judicial reform and the municipal reform passed during the Zedillo administration (1994–2000). However, the proposals for reform introduced after 2000 were much more ambitious and fundamental.

Two weeks before the 2000 presidential election, Fox asked Porfirio Muñoz Ledo to organize working groups to study the reform or replacement of the Constitution. Muñoz Ledo, a federal deputy and former president of the Democratic Revolutionary Party (PRD), had recently declined to run for the presidency in favor of Fox's candidacy. On August 21, 2000, the president-elect inaugurated the Commission for the Study of State Reform (Comisión de Estudios para la Reforma del Estado, or CERE), which was made up of scores of academics and a number of former and current politicians. The commission's preliminary conclusions were presented to president-elect Fox on November 22, 2000, only three months after its creation, and the commission's report was published the following year.[1]

On February 5, 2001, Constitution Day, President Fox reiterated his commitment to state reform. On March 9, he established a second study group within the Interior Ministry. This project was organized by the National Institute for the Historical Study of the Mexican Revolution (Instituto Nacional de Estudios Históricos de la Revolución Mexicana, or INEHRM), headed at the time by Francisco Valdés Ugalde, who was appointed director general by Interior Minister Santiago Creel. The INEHRM conducted nine forums between March and August 2001, whose participants expressed a wider range of opinions than those at the CERE forums; the conclusions reached by the INEHRM forums also tended to be more radical.

One of the objectives of the INEHRM forums was to gather information to be used for formulating a comprehensive state reform within the Interior Ministry that the president would introduce as a set of bills in Congress. However, the executive branch introduced no bills to that effect in 2002 or 2003. In April 2004, Interior Minister Creel and Francisco Paoli Bolio, then the deputy minister for political development, presented a draft of the ministry's moderate state reform proposals at the Center for U.S.-Mexican Studies in La Jolla, California.[2] Again, it appeared that the Interior Ministry was ready to introduce legislation intended to lead to state reforms. However, by November 2004, the executive branch had not formally introduced a comprehensive reform to Congress; instead, the administration had submitted reforms only in certain areas (for example, modifications of budget procedures and the measures dealing with the autonomy of the Office of the Attorney General, or PGR).

Meanwhile, the Congress has taken up the slack, presenting hundreds of bills that can be classified as state reform measures. Both houses of Congress have established a State Reform Special Committee to review such legislation. The key committees—those with the veto power—are the more conservative Constitution Committees. By November 2004, only a few state reforms had been approved. A partial reform of budget procedures has been approved, and the spring congressional term has been lengthened; but major issues such as relations between the executive and legislative branches of government have not yet been resolved, and approval of significant electoral reforms appears unlikely.

This chapter examines four general areas of the state reform project:

- electoral reforms,
- adjustments to relations between the executive and legislative branches,
- the strengthening of the legislative branch, and
- budget reforms.

All four areas have received special attention from the three major parties, and each party has introduced at least one comprehensive reform bill related to each of these areas.

This study will analyze all state reform bills in these four areas that were introduced in the 57th (1997–2000) and 58th (2000–2003) Legislatures, as well as the proposals presented by the CERE and the INEHRM forums. If bills have been reported out of committee or voted on during the 59th Legislature (2003–2006), then these have also been included.[3]

ELECTORAL REFORMS
The Chamber of Deputies

Status Quo. The constitutional provisions that define the formula used for electing members of the Federal Chamber of Deputies are found in Articles 52, 53, and 54. The 500-member Chamber of Deputies is elected through a mixed-member system: 300 deputies, referred to as district deputies, are elected by plurality ("first-past-the-post") vote in single-member districts; and an additional 200, known as list deputies, are elected from lists compiled by parties based on proportional representation in five 40-member regional districts.[4]

The rule requires that the list deputies be elected independently and separately from the district deputies with two exceptions: (1) no party can have more than 300 deputies, and (2) no party can have as a share of the whole chamber more than 8 percent more than its share of the valid vote. Therefore, the total amount of disproportionality can add up to only 8 percent, which is very low by international standards for systems based on proportional representation. Only parties that garner 2 percent of the vote are eligible to nominate candidates to run for list deputies.

Diagnosis. There is a general consensus, perhaps mistaken, that both chambers of the Mexican Congress are excessively large. The national press began to attack the size of Congress after the fiscal reform debacle in early 2002. The reason most often cited in the press was that it was too costly and too inefficient to have so many deputies and senators. Observers also argued that proportional representation increased the legislative strength of the Left and made it more difficult to pass fiscal reforms.[5] Legislators argued that it might be easier to coordinate the work of smaller chambers, although it is hard to imagine that coordinating the work of 500 deputies is really much more difficult than coordinating the work of 300. At any rate, there has been pressure to decrease the number of national legislators.

Some political parties prefer less proportionality in Congress. This assessment was especially true for the Institutional Revolutionary Party (PRI) before 2000, somewhat true for the National Action Party (PAN) during the 58th Legislature (2000–2003), and true again for the PRI during the 59th Legislature (2003–2006). Other parties, especially the PRD and some of the small political parties, prefer greater proportionality; for example, some lean toward allowing no overrepresentation of parties in the Chamber of Deputies.

In addition, some have complained that the 2 percent rule (increased from 1.5 percent in 1996) as the minimum ceiling for a party's eligibility for proportional representation seats is too low. These critics have proposed increasing the threshold to 4 or 5 percent.

Proposals for Reform. No other theme in the government's state reform agenda affects political parties more directly and more differently than modifying the formulas for election to Congress. Therefore, it is logical that there has been more variation in these proposals than in any other part of the state reform.[6] (Table 2.1 presents a summary of all the bills submitted dealing with electoral reforms for the Chamber of Deputies.)

The 57th Legislature considered five bills to modify the composition of the Chamber of Deputies. One bill, presented by the PRI, would have completely eliminated the list deputies elected by proportional representation, leaving the lower chamber with only the 300 deputies elected in single-member districts. In the 1997 election, the PRI had won 165 of the 300 districts; thus, if the chamber had not included list deputies, the party would have had a small majority. However, because the PRI had won just less than 40 percent of the valid vote, the law limited the party to a total of only 239 deputies in the chamber. Eliminating the list deputies made sense to the PRI at the time, because it would have been overrepresented by 15 percentage points.

The Green Party of Mexico (PVEM), which had won less than 4 percent of the vote and held only five seats in the lower chamber during most of the 57th Legislature, called for the elimination of single-member districts. The party proposed that all 500 members be elected in five regional districts based on proportional representation (PR) lists, and that each party's share of congressional seats should match its

Table 2.1
Bills that Modify the Electoral Formulas for the Chamber of Deputies

Legislator	Chamber	Party	Date	Single-Member District Deputies	List Deputies	Total Deputies	Total Limit	Proportional Representation Limit[1]
Héctor F. Castañeda Jiménez	Deputies	PRI	Oct. 27, 1998	300	0	300	No Limit	No limit
Jorge Emilio González Martínez	Deputies	PVEM	Jan. 20, 1999	0	500	500[2]	300	0%
Jesús Samuel Maldonado Bautista	Deputies	PRD	Apr. 13, 2000	300	200[3]	500	300	8%
Marcelino Díaz de Jesús	Deputies	PRD	Apr. 27, 2000	300	240[4]	540	300	8%
Felipe de Jesús Preciado Coronado	Deputies	PAN	Apr. 27, 2000	300	200[5]	500	300	8%
Magdalena del Socorro Núñez Monreal	Deputies	PRD	Sept. 20, 2000	300	200	500	300	0%
Amador Rodríguez Lozano	Deputies	PRI	Mar. 27, 2001	300	100	400	240	8%
Gregorio Urías Germán	Deputies	PRD	Oct. 5, 2001	300	240[6]	540	340	8%
José Soto Martínez	Deputies	PRI	Oct. 18, 2001	300	0	300	No limit	No limit
Rufino Rodríguez Cabrera	Deputies	PRD	Nov. 27, 2001	300	200[7]	500	300	8%

(continued next page)

JEFFREY A. WELDON 33

(Table 2.1, continued)

Legislator	Chamber	Party	Date	Single-Member District Deputies	List Deputies	Total Deputies	Total Limit	Proportional Representation Limit[1]
Uuc-kib Espadas Ancona	Deputies	PRD	Dec. 14, 2001	250	250	500	No limit	8%
Martí Batres Guadarrama	Deputies	PRD	Apr. 23, 2002	0	500[8]	500	No limit	0%
Miguel Bortolini Castillo	Deputies	PRD	July 24, 2002	300	300[9]	600	400	8%
Luis Miguel Barbosa Huerta	Deputies	PRD	Aug. 21, 2002	300[10]	200	500	300	8%
Diego Alonso Hinojosa Aguerrevere	Deputies	PAN	Oct. 10, 2002	300	200[11]	500	300	8%
Francisco Ricardo Sheffield Padilla	Deputies	PAN	Dec. 3, 2002	300	100	400	300	8%
Francisco Agundis Árias	Deputies	PVEM	Dec. 10, 2002	150	150	300	200[12]	8%
José Antonio Calderón Cardoso	Deputies	PAS	Dec. 13, 2002	0	300	300	No limit	0%
Cutberto Cantorán Espinosa	Deputies	PRI	Dec. 15, 2002	300	200[13]	500	No limit	0%
Adrián Alanís Quiñones	Senate	PRI	Feb. 26, 2003	300	100[14]	400	No limit	No limit
Omar Fayad Meneses	Deputies	PRI	Apr. 3, 2003	300	200[15]	500	300	8%
Juan Ramón Soto Reséndiz	Deputies	PAN	Apr. 10, 2003	210	140[16]	350	210	5%

(continued next page)

(Table 2.1, continued)

Legislator	Chamber	Party	Date	Single-Member District Deputies	List Deputies	Total Deputies	Total Limit	Proportional Representation Limit[1]
Luis Miguel Barbosa Huerta	Deputies	PRD	Apr. 23, 2003	300	240[17]	540	340	8%
Raymundo Cárdenas Hernández	Senate	PRD	Apr. 30, 2003	200	200[18]	400	240	0%
David Augusto Sotelo Rosas	Deputies	PRD	June 25, 2003	300	200[19]	500	300	8%

Notes: (1) The total disproportionality legally tolerated. (2) Seats assigned to deputies elected by proportional representation from five regional lists (PR seats). (3) Includes no PR seats; losing candidates in single-member districts who won the largest percentage of the vote win the PR seats. (4) Includes 40 PR seats assigned to an indigenous list. (5) Includes 10 PR seats assigned to a foreign list. (6) Includes 40 PR seats assigned to Mexicans living abroad. (7) Includes no PR lists; losing candidates in single-member districts who garner the largest share of the vote win the PR seats. (8) Includes state PR lists. (9) Includes 60 PR seats from an indigenous list and 40 PR seats from a foreign list. (10) The 300 district seats would be elected by absolute majority of votes instead of a plurality; thus there would be runoff elections at least 30 days later if no candidate won an absolute majority in the first round of balloting. (11) The threshold to qualify as PR deputies would increase from 2 percent to 3 percent. (12) The proposed limit is found in the electoral code, not in the Constitution, making the statutory reform unconstitutional. (13) The first five candidates on each of the five regional party lists must be indigenous persons. (14) Includes 50 seats assigned to the 10 highest second-place winners (determined by the number of votes received) for each party in each of the five regions; 30 elected by proportional representation; 10 designated from open citizen lists assigned to "national political groups"; and 10 assigned to Mexicans living abroad. (15) Members of the Chamber of Deputies are elected to serve six-year terms. The bill proposed that parties should ratify or substitute deputies elected by proportional representation halfway through their terms without a federal election. (16) Increases the threshold to qualify for PR seats to 4 percent. (17) Includes 40 PR seats from a foreign list. (18) Increases the threshold to qualify for PR seats to 3 percent and provides for Mexican citizens residing abroad to be elected according to PR lists. (19) Members of the Chamber of Deputies are elected for six-year terms. The bill increases the minimum threshold to qualify for PR seats to 10 percent and eliminates PR lists, proposing instead that the losing candidates in the district races with the highest number of votes be elected.

share of the valid vote it had won in the election. Had this system been used in 1997, the PVEM would have held 19 or 20 seats in the Chamber of Deputies.

One proposal offered by the PRD would have kept the current system in general but modified the way list deputies would be elected. The party proposed assigning the same proportions to the 200 deputies elected by proportional representation as those provided in the current law and eliminating the multimember lists. Instead, each party's list deputies would be that party's losing candidates who had won the highest share of the vote in their losing cause in the district races; the parties would nominate only district candidates. The winning candidates would go directly to the chamber, as would the losing candidates with the most votes. This system, which was used in the 1960s and 1970s to elect deputies from minority parties, would create greater internal competition but would offer two strange possibilities. First, some districts, especially those where the competition was high, would elect three, four, or more deputies. Second, if the party reached the 300-seat ceiling, all of its candidates—every winner and every loser— would automatically be seated in the Chamber of Deputies. These candidates would not have to work very hard to get into office. The PRD submitted similar bills in November 2001 and June 2003.

Late in the 57th Legislature, the PRD introduced another bill that would create 40 additional seats for list deputies that would be reserved for indigenous candidates. The 8 percent rule and the 300-seat ceiling would remain in effect, thus limiting the party with the most seats to less than 56 percent of the whole chamber, regardless of its share of the votes.[7] Felipe de Jesús Preciado, a PAN deputy, introduced a similar bill at the end of the 57th Legislature. This proposal called for 200 list deputies, 10 of whom would be reserved for Mexicans living abroad.[8]

In 2001, CERE proposed reducing the Chamber of Deputies to 400 deputies, all to be elected by proportional representation.[9] According to the CERE plan, each party would receive exactly the same share of seats as its share of the valid vote. The list of deputies to be elected on the basis of proportional representation would be open, allowing voters to choose the candidates from among the lists provided by the parties. This proposal was dead on arrival, however. There is very little support—except on the part of some PRD members and the very small parties—for abandoning single-member districts. It is also very unlikely that the parties would accept open lists, because this system could lead to excluding key party leaders from the legislature.

The INEHRM forums also recommended reducing the number of deputies, but the proposals provided no specifics. At the same time, INEHRM suggested creating more list deputies to provide for representation for indigenous groups and for Mexicans abroad. The forums also called for raising the minimum threshold for representation but did not provide a specific number.

The 58th Legislature took up 18 bills that modify the formulas for electing members of the Chamber of Deputies. A PRD proposal presented in the first month of the legislative session called for perfect proportionality under the mixed-member format. The formula would retain 300 district deputies and 200 list deputies as well as the 300-seat ceiling. However, the limit on a party's overrepresentation in the chamber would be decreased from 8 percent to 0 percent. In other words, each party above the minimum threshold would have the same share of seats as the share of the vote it had garnered. Had this system been used in the 2000 elections, the number of seats won by the PRD's coalition would have increased by 50 percent.

Amador Rodríguez Lozano, then a PRI member, introduced a bill that would reduce the number of list deputies to 100 and maintain the ceiling at 60 percent of the seats in the chamber, or 240 seats out of a total of 400. The proposal also called for maintaining the 8 percent rule. This system would introduce some inconsistencies, however, when the winning party had a substantial electoral advantage (more than 20 points) and the opposition was evenly divided. In these cases, the winning party could easily win more districts than the 240-seat limit. In fact, if the opposition were divided, a party with about 50 percent of the total vote could win in more than 267 districts, which would be more than two-thirds of the chamber.[10] The main reason for the 60 percent rule is to guarantee that no single party has the two-thirds majority needed to amend the Constitution. In October 2001, the PRI submitted another bill to eliminate the list deputies and has sponsored similar bills in the 59th Legislature.

During the second year of the 58th Legislature, the PRD introduced a bill that would provide for 250 district deputies and 250 list deputies. The 8 percent overrepresentation rule would be continued, and the limit on a party's seats would be abandoned. Martí Batres, the leader of the PRD faction in the lower chamber, proposed abandoning single-member districts and replacing them with 32 state lists, assigned by proportional representation. The system would still involve electing 500 deputies, but all would be elected by proportional representation within their respective states. Many Latin American countries elect their legislators in this manner. According to the proposal, greater proportionality would be maintained and state (if not district) representation would be preserved. The rule would guarantee that each party would have the same share of total seats in the chamber as its share of the valid vote.[11] Three additional bills proposed representation for special groups. One bill submitted by the PRD would add 40 list deputies to represent Mexicans abroad, resulting in a total of 540 deputies in the lower house. This time, the ceiling on representation in the chamber would be increased to 340—about 63 percent of the house. Another PRD proposal, even more ambitious, would provide for 60 additional list deputies for indigenous groups and 40 additional list deputies for Mexicans living in foreign countries. The proposal would increase the size of the chamber to 600 and set the ceiling for party representation at 400.

Finally, a bill presented by the PRI at the end of the fall 2002 legislative session would require each party to nominate indigenous persons to the top five spots on their five regional lists. As a result, the PRI and the PAN would each have at least 25 indigenous deputies, taking seats away from party leaders at the top of the lists. (If a party were to win about 35 percent–40 percent of the vote, it would be able to elect an average of 14–16 deputies per regional list.) According to the PRI proposal, most, if not all, of the PRD's expected list deputies would be indigenous persons, leaving little or no room for party leaders on the party lists. In addition, every member of the small parties, such as the PVEM, the Labor Party (PT), and Convergencia, would be an indigenous person.[12]

In August 2002, the PRD introduced a bill that would call for runoff elections in the 300 districts if no candidate won an absolute majority in the first round of voting. Candidates who had won at least 10 percent of the vote in the first round would qualify for the second round, which would be held about a month later. Parties would be allowed to substitute their candidates for others, supposedly to permit coalitions to stand for election in the second round. This proposal, inspired by the system that elects France's National Assembly, would establish a system that tends to achieve greater proportionality at the single-member district level if there are coalitions. However, the PRD continues to insist on keeping the lists of candidates to be elected by proportional representation within this system. In this case, it is not clear when the list deputies should be selected—in the first round or in the second round (to allow for the ceilings to take effect). This proposal would lead to greater dispersion in the electoral system. Runoff systems tend to increase marginal parties' share of the vote as they seek to be qualified to proceed to the second round. Any system of proportional representation also tends to increase the centrifugal forces in an electoral system.

The PAN presented two proposals to decrease the proportionality allowed by the system. The first, introduced in October 2002, would increase the threshold for a party's eligibility to nominate candidates to run as list deputies from 2 percent to 3 percent of the vote received. This reform would have two consequences: (1) it would make it more difficult for small parties running alone to achieve representation and maintain party registration; and (2) it would be more costly for large parties to include small parties in their coalitions. For all the parties in a five-party coalition to maintain their party registration today (for example, the PRD-led Alliance for Mexico included a total of five parties in the 2003 midterm election), the coalition needs 10 percent of the vote—that is, five parties multiplied by 2 percent each. If the threshold is increased to 3 percent, then the total vote required for all five parties to maintain registration would increase to 15 percent. Because other bills would require a more equitable share of the vote for the purposes of campaign financing, a larger threshold would make coalitions more costly in financial terms.[13]

The PAN made the news in early December 2002, however, when it submitted its second proposal, which would decrease the number of proportional representation seats to 100. The party argued that this reduction would save money (by reducing the number of deputies from 500 to 400) and make it easier to coordinate the work of the chamber. This bill would maintain both the 300-seat limit and the 8 percent rule. It also eliminates one of the mathematical inconsistencies of Rodríguez Lozano's similar bill, which proposed a 240-seat ceiling with

300 districts. But in both cases, a strong first-place finish could result in the election of enough delegates from single-member districts to give them a two-thirds majority in the chamber, despite the 8 percent rule. Not surprisingly, the PRD opposed the bill, given that all other PRD proposals tend to increase proportionality. However, the PRI also came out strongly against reducing the number of deputies and possibly increasing disproportionality. The PRI claimed that Vicente Fox was behind the PAN's bill and that the executive branch had proposed the legislation as a way to punish Congress. This accusation was not likely, but the PRI's discomfort in the face of a weakened system of proportional representation was an indicator that the party was uncertain about its position among the electorate.

Media reaction to the PAN's bill was very favorable, but the opposition accused the PAN of turning the question into a publicity stunt. This criticism is probably not too far from the truth. In the past, the PAN has been uneasy about reducing proportional representation. Other reforms floating around the PAN's parliamentary group would decrease the total number of deputies without reducing the proportionality of the chamber—some formulas calling for 240 district deputies and 160 list seats, others calling for 200 districts and 200 list seats. However, the PAN in particular might lose single-member districts as the districts become larger and more rural.

Other parties were quick to respond to the challenge to lower the number of deputies. On December 10, 2002, the PVEM proposed a further reduction in the number of deputies—to 300. The bill proposed 150 single-member districts and 150 party list seats and a ceiling of 200 seats; in addition, the 8 percent overrepresentation rule would be maintained.[14] This proposal presents two major problems. First, the smallest states would be guaranteed at least two districts; therefore, Baja California Sur, Colima, and a few other states would be very highly overrepresented in the Chamber of Deputies. Second, dividing the country into 150 districts would make the average district size in Mexico larger than the size of districts represented in the U.S. House of Representatives or in the Russian Duma.

On December 13, 2002, the Social Alliance Party (PAS), a far-right party with absolutely no electoral support, proposed reducing the number of seats in the Chamber of Deputies to 300. This change would be accomplished by abolishing single-member districts and creating only five multimember constituencies, which would elect a total of 300 deputies on the basis of proportional representation; this system would eliminate overrepresentation in the chamber because of the absence of districts. The PAS is too small to elect list deputies in state constituencies (as the PRD proposed). In 60-member constituencies, however, the PAS could elect six deputies with only 2 percent of the vote. Five deputies are required to form a parliamentary group in the Chamber of Deputies (current electoral rules provide for electing only four deputies with a minimum threshold of 2 percent).

Even the PRD joined in the race to reduce the number of deputies in the lower house. In April 2003 in the Senate, the party introduced a bill to reduce the number of districts to 200 and retain the 200 seats for list deputies. The maximum number of seats that a party could win was set at 240, with no overrepresentation tolerated.

Also in the spring 2003 term, the PAN introduced another bill to reduce the number of deputies, this time to 350. The bill called for 210 district deputies and 140 list deputies and set limits of 210 total seats to be held by one party and 5 percent overrepresentation by one party.

Earlier, in February 2003, the PRI introduced a mathematically complicated bill in the Senate. The bill proposed a system of 300 districts, 50 deputies assigned according to the best second-place finish for each party, 30 assigned by proportional representation, 10 designated from citizen lists provided by National Political Groups (quasi-parties), and 10 elected from lists of citizens living abroad. No limits were placed on total representation or overrepresentation by one party, making this a formula that favors the majority.

Two bills proposed increasing the term of deputies to six years. One proposal, submitted by the PRI, would allow the parties to ratify or replace their list deputies after the first three years, supposedly as a way to enforce party discipline or to remove those who had defected to other parties.

Likelihood of Reform. In light of the popularity of the calls for decreasing the size of the Chamber of Deputies, proposals to increase the number of deputies so as to include representation of special groups are not likely to prosper. The idea of requiring the first five deputies on a party's regional lists to be members of indigenous groups is also dead on arrival. A quota for indigenous groups or for youth (the latter proposed by the PVEM) may have greater success, however, as did the gender quota approved in spring 2002; quotas for indigenous persons or youth are unlikely to require too many places at the top of the party lists.

Other parties are likely to veto radical proposals, such those that call for only single-member districts or only proportional representation. Decreasing the size of the chamber to 400 is somewhat more likely. Reducing the number of list deputies to 100 is likely to run into mathematical problems.

Another proposal that was floating around would reduce the number of districts to 240 and the number of list deputies to 160. According to this plan, the 60 percent ceiling for the total number of seats held by one party would conveniently be set at 240, and the 8 percent rule could easily be maintained. This formula would introduce a problem of redistricting and minor malapportionment of seats among the states.

Nevertheless, reducing the size of the Chamber of Deputies to 300 or 400 deputies is a lot of sound and fury, signifying an insignificant decrease in the problems of coordinating the work of the chamber. The Chamber of Deputies is not "disorderly" because of its size but because of the parties that inhabit it. Each of those parties is almost perfectly disciplined, demonstrating that size is not the problem. Even reducing the proportionality of party representation in the chamber will not significantly reduce polarization within the lower house. Voter coordination—not deputy coordination—is the key to solving this particular problem.

The Senate

Status Quo. The electoral formula for the Senate is set out in Article 56 of the Constitution. The 128-member Senate is also chosen by means of a mixed-member electoral system that is even more complicated than the system used to elect members of the Chamber of Deputies. In each of the 32 states, every party nominates a ranked slate of two candidates for the Senate. The slate winning a plurality elects both of its candidates, and the slate that places second elects the first candidate on its list (known as the "first minority principle"). In addition, 32 senators are elected by proportional representation. Therefore, 64 senators are elected by plurality, 32 by the first minority principle and 32 by a national party list.[15]

Diagnosis. In the case of the Senate, there are widespread complaints that the inclusion of senators elected by means of a national party list violates the federal character of the upper house. Critics claim that Mexico's federal pact requires that all states be represented equally. In addition, observers believe that the size of the Senate should be reduced to 64 or 96 members as a way of making the body more efficient.

Proposals for Reform. The Senate has been the subject of numerous reform proposals. (Details of these bills are summarized in table 2.2.) Three bills were presented in the 57th Legislature. Two—one submitted by the PRD and the other by the PVEM—dealt with the problem of the unpopularity of list senators by replacing them with a system in which the losing Senate candidates with the highest share of the vote would win seats (32 senators would still be assigned by proportional representation to the parties that win at least 2 percent of the vote). The difficulty with this system is that it does not distinguish between a candidate for the Senate who lost because he or she came in second on the list of a party that placed second in a state and a candidate who lost because he or she headed the list of a party that placed third or lower in a state.

Another bill that the PRD introduced during the 57th Legislature would append an additional 16 seats reserved for indigenous senators. Also, a PRD bill submitted to the 58th Legislature would add 10 more list senators to represent Mexicans living abroad.

In an effort to defend the federal character of the Senate, CERE proposed eliminating the 32 list senators.[16] The system would retain the 64 senators who were elected by plurality and the 32 who were elected by placing second in their states. This proposal does not recognize the serious electoral consequences that the first minority system entails, however. For the PRI, there is no better system possible; in 2000, the party placed first or second in every state except the Federal District. Simulations demonstrate that the PRI could win a majority of seats with a similar distribution but still have fewer votes than the PAN has.[17] This system is exceptionally unfavorable for the PAN and the

Table 2.2
Bills that Modify the Electoral Formulas for the Senate

Legislator	Chamber	Party	Date	Plurality Seats	Second-place Seats	List Seats	Total
Jorge Emilio González Martínez	Deputies	PVEM	Jan. 20, 1999	64	32	32[1]	128
Jesús Samuel Maldonado Bautista	Deputies	PRD	Apr. 13, 2000	64	32	32[2]	128
Marcelino Díaz de Jesús	Deputies	PRD	Apr. 27, 2000	64	32	48[3]	144
Amador Rodríguez Lozano	Deputies	PRI	Mar. 27, 2001	64	32	0	96
Gregorio Urías Germán	Deputies	PRD	Oct. 5, 2001	64	32	42[4]	138
José Soto Martínez	Deputies	PRI	Oct. 18, 2001	96	0	0	96
Rufino Rodríguez Cabrera	Deputies	PRD	Nov. 27, 2001	64	32	32[5]	128
Uuc-kib Espadas Ancona	Deputies	PRD	Dec. 14, 2001	0	0	128[6]	128
Luis Miguel Barbosa Huerta	Deputies	PRD	Aug. 21, 2002	64[7]	32	32	128
Adrián Alanís Quiñones	Senate	PRI	Feb. 26, 2003	64	32	0	96
Juan Ramón Soto Reséndiz	Deputies	PAN	Apr. 10, 2003	64	32	0	96
Raymundo Cárdenas Hernández	Senate	PRD	Apr. 30, 2003	0	0	128[8]	128
David Augusto Sotelo Rosas	Deputies	PRD	June 25, 2003	32	0	32[9]	64

Notes: (1) Includes no PR seats; losing candidates based on plurality voting who have the highest percentages of the vote would win the PR seats. (2) Includes no PR seats; losing candidates based on plurality voting who have the highest percentages of the vote would win the PR seats. (3) Includes 16 PR seats from an indigenous list. (4) Includes 10 PR seats from a list assigned to Mexicans living abroad. (5) Includes no PR seats; losing candidates based on plurality voting who have the highest percentages of the vote would win the PR seats. (6) Includes four senators per state, elected by closed-list proportional representation (Hare quota with largest remainders). (7) The 64 first-place seats would require an absolute majority, instead of a plurality, of votes in the first round of balloting; thus the bill calls for runoff elections at least 30 days later if no candidate wins an absolute majority in the first round. (8) Includes four senators per state, elected by closed-list proportional representation (Hare quota with largest remainders). (9) Includes no PR seats; instead, losing candidates with the highest share of votes would be elected.

PRD, because there are a number of states in which each party is very unlikely to emerge from third place anytime soon. For example, the PAN would need to increase its vote margin over the PRI by more than 14 percentage points before the PAN could win a majority under this system. In fact, the PAN is much better off with a pure plurality system than with the plurality/first minority system.

The INEHRM forums proposed electing senators from each state on the basis of proportional representation and eliminating senators elected by the national proportional representation list. This system, even with three senators per state, is much more equitable than election based on the plurality/first minority principle. The main problem is that the system proposed by INEHRM is a bit too proportional; it makes it very difficult for any party to ever win a Senate majority.

During the 58th Legislature, Amador Rodríguez Lozano proposed eliminating the national list senators. Another PRI member proposed electing all senators by plurality vote and providing for three senators per state, evidently based on a party slate, with the winning slate electing all three senators.[18] In spring 2003, the PRI introduced another bill to eliminate the list senators, and the PAN quickly followed suit.

A bill introduced by Uuc-Kib Espadas of the PRD would provide for four senators per state, all elected by proportional representation within each state. During summer 2002, this proposal emerged as a strong consensus solution because the system would preserve proportionality and federal representation simultaneously. The PRD introduced a similar bill in the Senate in the spring 2003 term as well as a bill in the Chamber of Deputies that would reduce the total number of senators to 64: 32 senators elected by plurality, and the other 32 assigned to the parties by proportional representation, with the seats assigned to the candidates who had won the most votes in the states.

Luis Miguel Barbosa, a PRD senator, introduced a bill in August 2002 that would require runoff elections for senators chosen by plurality vote and those by the first minority principle if the winning slate did not win an absolute majority in the first round of voting. In this case, the slates winning at least 10 percent of the vote would appear on a runoff ballot about a month after the first round. It is odd that this reform would appear at the same time that the PRD was concentrating on a proportional solution to the formula for elections to the Senate. Perhaps the PRD is most interested in implementing the runoff system in elections for president, and possibly for deputies, but only made the proposal for senatorial elections as a way to maintain the proposition's congruency. There is no doubt that the PRD prefers full proportional representation based on state-level constituencies for the upper chamber.

Likelihood of Reform. Rules for the election of senators are more likely to be modified than are those for the election of chamber deputies. The PRD would clearly prefer proportional representation at the state level, with each state represented by four senators. The PRI and the PAN would prefer either maintaining the status quo or eliminating the list senators altogether. The PAN is likely to suffer under a more majoritarian system. The goal of reducing the number of senators without increasing disproportionality would be achieved by electing three senators per state, each by proportional representation.

Given that the Senate already tends toward disproportionality—because the small states have representation equal to that of the large states—it might be preferable to trade for greater proportionality in the upper chamber and somewhat less proportionality in the lower chamber. It is better to allow for artificial majorities in the lower chamber because a party won many more districts than to permit a party to win a majority in the Senate because it fared better in elections in the smaller states.

State Legislatures

Status Quo. Article 116 of the Constitution requires the states to have a minimum number of deputies in the state legislature, according to the population of the state. All states, however, have many more deputies than the minimum required. Furthermore, according to the Constitution, the legislators must be elected by means of a mixed-member system of single-member districts and proportional representation, though the Constitution provides no details on the proportion of seats in the whole legislature that are assigned by each formula. However, the Supreme Court and the Federal Electoral Tribunal have ruled that certain state electoral rules are insufficiently proportional and are therefore unconstitutional.

Diagnosis. There is no clear consensus that the system of election to state legislatures needs to be reformed. In this case, reform depends on the position in which a party finds itself. Parties that have large advantages in single-member districts tend to prefer weaker proportional representation and vice versa. Because each of the three parties' circumstances vary across the states, there is little consensus even within the parties about what should be done.

However, in November 1998, the Supreme Court ruled that a state law was unconstitutional because it was not sufficiently proportional. The Court set the following guidelines for what a state's mixed electoral system should look like:

- Parties must run candidates in a certain number of districts to qualify for seats assigned by proportional representation (PR seats).

- A party must attain a minimum threshold in order to qualify for PR seats.

- The PR seats are assigned additionally and independently of the seats won in districts.[19]

- The law must specify the order in which deputies are chosen from the lists assigned by proportional representation.

- The maximum number of seats that can be won by a party must not be greater than the number of electoral districts.

- A single party's overrepresentation in the legislature should be limited.

- The electoral rules should conform to the results of the election.[20]

Proposals for Reform. A number of bills have been introduced that attempt to regulate the formulas for electing members of state legislatures as established in the federal Constitution. (The bills are summarized in table 2.3.) All the state legislatures use mixed-member systems that include both district and list deputies. However, the formula for each state is different in terms of varying proportions of list deputies, distinct thresholds for list representation, dissimilar ceilings, different or no stipulations for overrepresentation, and so on. Furthermore, malapportionment and gerrymandering are more serious problems at the state level than they are at the federal level.

One bill, introduced early in the 57th Legislature by two small parties (the PT and the PVEM) would require list representation in the state legislature for any party that had won at least 2 percent of the vote

Table 2.3
Bills that Modify the Electoral Formulas for the State Legislatures
(All introduced in the Chamber of Deputies)

Legislator/ Party/Date	Single- member Districts	List Deputies	Total	Total Limit	Proportional Representation Limit[1]
Aurora Bazán López and Ricardo Cantú Garza PVEM and PT Dec. 8, 1997	NA	NA	NA[2]	NA	NA
Abraham Bagdadi Estrella PRD Nov. 18, 1999	No more than 60%	At least 40%	At least 15	NA	0%
Magdalena del Socorro Núñez Monreal PRD Sept. 20, 2000	Half	Half	At least 24[3]	NA	0%
José Soto Martínez PRI Oct. 18, 2001	All	None	NA	No limit	No limit
Luis Miguel Barbosa Huerta PRD Apr. 4, 2002	NA	NA[4]	NA	Number of districts	8%
Martí Batres Guadarrama PRD Apr. 23, 2002	None	All	NA	NA	0%

Notes: (1) The total disproportionality legally tolerated. (2) Any party with 2 percent of the electoral vote would be guaranteed list seats. (3) Includes the Federal District. (4) Any party with 2 percent of the electoral vote would be eligible for list seats.

in a state. Often, the formulas only make these parties eligible for list representation; whether they actually win seats depends on the parties' quotas.[21]

Another bill from the 57th Legislature introduced by the PRD would put a floor on the share of total seats that would be assigned by proportional representation. At least 40 percent of the legislature would have to be assigned by lists. Of course, the greater the ratio of list seats to districts, the more proportional the legislature would be.[22] Early in the 58th Legislature, the PRD submitted another bill that would require assigning half of the seats in each state legislature to deputies from single-member districts and the other half to proportional representation list deputies. In this case, the minimum size of the total legislature would be set at 24—currently the median size of the state legislatures.

A PRI bill introduced in October 2001 would eliminate all list deputies not only from the federal Chamber of Deputies and Senate but also from the state legislatures. This formula would retain only deputies who had been elected by plurality vote in single-member districts.

In April 2002, the PRD's Luis Miguel Barbosa submitted a bill to the lower chamber that would require state legislatures to adopt the rules that govern the composition of the federal Chamber of Deputies. Any party with 2 percent of the vote would be eligible for list representation. The ceiling on the number of seats would be limited to the number of districts in the state, and the limit on overrepresentation would be set at 8 percent. The bill, however, did not fix the percentage of seats that must be elected from the lists. Therefore, in Jalisco, where half the seats are from districts and half from the lists, the rule would prevent any party from ever having an absolute majority in the chamber (because the ceiling would be the number of plurality seats).

Finally, Martí Batres of the PRD presented a bill near the end of the spring 2002 session. The proposal would eliminate all districts from the state legislatures and impose pure proportional representation from a single statewide list.

Likelihood of Reform. It is interesting to note how some legislators introduce bills to strengthen federalism and state's rights on the one hand, and, on the other, present bills to force states to adopt electoral systems that the legislators prefer. It is unlikely that the Constitution will be further modified to compel the states to change their electoral systems. What is more likely is that the Supreme Court will mold the state electoral laws to conform to the Court's own ideas of proportional representation.

Moreover, an important component of electoral reform is missing from these proposals. A major problem recently has been the high levels of malapportionment in some state legislatures in which rural areas are strongly overrepresented. This situation directly affects the PAN and PRD, which tend to do better in urban areas. Nothing in the Constitution requires that districts be roughly the same size, and even the Federal Electoral Institute tolerates a variation of about 15 percentage points.

Presidential Runoff Elections

Status Quo. Article 81 of the Constitution deals with presidential elections but stipulates only that there be a direct election for the presidency, adding that details are to be found in the electoral code. The law provides for a plurality, first-past-the-post election of the president.

Diagnosis. Whether presidential elections should have runoffs when no candidate wins an absolute majority of the vote is a very controversial point among political scientists. Usually, runoff elections involve the two candidates with the highest vote totals in the preliminary round of voting. On the one hand, most consider it desirable for the incoming president to have the support of at least half of the voting population. Under some circumstances, a candidate might have a plurality with less than 35 percent of the total votes cast, and some could feel that such a president would lack a mandate to govern.

On the other hand, permitting runoff elections might create greater incentives for more parties to participate, in the hope either of finishing as one of the top two contenders, or, failing that, of negotiating support for one of the finalists in return for other benefits, such as legislative initiatives or cabinet positions in the administration. Rather than reducing the number of parties seeking the presidency, runoff elections might lead to greater fractionalization of the vote. Duverger's law strongly suggests that plurality elections, without runoffs, over time lead to two-party systems.

Moreover, it is not clear that a candidate who wins in a second round of balloting really has a greater mandate than a candidate who wins by a plurality in a single-round election does. It remains the case that most voters cast their ballots against the winning candidate in the first round, and it is possible that a candidate who placed third or lower in the first round might have been able to defeat the eventual winner if that candidate had qualified for the runoff election.

Proposals for Reform. In 1998, during the 57th Legislature, the PAN introduced a bill in the Chamber of Deputies that would reform Article 81 to require a runoff election between the top two presidential contenders if no candidate won an absolute majority in the first round of voting. CERE proposed instituting runoff elections but left open the possibility of an alternative vote, which would require every voter to

Table 2.4
Bills that Provide for Runoffs in Presidential Elections
(All bills introduced in the Chamber of Deputies)

Legislator	Party	Date	Details
Rafael Alberto Castilla Peniche	PAN	Mar. 17, 1998	If no candidate wins a majority, a runoff election is held between the top two contenders.
Fernando Ortiz Arana	PRI	Apr. 19, 2001	If a candidate wins a plurality by more than 5 percentage points, that candidate is elected; otherwise, a runoff election is held between the top two contenders 30 days later.
Luis Miguel Barbosa Huert	PRD	Aug. 21, 2002	If no candidate wins a majority, a runoff election is held between the top two contenders 30 days later.

rank all the candidates on the ballot.[23] The INEHRM forums also called for runoff elections in case no candidate won an absolute majority of the vote in the first round.

Two bills were introduced in the 58th Legislature to allow for possible runoff elections. The PRI proposal, submitted by Fernando Ortiz Arana, provides that a first round victory would require an absolute majority or a plurality with at least 5 percentage points separating first place from second; otherwise, a runoff election would be held a month later. The second bill, introduced by Luis Miguel Barbosa of the PRD, would require a runoff election between the top two contenders to be held a month later if no candidate won at least 50 percent of the vote in the first round of balloting. (Table 2.4 presents a summary of the bills dealing with the runoff elections.)

Likelihood of Reform. The likelihood of instituting a runoff election for the presidency is uncertain. The smaller parties should favor the change because the system would increase their political influence. The two largest parties will tend to prefer retaining the current rules, unless one of the two parties believes that it is likely that it will finish in second place. Because the runoff election can be established in the electoral code (which requires only a majority vote in both chambers for approval), a reform of this sort could occur up to one year before any election in which the expected partisan alignments make it convenient.

RELATIONS BETWEEN THE EXECUTIVE AND LEGISLATIVE BRANCHES

Presidential Veto Powers

Status Quo. Provisions for the presidential veto powers are found in Article 72 (and implicitly in Article 89) of the Constitution.[24] Currently, the president may veto any legislation whose approval requires the consent of both chambers of Congress. After the second chamber has voted to approve a bill, the president has 10 days to consider the legislation, and then must either publish it or return it to the chamber of origin along with objections. If Congress is no longer in session, the president can return the bill to Congress when it next meets in regular session (this period can be as short as two and a half months or as long as five months). Thus, Mexico has no provision for a pocket veto, as is the case in the United States. Finally, a two-thirds vote in each chamber is required to override a veto.

Most constitutional scholars claim that the president cannot veto the budget because it is approved by only one chamber. However, Article 72-J states that the president cannot veto resolutions approved by a single chamber when the chamber acts during electoral or impeachment proceedings. This would leave open the contrary hypothesis that the president can veto other types of legislation, such as the budget, that are approved by a single chamber. It would seem that the framers of Mexico's Constitution intended to give the president a veto over the budget, and when some of the framers occupied the Chamber of Deputies in the first years after the 1917 Constitution was promulgated, they sustained, amended, or overrode vetoes of the budget, but did not dispute the constitutionality of those vetoes.

Diagnosis. Article 72 is certainly one of the more contradictory articles of Mexico's Constitution and is in dire need of clarification. The main problem is that the Constitution does not provide any sanctions if the president does not publish a bill after the 10-day period has expired; in fact, there are no sanctions if the president does not publish a veto override. (Both of these cases are called "pocket vetoes" in Mexican politics, though they are certainly different from the pocket veto used in the United States).[25] In the United States, Congress has the power to publish bills if the president does not do so within the required period; but in Mexico, the power to promulgate legislation is considered exclusively an executive power.

In addition, legislative uncertainty arises in cases when a bill has been approved but Congress is no longer in session. By far, most legislation is approved within the last 10 days of a legislative term—most bills, in fact, in the last two days of the session. This timing causes two problems. First, the executive branch is swamped with legislation to review; therefore the 10-day limit for accepting the bill or returning it to Congress is perhaps unreasonable. Second, the president does not have to hurry to publish the legislation; it is possible to wait until the last day before the next session begins to either publish the law or veto it. For example, Congress received Vicente Fox's veto of the Rural Development Law on the first day of the spring 2001 legislative session. The second bill vetoed by Fox (the Administrative Accountability Law) was finally published with amendments only two days before the beginning of the spring 2002 legislative session—nearly three months after both chambers had accepted the observations in the veto. Other laws tend to take weeks or months to be published, even when the president has no intention of vetoing them.

There is also the question of whether the president can veto constitutional reforms. Because these reforms require approval by a two-thirds vote in both chambers, an override should be expected. However, both chambers approve legislation dealing with constitutional reforms (falling in general under the guidelines set out in Article 72), and nothing in the Constitution expressly prohibits a veto of this kind of legislation.

In light of these problems and seeming contradictions, the constitutional provisions that apply to the president's veto powers require clarification. Some actor other than the president must be empowered to publish legislation after the time limit set forth in the Constitution has expired.

Proposals for Reform. Only one bill considered by the 57th Legislature (1997–2000) addressed the presidential veto: Pablo Gómez's bill denying the president the power to veto the budget. The CERE report did not mention the veto power in general, though it did recommend further study on whether the president should have the power to veto the budget.[26] The INEHRM forums called for giving the president line-item veto power, arguing that this approach was more efficient but omitting the fact that it would create much stronger veto power and a stronger presidency. (Table 2.5 provides a summary of all the bills dealing with the presidential veto that Congress has considered since 1999.)

The 58th Legislature (2000–2003) took up 10 bills that attempt to modify or clarify the president's veto power. First, in March 2001, the PAN's Adalberto Madero introduced a bill in the Senate that allowed the president to examine bills for 20 days (instead of 10). This proposal is reasonable in that it gives the executive branch more time for review, but it does not resolve the problem of who should publish the bill if the president refuses to do so.

On April 5, 2001, two bills proposed major changes in the president's veto power in opposite directions. The bill submitted by the executive branch would give the president "super veto" power—a line-item veto for both the budget and the revenue law.[27] According to this proposal, if Congress failed to override a presidential veto, the original text of the president's bill would remain in effect. A few weeks earlier, Fox had vetoed the first legislation in 30 years (the Rural Development Law). In Congress, the PRI and the PRD reacted negatively to his veto, claiming that it was undemocratic. In response partly to Fox's veto and partly to the administration's radical proposal for veto reform, the PRD's Luis Miguel Barbosa presented a bill that explicitly denied the president the power to veto the federal budget, the revenue law, and constitutional reforms. Furthermore, the proposal provided that Congress could override vetoes of regular legislation by a majority vote instead of a two-thirds vote. This legislation would essentially eliminate the presidential veto, allowing a veto only to suspend legislation rather than block it.[28] Two weeks later, the PT introduced a bill that also provided for a majority vote to override a presidential veto. And in March 2003, the PRI submitted bills in each of the chambers to provide for an override if the number of legislators voting to do so was equal to or greater than the absolute majority of the number of members of the chamber (251 out of 500 in the lower chamber, and 65 out of 128 in the Senate).

Luis Miguel Barbosa compromised somewhat from his original stance in a bill he submitted in May 2001. This bill did not directly

Table 2.5
Bills Amending the Presidential Veto

Legislator	Chamber	Party	Date	Details
Pablo Gómez Alvarez	Deputies	PRD	Apr. 29, 1999	No veto of the budget.
Adalberto Madero Quiroga	Senate	PAN	Mar. 27, 2001	President must veto a bill or publish it within 20 days; no congressional publication of the bill.
Executive	Deputies	PAN	Apr. 5, 2001	Line-item veto for the federal budget and the revenue law.
Luis Miguel Barbosa Huerta	Deputies	PRD	Apr. 5, 2001	Majority can override vetoes; no vetoes of constitutional reforms, the federal budget or the revenue law.
Félix Castellanos Hernández	Deputies	PT	Apr. 19, 2001	Majority can override vetoes.
Luis Miguel Barbosa Huerta	Deputies	PRD	May 23, 2001	No vetoes of constitutional reforms or the federal revenue and expenditures budget (one law in this bill).
State of Chihuahua	Deputies	NA	May 30, 2001	Either chamber can publish laws if the president refuses to do so.
Eduardo Rivera Pérez	Deputies	PAN	Mar. 22, 2002	President of the Congress can publish laws after the time limit has passed.
Uuc-kib Espadas Ancona	Deputies	PRD	Apr. 4, 2002	President must publish bills within 15 days.
Demetrio Sodi de la Tijera	Senate	PRD	July 10, 2002	No veto of the budget.
Lucio Fernández González	Deputies	PAN	Oct. 10, 2002	President must publish or veto a bill within 45 days.
Alberto Amador Leal	Deputies	PRI	Mar. 25, 2003	Line-item veto permitted; Congress can override vetoes by a vote of more than half of the whole membership of each chamber (251 in the hamber of Deputies and 65 in the Senate).
Antonio García Torres	Senate	PRI	Mar. 27, 2003	Congress can override vetoes by a vote of more than half of the whole membership of each chamber; no veto of the budget; the president of the Chamber of Deputies can publish laws after the time limit has passed.
Committee Report	Deputies	NA	Apr. 15, 2003	The president must publish or veto a bill within 30 days; if the bill is not approved on time, the president of the chamber of origin can publish the bill.

(continued next page)

(Table 2.5, continued)

Legislator	Chamber	Party	Date	Details
Luis Miguel Barbosa Huerta	Deputies	PRD	Apr. 29, 2003	Veto of the budget allowed by the combination of the revenue law and the appropriations law in a single bill if approved by both chambers.
Raymundo Cárdenas Hernández	Senate	PRD	July 30, 2003	The president of the chamber of origin can publish bills after the time limit has passed; if a bill is vetoed for reasons of constitutionality and Congress rejects the veto, the Supreme Court must resolve the question within 30 days.

change the override requirement but still prohibited vetoes of the annual appropriations and revenue legislation and of constitutional amendments. In the bill he argued that Article 72 was never meant to create a veto; it was just a means to slow down legislation and correct technical errors that the executive branch might find.

Several other bills addressed the time limits and the president's refusal to publish bills or to delay doing so. The state legislature of Chihuahua introduced a bill that allowed Congress or either chamber to publish laws if the president refused to do so. The PAN's principal bill dealing with reform of the executive branch would allow the president of Congress to publish bills after the time limit had elapsed. Another bill submitted by the PRD in the spring 2002 legislative session would require the president to publish bills within 15 days. Yet another bill, this one introduced by the PAN, regulated the amount of time that the second chamber should take to resolve votes on the veto. For example, if the Chamber of Deputies voted to affirm or overturn a veto, the Senate would be required to take a vote on the issue within 60 days.[29] The president would also have a total of 60 days to decide to veto a bill or publish it. Another bill from the PRD would allow Congress to publish bills that the president held for too long. Furthermore, if the president were to argue that a bill was unconstitutional when vetoing it and the Congress were to override the veto, the Supreme Court would resolve the question within 30 days.

In April 2003, the Chamber of Deputies approved a committee report that combined ideas from the four bills that Congress had considered in 2002. The reform would require the president to publish or veto a bill within 30 days. If the bill is not approved within that period, the bill could be published by the president of the chamber that had forwarded the bill to the executive branch. The reform bill was approved by a vote of 389 to 2, with one abstention. By the end of the first year of the 59th Legislature, the Senate had still not voted on the reform.

Likelihood of Further Reform. Article 72 is one of the most confusing articles in the Constitution. Yet, given its explanation of the procedures required for lawmaking, it is one of the most basic provisions. Unfortunately, there appears to be little consensus on what kind of reform is required. All the political parties would prefer some form of alternative publication of bills and would prefer the president to veto or publish them within a reasonable time. But there does not seem to be any agreement yet on the basic rules of the veto (such as what can be vetoed, what the override requirements are, and so forth).

Presidential Appointment Powers

Status Quo. The appointment powers of the Mexican president are found in the Constitution's Articles 76, 89 (for the cabinet), and 96 (for the Supreme Court). Currently, the president can appoint every member of the cabinet without congressional confirmation with the exception of the attorney general, whose appointment requires majority approval by the Senate.

The president nominates three finalists for each position on the Supreme Court. The Senate then elects one new justice from the list by a two-thirds vote. If the Senate rejects the entire list, the president sends a second list. If the Senate rejects the second list, the president designates one member from that list to serve on the Supreme Court.

Diagnosis. This system minimizes the legislative branch's checks and balances over the executive branch. If the system provided for congressional confirmation of presidential nominations for cabinet posts, cabinet ministers would be responsible not only to the president but also to Congress. The procedures for electing justices to the Supreme Court allow for ultimate election by the Senate but from nominees submitted by the executive branch (in the past, Congress elected Supreme Court justices directly). Even if a majority of the Senate does not like the executive branch's selection, the president can prevail if the administration's list includes a favorite nominee and two very weak ones. The Senate must act within 30 days; therefore, if the president controls one-third of the chamber, these members can block any other nominee, thus essentially allowing the president to designate the justice. In winter 2003–2004, the Senate required the president to submit a second list of candidates in order to reach the two-thirds vote required to elect a justice.

Proposals for Reform. In the 57th Legislature, five proposals were submitted dealing with modifications of the president's appointment powers. (Table 2.6 provides a summary of the bills dealing with the president's appointment powers.) One bill, presented by the coordinator of the PT in 1998, proposed that the Chamber of Deputies elect the attorney general from a list of three nominees submitted by the chamber. This system would totally remove the president's power to appoint the attorney general, arguably the cabinet member most responsible for implementing the law within the executive branch. The idea behind the proposal was to turn over responsibility for all federal prosecutors to an autonomous agency that is independent of the president. The PRD introduced a bill in 1999 that proposed that the Chamber of Deputies nominate the attorney general from a list of three finalists submitted by the president; the Senate would then confirm the nomination. This approach, which involves the executive branch and both chambers of Congress, used a selection mechanism similar to the one the Senate uses to elect Supreme Court justices.

In the most comprehensive state reform bill introduced in the 57th Legislature, Mauricio Rossell of the PRI proposed that the Senate confirm all cabinet appointments. In January 2000, the PRD submitted a bill that would require the Chamber of Deputies to confirm all cabinet members except the minister of the interior and the foreign minister.

The last bill on this topic introduced during the 57th Legislature was a PRD proposal to allow the Senate to directly elect Supreme Court justices by a two-thirds vote, designating the nominees directly without intervention by the president. The PRD introduced another bill to the same effect in the 58th Legislature, but these are the only two bills that would modify the manner in which justices are selected.

The CERE report did not resolve the question of the president's appointment powers.[30] The INEHRM forums called for confirmation of

Table 2.6
Bills Amending the President's Appointment Powers

Legislator	Chamber	Party	Date	Details
Ricardo Cantú Garza	Deputies	PT	Apr. 30, 1998	The Chamber of Deputies elects the attorney general from a list of three candidates submitted by the chamber.
María Guadalupe Sánchez Martínez	Deputies	PRD	Mar. 25, 1999	The Chamber of Deputies nominates the attorney general from a list of three candidates submitted by the president; the Senate confirms the nomination.
Mauricio Rossell Abitia	Deputies	PRI	Apr. 27, 1999	The Senate must confirm all cabinet appointments.
Isael Petronio Cantú Najera	Deputies	PRD	Jan. 12, 2000	The Chamber of Deputies must confirm all cabinet appointments, except interior and foreign ministers.
Lenia Batres Guadarrama	Deputies	PRD	Apr. 29, 2000	The Senate directly elects justices of the Supreme Court by a two-thirds vote.
Ricardo Moreno Bastida	Deputies	PRD	Sept. 26, 2000	Both chambers confirm the appointment of the attorney general.
Jesús Ortega Martínez	Senate	PRD	Oct. 31, 2000	The Senate must confirm all cabinet appointments; if the Senate does not confirm a nomination, the president sends another until one is confirmed.
Amador Rodríguez Lozano	Deputies	PRI	Mar. 27, 2001	The Senate must confirm foreign and finance ministers.
Tomás Torres Mercado	Deputies	PRD	Aug. 8, 2001	The Senate directly elects justices of the Supreme Court by a two-thirds vote.
Emilia Patricia Gómez Bravo	Senate	PVEM	Nov. 29, 2001	The Senate must confirm all cabinet appointments within eight days; if the Senate does not confirm a nomination, the president sends another until one is confirmed.
Eric Eber Villanueva Mukul	Deputies	PRD	Dec. 4, 2001	The president nominates the head of government; the Chamber of Deputies confirms the appointment.
Rosario Tapia Medina	Deputies	PRD	Feb. 13, 2002	The Senate elects the directors general of the state electricity firms from a list of three candidates submitted by the president; the Senate confirms the director of the Energy Regulatory Commission.

(continued on next page)

(Table 2.6, continued)

Legislator	Chamber	Party	Date	Details
Martí Batres Guadarrama	Deputies	PRD	Apr. 4, 2002	Both chambers confirm all cabinet nominations.
Uuc-kib Espadas Ancona	Deputies	PRD	Apr. 4, 2002	The Senate must confirm the appointment of the finance minister, the foreign minister, the attorney general, ambassadors, consuls, and so forth by a two-thirds vote; the Chamber of Deputies confirms all other nominations by a two-thirds vote.
Enrique Garza Tamez	Deputies	PRI	Apr. 16, 2002	The Senate must confirm all cabinet and diplomatic appointments by a two-thirds vote.
Demetrio Sodi de la Tijera	Senate	PRD	July 10, 2002	The Senate must confirm by all cabinet appointments.
Manuel Espino Barrientos	Deputies	PAN	Oct. 22, 2002	The Senate confirms the director of INEGI.
Fidel Herrera Beltrán	Senate	PRI	Mar. 12, 2003	Both chambers confirm the head of cabinet by a two-thirds vote.
Omar Fayad Meneses	Deputies	PRI	Mar. 20, 2003	The Chamber of Deputies nominates the attorney general; the Senate confirms the nomination.
Dulce María Sauri Riancho	Senate	PRI	July 2, 2003	The president nominates the seven-member governing board of INEGI; the Chamber of Deputies confirms by a two-thirds vote.
State of Mexico	Senate	NA	July 16, 2003	The Senate elects the head of the National Water Commission by a majority vote from a list of three candidates submitted by the president.
Raymundo Cárdenas Hernández	Senate	PRD	July 30, 2003	The Senate confirms the finance, public security, defense, navy, interior, and foreign ministers; the Chamber of Deputies confirms the other ministers; the Senate designates the attorney general and elects members of the Supreme Court from proposals submitted by the bar and law schools.

cabinet appointments by Congress and the direct election of Supreme Court justices by Congress (with no intervention by the executive branch). The 58th Legislature took up eight proposals that would modify the method of selection and confirmation of cabinet ministers.

A bill introduced by the PRD would require both chambers of Congress to confirm the attorney general. The PRI later countered with a bill proposing that the Chamber of Deputies nominate the attorney general and that the Senate confirm the appointment. Bills to create an autonomous Office of the Attorney General have proliferated in the 59th Legislature, including a bill submitted by the executive branch.

Another bill, presented by Jesús Ortega, the leader of the PRD faction in the upper chamber, would require the Senate to confirm all cabinet ministers. If the Senate rejected an appointment, the president would submit more nominations successively until one nomination was confirmed (the method used in the United States). The PVEM introduced a similar bill in the Senate, adding a time limit of eight days for the Senate to confirm the appointment. Another bill—from the PRI—would require Senate confirmation of all cabinet members by a two-thirds vote. Finally, a bill submitted by Martí Batres, the coordinator of the PRD in the Chamber of Deputies, called for a majority in both houses of Congress to confirm all cabinet ministers.

Other bills selected only certain members of the cabinet for confirmation. One of the more comprehensive state reform bills, introduced by Amador Rodríguez Lozano, would call for the Senate to confirm the foreign minister and the finance minister. A bill proposed by Uuc-Kib Espadas, one of the PRD specialists in state reform, would have two-thirds of the Senate confirm the finance minister, the foreign minister, and the attorney general, as well as ambassadors (the latter are currently confirmed by a majority vote in the Senate). The Chamber of Deputies would confirm the nominations of all other members of the cabinet. A Senate bill submitted by the PRD would provide for Senate confirmation of the finance, public security, defense, navy, interior, and foreign ministers, with the Chamber of Deputies confirming the rest of the cabinet.

Other bills called for congressional confirmation of nominees for director of the Instituto Nacional de Estadística, Geografía, e Informática (INEGI, Mexico's census and statistics agency). Another bill would have the Senate directly elect the heads of the federal electricity agencies from lists submitted by the president. Yet another proposal would allow for the appointment of the head of the National Water Commission from the president's list of candidates.

In March 2003, the PRI introduced a bill to create a position of head of the cabinet to coordinate the cabinet, with the president remaining as the head of the government. The proposal called for both chambers to confirm this appointment by a two-thirds vote.

In December 2001, the PRD introduced a bill to create the position of head of government to be nominated by the president and confirmed by the Chamber of Deputies. The head of government would be the chief officer of the cabinet and share executive powers with the president. The section on parliamentary government describes this office in greater detail.

Likelihood of Reform. It is relatively likely that there will be some modifications of the president's appointment powers. One approach would be to allow the legislative branch—probably the Senate—to confirm certain key members of the cabinet, most likely the foreign minister and the finance minister. The other likely solution would be for Congress—again probably the Senate—to confirm all nominees for cabinet positions, as is done in the United States.

There has been some movement toward homogenizing the powers of the two chambers—to have both approve the budget and treaties, leading to having both chambers confirm nominations. This change would increase the likelihood of conflicts arising between both branches of government and would probably lead to longer delays in confirmation of appointments. Perhaps the PRD's proposal—to divide the cabinet so that each chamber confirms a different subset of ministers—offers a viable solution. Nonetheless, the idea that a two-thirds vote is needed to confirm cabinet appointments is an excessive restriction on the executive branch. One minority party—with just over one-third of the vote—could essentially control nominations for cabinet posts.

Greater attention, however, should be paid to the method used for nominating Supreme Court justices. The current system gives the executive branch too much influence, but the proposal to have the Senate elect the justices directly further weakens the system of checks and balances because it eliminates the president from the process. In this case, the model used in the United States would involve giving both branches of government an equivalent veto over the selection (except that one is ex ante and the other is ex post): the president nominates a single candidate, whom the Senate must accept or reject, and in the latter case, the process is repeated until a nominee is confirmed.

Parliamentary Government

Status Quo. The section of the Constitution that relates to parliamentary government is found in Article 80, and the method of election of the president is included in Article 81. The Constitution states that the executive branch resides solely in the president of Mexico, who is elected directly by the people. The cabinet ministers and the rest of the executive branch are agents of the president, who can freely appoint and remove every member of the cabinet except the attorney general, whose appointment requires Senate confirmation; however, the president faces no restrictions on removing the attorney general from office.

Diagnosis. The president of Mexico played the predominant role in the country's political system from the late 1930s until the late 1990s.[31] Even though some analysts have blamed the excessive powers of the president on the Constitution, an examination of the document demonstrates that the legal powers of the presidency are relatively weak compared with those assigned to the chief executive in many other presidential systems.[32] A closer look reveals that most of the real power of Mexico's chief executive in the twentieth century was attributable to the partisan powers of the presidency, particularly as head of the party.[33]

Some analysts have proposed that Mexico abandon the presidential system and replace it with a premier-presidential system or a semi-presidential system.[34] These types of political systems have a president who is elected directly by the people and acts as head of state. However, these systems also include a prime minister, who is elected by the legislative branch and serves as the head of government. These systems place great emphasis on the difference between the state and the government (a distinction that is relatively incomprehensible in both the United States and Mexico).

Proposals for Reform. Proposals related to parliamentary government deal with establishing a system in which one or both chambers of Congress can remove members of the cabinet by a vote of no confidence. In addition, some propositions along these lines call for implementing parliamentary question periods. (Table 2.7 presents a summary of the bills related to parliamentary government.)

Only one proposal of this type was introduced in the 57th Legislature. The PRD bill would require the Chamber of Deputies to confirm the nominees for all cabinet positions except interior minister and foreign minister; similarly, approval by the lower chamber would be required for the removal of cabinet ministers except the two whom the chamber did not confirm. Furthermore, either chamber of Congress could "reject" reports from cabinet ministers that were not approved by two-thirds of the chamber. Even though this clause appears rather cryptic, it refers to the reports that cabinet ministers submit to Congress or its committees under Article 93 of the Constitution. Rejecting the report is a form of censure, but it does not directly entail removing the minister from office.

The CERE report came down strongly in favor of maintaining the basic presidential system but equally supported increasing the use of parliamentary procedures.[35] CERE recommended creating a Head of Cabinet office, whose director would be nominated by the president and confirmed by the Congress, with the president free to remove the person from office. The CERE report ruled against motions of no confidence. The INEHRM forums also strongly supported the idea of a head of cabinet to represent the public administration before Congress. INEHRM also proposed giving Congress the power to call the president to the chambers to explain national affairs.

The 58th Legislature considered seven bills, five from the PRD and one each from the PRI and the PAS, that would move Mexico in the direction of a parliamentary government. The most comprehensive bill is the one introduced by Eric Eber Villanueva in December 2001 proposing the creation of the office of Head of Government, with the head nominated by the president and confirmed by the Chamber of Deputies. The bill would give the lower house the power to remove the head of government by a majority vote of no confidence. The head of government would execute the law, lead the federal public administration, and submit the federal budget. The president would be the head of state, command the armed forces, and conduct foreign policy (although some PRD bills called for the president to be highly constrained by Congress on issues of foreign policy). By amending Article 80 of the Constitution, this bill also would create a plural executive, namely, the president and head of government. Raymundo Cárdenas of the PRD introduced a similar bill in the Senate near the end of the

Table 2.7
Bills that Lead toward Parliamentary Government
(independent of confirmation of cabinet appoinments)

Legislator	Chamber	Party	Date	Executive	Details
Isael Petronio Cantú Najera	Deputies	PRD	Jan. 12, 2000	President	The Chamber of Deputies must confirm all cabinet appointments and approve all cabinet removals, except for interior and foreign ministers; Congress can "reject" cabinet ministers' reports that are not approved by a two-thirds vote.
Eric Eber Villanueva Mukul	Deputies	PRD	Dec. 4, 2001	President and head of government	The head of government is nominated by the president and confirmed by the Chamber of Deputies and can be removed by the Chamber of Deputies by a vote of censure. The head of government executes the law, heads the federal public administration, and submits the budget.
Marti Batres Guadarrama	Deputies	PRD	Apr. 4, 2002	President and cabinet[1]	Both chambers confirm all cabinet nominations and can remove cabinet members; Congress must consent to the president's dismissal of cabinet members.
Uuc-kib Espadas Ancona	Deputies	PRD	Apr. 4, 2002	President	The Senate must confirm the appointment of the finance minister, the foreign minister, the attorney general, ambassadors, consuls, and so forth, by a two-thirds vote and can censure and remove any of these by a two-thirds vote; the Chamber of Deputies confirms all other nominations by a two-thirds vote and may censure and remove them by a two-thirds vote.

(continued next page)

(Table 2.7, continued)

Legislator	Chamber	Party	Date	Executive	Details
Luis Miguel Barbosa Huerta	Deputies	PRD	July 24, 2002	President	The chambers can call on members of the cabinet and require them to engage in a question period.
Beatriz Patricia Lorenzo Juárez	Deputies	PAS	Dec. 13, 2002	President	The members of the cabinet are politically responsible to the Chamber of Deputies, which can remove them if they have lost the confidence of the chamber.
Fidel Herrera Beltrán	Senate	PRI	Mar. 12, 2003	President and head of cabinet	The president nominates the head of cabinet; both chambers confirm the appointment by a two-thirds vote.
Raymundo Cárdenas Hernádez	Senate	PRD	July 30, 2003	President and head of government	The president nominates the head of government; both chambers confirm the appointment by majority vote. The head of government executes the law, heads the federal public administration, nominates members of the cabinet, and submits the budget.

Notes: (1) This bill suppresses Article 81's stipulation that the president must be elected in a direct election.

58th Legislature; the main difference in the Senate bill was the requirement for both chambers to confirm the head of government.

In April 2002, Martí Batres, the leader of the PRD faction in the lower chamber, introduced a bill to create a plural executive position made up of the president and the cabinet. This bill called for both chambers of Congress to confirm all cabinet appointments and gave both houses the right to remove cabinet ministers with a vote of censure. Furthermore, the consent of Congress would be required before the president could dismiss any cabinet ministers. In addition, the bill would modify Article 81 of the Constitution by eliminating the requirement for the president to be elected by a direct vote of the people (although the bill did not provide any details on what form the election should take).

On the same day, the PRD's Uuc-Kib Espadas presented a bill proposing that the Senate confirm the foreign minister and the finance minister by a two-thirds vote and that the Chamber of Deputies confirm all other cabinet appointments by the same margin. Furthermore, the bill would give the Senate the power to remove the two ministers it appointed as well as ambassadors, consuls, and so forth, by a two-thirds vote. The Chamber of Deputies could remove by censure any of the cabinet ministers that deputies had confirmed by the same margin. Espadas's bill, however, maintained the president as the head of the executive branch.

In July 2002, Luis Miguel Barbosa (PRD) introduced a bill that would implement a period of time set aside for parliamentary questions. In fully parliamentary systems, the legislature can call on members of the cabinet, who are agents of the members of parliament and are elected by them, to appear on the floor and explain policy and current events. Luis Miguel Barbosa proposed using the same system in Mexico. However, in Mexico, cabinet ministers are agents of the executive branch and are not directly accountable to Congress. This does not mean that Congress should not have the power to subpoena members of the cabinet under certain circumstances, but the idea of answering their questions, Westminster-style, would seriously violate the Mexican government's system of separation of powers.

Finally, in December 2002, the Social Alliance Party introduced a bill that would make the members of the cabinet politically accountable to the Chamber of Deputies. The lower chamber would have the power to remove any minister—by an unspecified extraordinary majority—if the cabinet member had lost the confidence of the deputies.

Likelihood of Reform. The likelihood that these reforms will be passed appears quite low. One would think that both the PRI and the PAN would attempt to block any proposal that creates a cabinet government responsible to the legislative branch instead of to the president. However, both the PAN and the PRI have introduced bills in the 59th Legislature to provide for a head of cabinet or a head of government, although these bills generally come up short in terms of parliamentary government. The PRD—whose power currently is concentrated in Congress, not in the executive branch—favors bills that transfer power from the latter to the former. However, the opinion of Andrés Manuel López Obrador—whose PRD government dominates the legislature of the Federal District, and whose sights are on the presidency—has yet to be heard on this matter.

The proposals that deal with parliamentary government place the entire political burden on the executive branch. Proponents forget that true parliamentary systems exhibit a total fusion of the executive and legislative branches as well as shared responsibility for government. In the proposals introduced in the Mexican Congress, a vote of no confidence would remove the proposed head of government or members of the cabinet. In most parliamentary systems, however, a vote of no confidence in the government not only would cause the government to fall but also would lead to the dissolution of parliament. In the hybrid system that some members of the Mexican Congress want to create, the legislative branch can attack the executive branch without risk. The likely outcome would be increased acrimony between the two branches, frequent dismissals of ministers who fall out of favor, greater deadlock, and less collaboration and cooperation between Mexico's chief executive and Congress.

State of the Union Address

Status Quo. Reference to the president's state of the union address is found in Article 69 of the Constitution. Most of the details on how the speech is to be given, however, including protocol, are found in the Organic Law of Congress. Currently, the president must appear before Congress on September 1 of each year (which is the date that the first session of Congress begins) and present a written report on the state of the union. The Organic Law of Congress allows each party to present its position before the president arrives. When the president arrives, he or she gives the state of the union address, although an oral presentation is optional.[36] The president of the Chamber of Deputies, who can be a member of an opposition party, then gives a short general response to the president's address.

Diagnosis. Some analysts believe there is not enough dialogue between Mexico's president and Congress. They propose that the president at least listen to the speeches of the opposition parties and perhaps even engage in a question-and-answer period after the president's address.

Proposals for Reform. No bills to amend Article 69 were submitted to the 57th Legislature, nor did the CERE report address the topic. On the other hand, the INEHRM forums concluded that Article 69 should be amended to provide for a question-and-answer period after the president's speech.

In a comprehensive state reform bill introduced by Rodríguez Lozano in March 2001, the president would deliver the state of the union address and then listen to the opinions offered by the parties in Congress. The proposal would have the parties make their presentations after the president's address, instead of before the president enters the chamber. In May 2001, the state legislature of Baja California introduced a bill in the Chamber of Deputies that would require the president to make a speech rather than just submit a written report; the proposal would only codify current practices.

President Fox presented a semiannual report on the state of his administration with his cabinet before the press in spring 2001; congressional leaders were not included in the session. Some claimed that the president did not have the right to report on the state of the union unless it was done before Congress. Thus, in reaction to Fox's semiannual report, two bills were introduced to require the president to present a semiannual report at the beginning of each session of Congress—one on September 1 and the second on March 15, when the spring session begins. The second of these bills, presented by the PVEM coordinator in the Senate, was reported out of committee on April 29, 2002, but by the end of 2004 it had yet to be voted on. (Table 2.8 presents a summary of the bills related to the state of the union address.)

Table 2.8
Bills that Amend the Procedures for the State of the Union Address

Legislator	Chamber	Party	Date	Constitutional Reform Details	Organic Law Details
Amador Rodríguez	Deputies	PRI	Mar. 27, 2001	President presents report and legislative plan in a speech; each party in Congress presents its opinion.	
Baja California	Deputies	NA	May 23, 2001	President presents report in a speech.	
Sen. Fidel Herrera Beltrán	Deputies	PRI	June 6, 2001	President presents report in a speech at the beginning of each session.	
Jorge Emilio González Martínez	Senate	PVEM	Aug.15, 2001*	President presents report in a speech at the beginning of each session.	President listens to the opinions of the parties in Congress, gives the speech, then participates in a question-and-answer session with the parties.
Julieta Prieto Fuhrken	Deputies	PVEM	Apr. 2, 2002	President presents report in a speech; Congress can subpoena the president for a more detailed report.	Question-and-answer session included as part of the report.
Juan Manuel Martínez Nava	Deputies	PRI	Apr. 2, 2002	President presents report in a speech.	Parties present their opinions after the president enters the chamber.
Uuc-kib Espadas Ancona	Deputies	PRD	Apr. 4, 2002	President submits written report eight days before presenting it in a speech, then listens to the opinions and questions of the parties in Congress, to which the president must respond.	
Jorge Carlos Ramírez Marín	Deputies	PRI	Apr. 25, 2002	President presents report in a speech on Dec. 1, except in inaugural years, when the report is delivered in a speech on Nov. 15; the	

(continued next page)

*The bill was reported out of committee on April 29, 2002.

(Table 2.8, continued)

Legislator	Chamber	Party	Date	Constitutional Reform Details	Organic Law Details
Jorge Carlos Ramirez Marín (continued)				parties in Congress may present opinions and questions, to which the president must respond.	
Genoveva Domínguez Rodríguez	Deputies	PRD	Apr. 29, 2002		President listens to the opinions of the parties, gives speech, then participates in a question-and-answer session with the parties.
Raymundo Cárdenas Hernández	Senate	PRD	July 30, 2003	Head of government presents report in a speech delivered before each term of Congress.	
Beatriz Paredes Rangel	Deputies	PRI	Aug. 7, 2003		President gives speech, then participates in a question-and-answer session with the parties.

Some of these bills would also modify the Organic Law of Congress by calling for the regulation of the form of the state of the union address and the responses by the parties. The Organic Law provides for the basic internal structures of both chambers and regulates many congressional procedures (except for debate and amendment procedures, which are covered in another law, the Rules of Congress). The PVEM bill, reported out of committee without amendments, would require the president to listen to the opinions of the parties before making the speech, then deliver the address, and finally enter into a question-and-answer period with the members of Congress. The Organic Law of Congress and the Rules of Congress regulate the internal order of the legislative branch, including the organization of the deputies in parliamentary groups and the rules of debate, but the rules of the legislative branch should not regulate the activities of the chief executive. According to Article 70 of the Constitution, the president cannot veto these bills. Therefore, amendments to the Organic Law, as reported out of committee, that increase the obligations of the president should turn out to be unconstitutional, because the president would have no way to influence this legislation.

In April 2002, additional bills were introduced to modify the format of the president's state of the union address. The most radical of these is from the PVEM and would require the chief executive to give the speech on September 1 and would give Congress the power to subpoena the president for a more detailed report; the modifications of the Organic Law would permit a question-and-answer period. It is unusual for the legislative branch in presidential systems to have the power to subpoena the president. Nonetheless, by including this provision in the Constitution, the amendments to the law would be sanctioned by Mexico's Constitution.

Five bills—three introduced by the PRI and two by the PRD—would also permit dialogue between the chief executive and the Congress. One PRI bill would only make these modifications in the Organic Law, whereas two PRI bills called for setting forth the rules for questions in the Constitution. One PRD bill would require the president to present the written report on the state of the union eight days before delivering the speech in order to give members of Congress time to formulate questions.

One bill proposed changing the date of the report. A common complaint has been that the state of the union address is delivered on September 1, only eight months after the start of the calendar year. The first report is given nine months into the administration's term (December 1 to September 1). After an administration's final report, three months pass for which no report is ever issued (September 1 through December 1, the date when the new president takes office). A bill presented by the PRI would move the date of the annual report to December 1, except in inaugural years, when the speech would be moved up to November 15. This would mean that every state of the union address would account for exactly one year of the administration's term of office, except for the final year, when the report would cover 11.5 months. The problem with this proposal is that December is the time when Congress is always busiest with legislation and is beginning to report out bills on the annual budget. The speech is always followed up by detailed reports in hearings with at least a half-dozen cabinet ministers (these hearings are sometimes held in committee, but most often on the floor of the chamber). Congress would not have time both to work on legislation and to provide oversight of the government in the 15 calendar days members are in session in December.

A proposal emerging from the Committee for State Reform in the Chamber of Deputies would establish a third regular session of Congress in the month of January, with the annual report delivered on January 15 and the rest of the session dedicated to the detailed reports submitted by cabinet ministries. According to press reports, there was consensus on this proposal, but it appears that the PRI has since dissented, and thus far nothing has been reported out of committee.[37]

In April 2004, during the 59th Legislature, the Chamber of Deputies approved a bill that would require the president to listen to the speeches delivered by the parties before giving the state of the union address but did not provide for questions and answers afterward. The Senate did not act on the bill before President Fox delivered his 2004 state of the union address.

Permission for the President to Leave the Country

Status Quo. According to Article 88 of the Constitution, the president cannot leave the country without the permission of both chambers of Congress.

Diagnosis. The rule seems anachronistic, more applicable to a time in the nineteenth century when presidents left the country in self-imposed exile with the hope of returning to power when their fortunes improved. Some believe that the rule also imposes a veto on presidential initiatives in foreign affairs. Finally, the rule creates uncertainty for countries that plan to host the Mexican president because of the possibility that Congress could reject the trip.

Before April 2002, the question of congressional approval for presidential trips abroad was academic. Then on April 9, the opposition parties in the Senate voted 71–41 to reject President Fox's request to travel to Calgary, Vancouver, Seattle, and San Francisco. The formal reasons given were that the trip did not involve state visits but had purely commercial objectives. The real reasons for congressional opposition involved differences of opinion between the legislative and executive branches on matters of foreign policy in general, and specifically relations with Cuba. As a result, Fox had to cancel the trip.

Proposals for Reform. The 57th Legislature took up two bills that would modify the rules for presidential travel. One of the comprehen-

Table 2.9
Bills that Amend the Procedures for Granting Permission for the President to Leave the Country
(All introduced in the Chamber of Deputies)

Legislator	Party	Date	Details
Mauricio Rossell Abitia	PRI	Nov. 19, 1998	Permission required for trips lasting longer than one month.
Committee on Foreign Relations	NA	Dec. 14, 1999	Permission required for trips lasting longer than 15 days.
Amador Rodríguez Lozano	PRI	Mar. 27, 2001	Permission required for trips lasting longer than one month.
State of Chihuahua	NA	May 30, 2001	Permission required for former presidents to travel for 24 months after leaving office.
Eric Eber Villanueva Mukul	PRD	Dec. 4, 2001	Permission to travel also required for the head of government.
Uuc-Kib Espadas Ancona	PRD	Apr. 3, 2002	President must submit request at least 20 days before departure; if authorization has not been denied 10 days before departure, the president may travel.

sive political reform bills, introduced by Mauricio Rossell in 1998, would require congressional approval for trips lasting longer than one month. For practical purposes, this modification would apply to trips for medical treatment only; thus, congressional permission would seem admissible. Another bill, introduced by the Committee on Foreign Relations of the Chamber of Deputies in 1999, would require congressional authorization of trips lasting longer than 15 days, which might include long trips to Europe or Asia, but not trips for most summits or for trade or state visits in the Americas. (Table 2.9 presents a summary of the bills related to presidential travel abroad.)

The CERE report did not address the issue, whereas the INEHRM forums proposed requiring congressional authorization for presidential trips lasting longer than 5 days—a period that is much shorter than the 15 or 30 days the deputies had proposed. INEHRM's proposal would still require authorization for most visits to more than one country. During the 58th Legislature, Amador Rodríguez Lozano introduced a bill that would require congressional authorization for trips lasting longer than one month. One radical bill from the PRI-controlled legislature in the state of Chihuahua would require Congress's permission for former presidents to travel for up to 24 months after leaving office—a proposal purportedly made to control lobbying by former presidents.[38] One PRD bill included a requirement for the proposed head of government to obtain congressional permission for travel abroad. Another PRD bill would require the president to submit a travel request at least 20 days before departure and would allow the president to travel if Congress has not denied authorization 10 days before the trip.

In general, the PRI has presented bills to weaken authorization requirements, the PRD has supported maintaining such requirements, and the PAN has been officially neutral but is likely to support requiring authorization only for longer trips.

STRENGTHENING THE LEGISLATIVE BRANCH

Balance of Power between the Senate and the Chamber of Deputies

Status Quo. The rules governing the balance of power between the upper and lower houses of Congress are found in Articles 73, 74, and 76 of the Constitution. The first deals with the functions of both chambers; Article 74 concerns the exclusive jurisdiction of the Chamber of Deputies; and Article 76 relates to the exclusive powers of the Senate.

Currently, although both chambers must approve all tax legislation and the annual revenue law, only the Chamber of Deputies approves the appropriations bill. Only the Senate approves international treaties, and it does so by majority vote. Neither chamber has the power to approve the six-year National Development Plan (PND). Until recently, neither chamber had the explicit power to legislate in matters of national security.

Diagnosis. There seems to be justification for allowing the Senate to participate in the appropriations process. This approach should induce greater equity in expenditures for the states, because each state sends three senators to the upper chamber.[39] Senate involvement in appropriations would also provide a backdoor for a presidential veto of the budget, unless a veto was otherwise expressly prohibited.

There is less justification for allowing the Chamber of Deputies to approve treaties, other than increasing the likelihood that treaties will be rejected. Proponents of reform often argue that Article 51 of the Constitution states that federal deputies represent the nation as a whole (not their respective districts or states), whereas the Senate represents the states.[40] Therefore, treaties are approved on the basis of Mexico's federal pact, but not by the nation.

The National Development Plan, which the president proposes early in the new administration's term of office, forms the general outline for the president's government. For example, all government activities, budget outlays, and the internal organization of the ministries should follow the framework of the plan. Some believe that Congress should have a say in the formulation of the plan, whereas others believe that the PND is essentially an executive plan and should be free of congressional meddling. It is important to note that, if Congress were granted the power to approve the PND, unless explicitly forbidden by the Constitution, Congress would automatically obtain the power to amend the PND. This development would lead to a major modification in the separation of powers.

Proposals for Reform. Balancing powers between the two chambers has been one of the areas with the greatest number of bills introduced, as has the proposal to allow congressional approval of the National Development Plan. (The bills submitted on this issue are detailed in table 2.10.) The 57th Legislature considered three such reforms. The PAN and the PRD each introduced a bill that would allow both chambers to approve treaties. The PRI presented a bill (Rossell's comprehensive reform) that provided for both chambers to approve treaties and the federal budget.

The CERE report proposed that both chambers approve both international treaties and the federal budget.[41] The Senate would be the first chamber to vote on treaties, and the Chamber of Deputies would be the chamber of origin for the budget. In the case of the budget, CERE did not recommend eliminating the presidential veto, which would emerge naturally. The INEHRM forums called for a bicameral process for passing the budget but expressly prohibited the veto. INEHRM also decided that both chambers should approve treaties, but it went further, suggesting that the Congress should instruct the president

Table 2.10
Bills to Amend the Powers of the Chambers of Congress

Legislator	Chamber	Party	Date	Details
Juan Bueno Torio	Deputies	PAN	Dec. 11, 1997	Both chambers approve treaties.
Mauricio Rossell Abitia	Deputies	PRI	Nov. 19, 1998	Both chambers approve treaties and the budget.
Luis Meneses Murillo	Deputies	PRD	Dec. 14, 1998	Both chambers approve treaties.
J. Jesús Garibay García	Deputies	PRD	Oct. 10, 2000	Both chambers approve the National Development Plan (PND).[1]
Ricardo Gerardo Higuera	Senate	PRD	Nov. 16, 2000	Both chambers approve the PND.
Amador Rodríguez Lozano	Deputies	PRI	Mar. 27, 2001	Both chambers approve the PND and the budget.
Luis Miguel Barbosa Huerta	Deputies	PRD	May 23, 2001	Both chambers approve the budget.
Martí Batres Guadarrama	Deputies	PRD	Oct. 9, 2001	Both chambers approve treaties.
Omar Fayad Meneses	Deputies	PRI	Nov. 8, 2001	Both chambers can legislate on national security matters.
Miroslava García Suárez	Deputies	PRD	Feb. 6, 2002	Both chambers approve treaties.
Uuc-kib Espadas Ancona	Deputies	PRD	Apr. 4, 2002	Both chambers approve the PND and treaties.
Luis Miguel Barbosa Huerta	Deputies	PRD	Apr. 4, 2002	Both chambers approve treaties.
Norma Patricia Riojas Santana	Deputies	PSN	Apr. 11, 2002	Both chambers approve treaties
Alberto Amador Leal	Deputies	PRI	Apr. 25, 2002	Both chambers can legislate on national security matters.
César Augusto Santiago Ramírez	Deputies	PRI	Apr. 29, 2002	Both chambers approve the PND.
Demetrio Sodi de la Tijera	Senate	PRD	July 10, 2002	Both chambers approve the PND and the budget.
Emilio Gamboa Patrón	Deputies	PRI	Aug 7, 2002	Both chambers approve the budget.

(continued next page)

[1] This is a six-year plan presented by the executive branch in the spring of the first year of the president's term.

(Table 2.10, continued)

Legislator	Chamber	Party	Date	Details
Enrique Martínez Orta Flores	Deputies	PRI	Apr. 28, 2003	Both chambers approve treaties.
Luis Miguel Barbosa Huerta	Deputies	PRD	Apr. 29, 2003	Both chambers approve the budget.
Jaime Cervantes Rivera	Deputies	PT	Apr. 29, 2003	Both chambers approve treaties.
Raymundo Cárdenas Hernández	Senate	PRD	July 30, 2003	Both chambers approve treaties, the budget, and the PND; basic or organic laws must be approved by a two-thirds vote.
Jorge Chávez Presa	Deputies	PRI	Aug. 27, 2003	The Chamber of Deputies approves the PND.

on peace negotiations (after the conclusion of a war) and approve the peace treaty.[42]

Eight bills presented during the 58th Legislature proposed that both chambers approve international treaties; all these bills, however, maintained the requirement for a majority rule for ratification.[43] Congressional opposition to Fox's international initiatives inspired the push for bicameral review of treaties. Six bills were introduced that would extend the approval of the budget to the Senate; two from the PRD expressly prohibited the veto. Five bills would allow for both chambers to approve the PND, with different rules for congressional participation in its formulation. Another bill would have the Chamber of Deputies alone approve the PND.

The PRI introduced three bills in the Chamber of Deputies dealing with national security. A proposal by César Augusto Santiago would create a National Security Council, with the participation of the executive and legislative branches, which would regulate national security planning and oversee executive investigative powers. Two other bills—one introduced by Omar Fayad and one by Alberto Amador—would simply empower Congress to pass legislation on matters of national security. In fact, it is surprising that this power did not exist, at least as an implied power, prior to 2005. These bills would also authorize executive powers in matters of national security. All three bills were introduced after September 11, 2001, and were partially motivated by the terrorist attacks. Nevertheless, all three bills generally seek to fill an important vacuum in federal constitutional law. They would provide a constitutional basis for a national security adviser, for example, or a legal foundation for the Center for Investigation and National Security (CISEN), Mexico's national intelligence agency.

On December 13, 2002, the Chamber of Deputies voted on a congressional committee report that included all three of the bills discussed above. The report would allow Congress to pass legislation on national security matters and establish limits on the president's investigative powers. The president would be formally empowered to preserve national security (as part of the president's duty to defend the nation). The bill was approved by a floor vote of 426 in favor, with 6 abstentions (all conservative *priístas*), and forwarded to the Senate, where it was approved unanimously at the end of the spring 2003 term.

Likelihood of Further Reform. Despite the evident wide support for bills that call for both chambers to share powers, in the end these proposals will face two strong sources of opposition. First, the PAN has not introduced any bills to this effect in the 58th Legislature. It is unlikely that the party is strongly opposed to any one of them, but the PAN does have other priorities, and these face some opposition from the other political parties. Perhaps some logrolling is in order. Second, these bills may fail because of each chamber's desire to protect its own prerogatives. Will the Senate really vote to give up its exclusive right to approve treaties? Will the Chamber of Deputies do the same on the budget? On the other hand, there is greater consensus on granting Congress the power to approve—and, by implication, amend—the National Development Plan presented by the executive branch. Another committee report called for granting autonomy to INEGI; the bill received a first reading in the Chamber of Deputies, but by the end of November 2004 had not yet been voted on.

Increasing the Length of the Spring Term of Congress

Status Quo. The length of congressional terms is dealt with in Articles 65 and 66 of the Constitution. The Permanent Committee, which represents the legislative branch during congressional recesses, is found in Article 78. Currently, the spring legislative session begins on March 15 and ends on April 30, allowing for only 47 days when Congress is in session. The fall term begins on September 1 and ends on December 15 (unless a special session is called because the budget is not approved until the end of the year); therefore, there is a three-month recess between the fall and spring terms and a four-month recess during the summer.

During the recesses, the Permanent Committee meets at least once a week. Standing congressional committees in each chamber can continue to meet. The Permanent Committee consists of 19 deputies and 18 senators elected by a majority vote of their respective chambers on the last day of the regular terms.[44] No rule addresses whether the committee members must be elected by proportional representation. The Permanent Committee has the power to confirm the appointments of the attorney general, ambassadors and other diplomatic officers, and treasury officials, as well as military promotions, but not appointments to the Supreme Court. The committee also can resolve authorizations for Mexican citizens to receive foreign medals or decorations and to work for foreign governments (usually in embassies).[45] In addition, the Permanent Committee can convoke special sessions of one or both chambers of Congress: the president can request such a session, as can members of Congress, but only the Permanent Committee can resolve the question. Because calling a special session requires a two-thirds vote, the question of how members of the Permanent Committee should be elected is crucial.[46]

Diagnosis. There is little doubt that the spring term of Congress is ridiculously short. Usually nothing gets approved until about April 20, leaving only 10 days for floor action on bills that have been introduced.

The Permanent Committee is also a curious institution that could be better replaced by some other body. It is important for some form of the legislative branch to exist when Congress is not actively in session for several reasons—protocol, for example, or to receive communications or call Congress back into session in emergencies. Nonetheless, the current system could lead to abuses, especially when one party holds a majority in a chamber. Recently, members of the Permanent Committee have been elected in a manner roughly proportional to each party's share of seats in Congress, but there is no constitutional or legal guarantee that this practice will always be followed.

Proposals for Reform. Between April 1998 and April 2003, a total of 14 bills to lengthen the spring term of Congress were introduced in Congress (these are detailed in table 2.11). This issue is considered one of the more innocuous reforms and is generally pleasing to all the political parties as well as the public. No one really likes the idea that federal legislators work only part-time. The deputies and senators in Congress also believe that they would be more productive if their terms were lengthened.

The CERE report endorsed lengthening the spring term to three and a half months.[47] The INEHRM forums also called for extending the term but did not provide specific recommendations. Between the 57th and 58th Legislatures, the four largest parties introduced nine bills to lengthen the spring term to anywhere between 91 and 167 days. The proposed starting dates ranged from January 15 to March 15, and the proposed ending dates from May 30 to June 30. All but three of these bills were presented during or soon after the spring term, demonstrating legislators' frustration with the short session. Also, there is a tendency over time to present bills calling for even longer terms. For example, a PRD bill introduced for Senate consideration in July 2002 called for the term to begin on January 15 and end on June 30. It should be remembered that a January opening date could also be used for the president's annual state of the union message.[48]

The Constitution stipulates that if both chambers want to end their terms early but cannot agree on the termination date, the president should set the date, a typical practice in systems that have separation of powers. The PRD has considered this option an unacceptable intrusion by the president in the affairs of the legislative branch.[49] The party has presented several bills that would end this presidential prerogative.

Two radical but plausible bills introduced by the PRD would create one year-long term, beginning in September, and completely eliminate all formal recesses, the Permanent Committee, and special sessions. This proposal does not mean that no recesses would be allowed, but that they would be informal; Congress would be required to meet at least three times each month. The idea of annual terms is not without precedent in Mexico: in 2001, the state of Baja California adopted a similar measure, which provides for three consecutive four-month terms during the year. Maintaining the shorter terms while remaining in session for the whole year is important for procedural reasons.[50]

Table 2.11
Bills to Modify the Length of the Spring Term of Congress

Legislator	Chamber	Party	Date	Begins	Ends	Total Days
José L. Gutiérrez Cureño	Deputies	PRD	Apr. 30, 1998	Mar. 1	June 30	122
Julio Castrillón Valdez	Deputies	PAN, PRD, PT, and PVEM	Oct. 29, 1998	Mar. 15	May 31	78
Isael Petronio Cantú Najera	Deputies	PRD	Jan. 12, 2000	Mar. 1	June 30[1]	122
David Rodríguez Torres	Deputies	PAN	Apr. 19, 2001	Mar. 1	May 31	92
Augusto Gómez Villanueva	Deputies	PRI	June 6, 2001	Mar. 1[2]	May 30[3]	91
Raymundo Cárdenas Hernández	Senate	PRD	Sept. 18, 2001	Jan. 15	June 30[4]	167
Martí Batres Guadarrama	Deputies	PRD	Mar. 20, 2002	NA[5]	NA	365
Felipe Calderón Hinojosa	Deputies	PAN	Mar. 20, 2002	Mar. 1	May 30	91
Uuc-kib Espadas Ancona	Deputies	PRD	Apr. 4, 2002	Feb. 1[6]	May 31[7]	120
Juan Manuel Martínez Nava	Deputies	PRI	Apr. 4, 2002	Mar. 15	June 15	93
Sara Castellanos Cortés	Senate	PVEM	Apr. 16, 2002	Mar. 15	June 30	108
José María Núñez Murillo	Deputies	PAN	Apr. 24, 2002	Mar. 1	June 30	122
Demetrio Sodi de la Tijera	Senate	PRD	July 10, 2002	Jan. 15	June 30[8]	167
Committee Report	Deputies	NA	Dec. 14, 2002	Feb. 1	Apr. 30	88
Uuc-Kib Espadas Ancona	Deputies	PRD	Apr. 28, 2003	NA[9]	NA	365

Notes: (1) The fall session would end on December 31. (2) The president would deliver his or her report at the beginning of each session. (3) The fall session would end on December 23. (4) The president would not resolve differences in closure dates. (5) Provides for one annual session, but Congress must meet at least three times per month; eliminates the Permanent Committee. (6) The president would present his or her report and answer questions at the opening of both sessions. (7) The president would not resolve differences in closure dates. (8) The president would not resolve differences in closure dates. (9) One annual session.

On December 14, 2002, the Chamber of Deputies voted on a bill to modify Article 65, moving the starting date of the spring term to February 1. A two-thirds vote is required to approve constitutional reforms. The committee report was approved on the floor by a vote of 339–75, with 22 abstentions. The PRI delegation voted 102 in favor and 57 against, with 9 abstentions (fewer than two-thirds of the priístas in the chamber voted in favor). The Senate did not approve the bill until December 15, 2003, one year after the lower chamber voted. By summer 2004, the state legislatures had approved the reform. As a result, the spring 2005 term of the 59th Legislature began on February 1.

Likelihood of Further Reform. The legislators in Congress could also consider the Baja California solution, according to which the collective presidency of each chamber, which consists of the president, vice presidents, and secretaries, would remain active during the vacations to receive correspondence and assume duties of protocol. These bodies could also call each of their respective houses into session when necessary. Unlike the members of the Permanent Committee, the officers of the chambers are all elected by a two-thirds vote.

Reelection of Federal and State Legislators

Status Quo. The prohibition on consecutive reelection of federal deputies and senators is spelled out in Article 59 of the Constitution. The rules for reelecting members of state legislatures are in Article 116 and those for members of the legislature of the Federal District are in Article 122.

Since 1933, senators, federal deputies, and state legislators have been prohibited from immediate reelection to the same post. To be reelected as a deputy, the candidate for the office is required to spend three years outside the chamber, although this time can be spent in another elected office.

Diagnosis. The prohibition on consecutive reelection is now considered one of the key explanations for the historical weakness of the Congress vis-à-vis the Mexican president.[51] In the first place, accountability is weakened in a situation in which the voters can neither reward a legislator for achievements in office nor punish a deputy for bad performance. Under these circumstances, the legislator never needs to be concerned with the opinions of the electorate and can look elsewhere for cues regarding legislative performance. For opposition legislators, the cues usually come from the National Executive Committee of their party. Before 2000, PRI deputies would also get their cues from the party leadership; but because the president of the republic was usually the real head of the party, all of the instructions came from the executive branch. When the same party controlled the presidency and majorities in both chambers of Congress, the combination of the prohibition on consecutive reelection to the legislature and the president's role as the de facto head of the party led to extreme forms of "presidentialism."[52]

Another problem with the prohibition of consecutive reelection is that it limits legislators' experience. The institutional history existing in a chamber at any time is relatively low, and the total number of federal deputies with any experience in the house has averaged 17.5 percent.[53] Consequently, few members of Congress know enough about the legislative process to pass laws without extraordinary support from the executive branch. Nor do legislators have enough experience to engage adequately in oversight of the executive branch of government.

It should be noted that the prohibition on legislative reelection does not follow from revolutionary ideology. Although the principle of banning the reelection of the president and other executive offices was an important component of the ethos of the Mexican Revolution, there was no talk at the time of prohibiting the reelection of legislators. In fact, the framers of the 1917 Constitution were emphatic about forbidding the reelection of the president but allowed the reelection of federal deputies and senators. It was only after the formation of the National Revolutionary Party (PNR), the precursor of the PRI, that the prohibition of consecutive reelection of members of Congress was proposed. At the time, this measure was probably not attributable to the need to subordinate Congress to the executive branch (with the end of divided government in 1929, most of the chief executive's bills were approved by Congress). Rather, the basic reason for banning consecutive reelection to Congress was more likely an attempt to weaken federal legislators' ties to their local political bosses. The geographical dispersion of power within the PNR was a greater threat to party leadership than lack of party discipline among federal deputies.[54]

Some analysts have objected to permitting the reelection of list deputies, because these are nominated directly by the party and do not have to run for office. Many have complained that, unlike the deputies elected in single-member districts, the list deputies are not "directly" elected.[55]

Proposals for Reform. In 1964, the Chamber of Deputies approved a bill that had been introduced by Vicente Lombardo Toledano of the Socialist Popular Party that called for reforming Article 59 to permit the reelection of deputies for a second consecutive term (but not more). The Senate (all of whom were PRI members) rejected the constitutional amendment, and the Chamber of Deputies tabled the bill after it was returned to the lower house.[56]

Juan Antonio García Villa (PAN) introduced the first recent bill to propose amending Article 59 in the 56th Legislature (1994–1997). The bill, part of a comprehensive reform submitted by the PAN to strengthen the legislative branch, called for allowing federal deputies to serve up to three consecutive terms in office (for a total of nine years) and senators to serve two (for a total of twelve years).

The 57th Legislature considered three bills that would allow for reelection of federal legislators. Mauricio Rossell (PRI) proposed that deputies be eligible to be elected for up to four consecutive terms, unless they had served as list deputies. He proposed that no candidate on the proportional representation lists could have served as a legislator in the previous legislature. Senators would be limited to two terms, but with the same limits on list senators as those placed on deputies.

A bill introduced by Julio Castrillón (PAN) and endorsed by all four opposition parties at the time proposed allowing district deputies to serve for up to four consecutive terms, list deputies for two terms, and senators for two terms. An additional bill, presented by the PRI's Miguel Quirós, proposed two terms for all deputies and two for senators. However, this bill would limit the number of deputies who could be reelected by prohibiting a party from nominating more than 20 percent of its candidates who had been deputies in the previous legislature. This restriction really runs contrary to the bills that limit reelection for list deputies. If a party can nominate only some of its members for reelection, these candidates are likely to come from the party's leadership rolls and are also more likely to be nominated on the proportional representation lists.

The CERE report dealt with the question of consecutive reelection during two roundtable discussions, each of which came to a different conclusion. The roundtable focusing on elections suggested that the reelection of district deputies and senators should be unlimited, but that list legislators could only be reelected if there were open lists. An open list system would allow voters to select candidates from the list, instead of selecting the winner from his or her place on the list. Thus, an open list system would result in weakening parties. The CERE roundtable that discussed separation of powers made two proposals. One would allow for consecutive reelection for up to 12 years for district deputies but require list deputies to run for reelection in districts. The second proposition would allow for unlimited reelection for district deputies and two consecutive terms for list deputies, who afterward would be required to run in a district. List senators would be ineligible for reelection to consecutive terms. The INEHRM forums endorsed consecutive reelection of federal legislators; however, a lack of consensus on the details led to the exclusion of specific terms of reelection in INEHRM's final recommendations.

During the 58th Legislature, five more bills proposed eliminating the ban on consecutive reelection. The PRI's Amador Rodríguez Lozano proposed three consecutive terms for deputies elected in districts but did not allow nominating a candidate who had served in the lower chamber in the previous term for list deputy. The proposal also would prohibit parties from nominating more than half of their candidates for deputy who had been deputies in the previous legislature. The bill also called for two consecutive terms for senators, with the same restriction. Furthermore, senators elected from the first minority slates would have to run in second place in the subsequent election.

The state legislature of Chihuahua proposed unlimited reelection of all deputies and senators. The bill is the simplest of all proposals dealing with the ban on consecutive reelection; it simply called for repealing Article 59.

José Francisco Yunes (PRI) proposed a liberal reelection scheme that provided for deputies to be reelected for up to six consecutive terms and senators for three terms in a row (18 years in each case). The PRI later introduced another bill that proposed a two-term limit. The leader of the PAN parliamentary group, Felipe Calderón, proposed that deputies serve four terms each and senators serve two, for a total of 12 years each. The PVEM introduced a bill in the Senate to permit the reelection of deputies for two consecutive terms but did not extend this measure to senators.

The PRD finally joined the reelection bandwagon in spring and summer 2003. The most important bill—introduced in the Senate by Demetrio Sodi (PRD) and cosponsored by PRI, PAN, and PRD senators—allowed for unlimited reelection of legislators. This bill was particularly consequential, because it was the first to be sponsored by all three political parties, and thus was not a part of their respective legislative reform bills, which otherwise tend to emphasize the particular party's vantage points. Later, during the summer 2003 recess, the PRD introduced two additional bills, one in each chamber, to allow for two or four consecutive terms for members of Congress. On February 10, 2005, the Senate voted on the Sodi bill (amended so that deputies and senators could serve up to 12 consecutive years). Many PRI senators publicly supported the bill (enough to approve the bill with the support of the PAN, PVEM, and part of the PRD), but there was also significant opposition in the PRI. To avoid a split in the party, the PRI decided to vote against the bill. The final vote was 50 in favor, 51 against, and one abstention. (Table 2.12 presents a summary of the bills introduced to permit consecutive reelection of federal legislators.)

Seven bills have been submitted that would permit the reelection of deputies in the state legislatures (see table 2.13). A bill introduced by Miguel Quirós of the PRI in June 2000 would permit one term for all deputies but allow a party to nominate only 20 percent of its delegation for reelection. The other six bills were presented during the 58th Legislature. Two—proposed by state legislatures in Baja California and San Luis Potosí—would allow reelection of state deputies under rules agreed to within each state. Bills introduced by Felipe Calderón and Demetrio Sodi would do the same. The PVEM bill presented to the Senate would allow for two consecutive terms for local legislators, as would a PRI bill that was introduced in the lower chamber.

Likelihood of Reform. The likelihood of permitting consecutive reelection of legislators is difficult to assess. Until late in the 58th Legislature, the PRD had been firmly against consecutive reelection. The PAN is generally in favor of the measure, and the PRI appears to be closely

Table 2.12
Bills to Permit the Consecutive Reelection of Federal Legislators

Legislator	Chamber	Party	Date	Consecutive Terms			Total Limit on Reelection[1]
				District Deputies	List Deputies	Senate	
Juan Antonio García Villa	Deputies	PAN	Apr. 2, 1996	3	3	2	None
Mauricio Rossell Abitia	Deputies	PRI	Oct. 29, 1998	4	1[2]	2	None
Julio Castrillón Valdez	Deputies	PAN, PRD, PT, PVEM	Oct. 29, 1998	4	2	2	None
Miguel Quirós Pérez	Deputies	PRI	June 1, 2000	2	2	2	20%
Amador Rodríguez Lozano	Deputies	PRI	Mar. 27, 2001	3	1[3]	2[4]	50%
State of Chihuahua	Deputies	NA	May 30, 2001	Unlimited	Unlimited	Unlimited	None
José Francisco Yunes Zorrilla	Deputies	PRI	Nov. 21, 2001	6	6	3	None
Felipe Calderón Hinojosa	Deputies	PAN	Mar. 20, 2002	4	4	2	None
Sara Cortés Castellanos	Senate	PVEM	Oct. 8, 2002	2	2	1	None
Omar Fayad Meneses	Deputies	PRI	Apr. 3, 2003	2	2[5]	2	None
Demetrio Sodi de la Tijera	Senate	PRD, PRI, PAN	Apr. 10, 2003	Unlimited	Unlimited	Unlimited	None
David Augusto Sotelo Rosas	Deputies	PRD	June 25, 2003	2	2	2	None
Raymundo Cárdenas Hernández	Senate	PRD	July 30, 2003	4	4	2	None

Notes: (1) Percentage of deputies of any party that can be nominated for reelection in the next legislature. (2) No one on the PR lists could have been a legislator in the next legislature. (3) No one on the PR lists could have been a legislator in the previous legislature. (4) First-minority senators must run second on their lists. (5) The previous legislature. (3) No one on the PR lists could have been a legislator in the previous legislature. (4) First-minority senators must run second on their lists. (5) The Chamber of Deputies is elected for a six-year term; halfway through the term, the PR deputies are ratified or substituted by the parties, with no federal election necessary.

Table 2.13
Bills that Permit Consecutive Reelection of State Deputies

Legislator	Chamber	Party	Date	Consecutive Terms		Details
				District Deputies	List Deputies	
Miguel Quirós Pérez	Deputies	PRI	June 1, 2000	2	2	No party can register more than 20 percent of its candidates for reelection.
Baja California	Deputies	NA	Feb. 21, 2001	U*	U*	Limits applied by states.
Felipe Calderón Hinojosa	Deputies	PAN	Mar. 20, 2002	U*	U*	Limits applied by states.
San Luis Potosí	Senate	NA	June 19, 2002	U*	U*	Limits applied by states.
Sara Cortes Castellanos	Senate	PVEM	Oct. 9, 2002	2	2	
Omar Fayad Meneses	Deputies	PRI	Apr. 3, 2003	2	2	
Demetrio Sodi de la Tijera	Senate	PRD, PRI, PAN	Apr. 10, 2003	U*	U*	

*Unlimited.

split. It is clear that a two-thirds majority cannot be found unless the PRI instructs its members to support the reform. Because the PRI has traditionally favored the no-reelection clause as a way of resolving internal party problems, it seems unlikely that the PRI will agree to the reform anytime soon. Opponents claim that any opening on the issue of consecutive reelection will inevitably lead them down a slippery slope toward the reelection of the president, which everyone opposes (at least in public).

It is possible that a very limited system of consecutive reelection could be approved, perhaps one that provides for two or three consecutive terms for members of each chamber. If any reform has a chance of being approved, the PAN's proposal seems the most viable. This step will not resolve the problems of accountability during the last term of Congress members, but perhaps this is a reform that is best taken in small steps.

It is encouraging that the last eight bills that were introduced eliminate restrictions on reelecting list deputies. This constraint has been a frequent concern among academics, who worry about strong parties, but is less problematic for the parties themselves. Limiting reelection for list deputies would have two consequences: first, it would make the list deputies second-class legislators; and, second, restricting the re-election of list deputies would hurt the smaller parties, because most of their delegation comes from the proportional representation lists. As a result, the smaller parties would be forced to send novices to every Congress whereas the larger parties could continue to reelect their deputies from districts.

Budget Reform

Status Quo. Articles 74 and 75 are the portions of the Constitution most relevant to the federal budget. The question of the veto of the budget is implied in Article 72.[57]

Before the 2004 reforms, the president had to submit the revenue law and his appropriations bill by November 15 of the year before the beginning of the new fiscal year. Because the congressional term usually ends by December 15, this schedule allowed for only one month to consider some of the most important legislation submitted every year. If Congress fails to approve the budget by December 15, members can call for a special session to approve the budget by the end of the year, as occurred when approving the budgets for fiscal years 1999, 2000, 2002, and 2004. The budget for fiscal year 2003 was approved on December 16, 2002, but because it was still considered the legislative day of December 15, a special session of Congress did not need to be called. In addition, in inaugural years the president takes office on December 1, inconveniently late in the budget season, yet the executive branch must still submit the budget by December 15 in those years. With the regular session of Congress ending on December 31 in inaugural years, the legislative branch has only two weeks—including the Christmas holidays—to review, amend, and approve the federal budget. (Similarly, in inaugural years the president has only 15 days to figure out how to modify the budget that has been prepared by the former president's Finance Ministry.)

The Finance Ministry is required to submit the public accounts to the Chamber of Deputies by June 10 of the year following the fiscal year in question. The congressional auditing agency then investigates the accounts, and the Chamber of Deputies usually passes the decree that approves the public accounts in December.

Only the Chamber of Deputies approves the appropriations bill, whereas both chambers approve the annual revenue law. There had been some controversy over whether the Chamber of Deputies can amend the budget, because the Constitution mentions only approval of the president's proposal, not modification. Nonetheless, since 1917, the lower chamber has frequently modified the bill— sometimes minimally, sometimes extensively.

Because only the Chamber of Deputies approves the budget, most constitutional scholars claim that the president cannot veto the budget, because Article 72 of the Constitution—the only article that mentions the veto—refers only to bills approved by both chambers.[58] Nonetheless, between 1917 and 1934, the president vetoed the budget 45 times.[59] And in those years, the Chamber of Deputies never complained that the president's veto was unconstitutional.

In December 2004, President Fox vetoed the 2005 budget after the opposition parties in Congress made substantial modifications to his proposal. The Chamber of Deputies refused to consider the veto, arguing (for the first time in history) that the veto was unconstitutional. The president submitted a constitutional controversy to the Supreme Court, requesting that the Court affirm his power to veto the budget and asking that certain line items be suspended until the controversy was resolved. The Supreme Court will decide on the constitutionality of the budget veto during 2005.

The Constitution is not clear on what should happen if the Chamber of Deputies does not approve the budget by the end of the year. According to Article 75 of the Constitution, the Chamber of Deputies cannot fail to pay salaries. The rest of the budget, however, would appear to be in a limbo of sorts on January 1 if the budget were not approved on time.

Diagnosis. Before the 2004 reforms were passed, the Chamber of Deputies had very little time to examine, amend, and approve the federal budget. Typically, the chamber would approve the budget bill on the last day of the fall session, after it had been reported out of committee a day earlier, at most. Thus, deputies felt rushed and unable to give the bill its due attention.

The current submission date of the public accounts is considered to be too late to prevent financial abuses.[60] Political analysts believe that an earlier date of submission is both feasible and desirable.

Before 2004, it was not clear whether the Chamber of Deputies could amend the budget or whether the president could veto the amendments made by the legislature. Over time, parliamentary practice has favored the interpretation that allows amendments to the budget. However, constitutional scholars are nearly unanimous in their rejection of a veto over the budget even when legislative procedures historically have been to the contrary. Regardless, it is important for the president to be able to veto the budget as a control over possible excesses proposed by the legislative branch.

The problem of the veto could be resolved if the Senate were allowed to approve the budget. With the budget approval process becoming bicameral, this modification could run the risk of further delay; but there is little reason to deny the Senate a role in the process. After all, the upper house already approves the federal revenue law.

Finally, many worry that economic and political instability could result from a lack of definition of financial issues because the budget has not been approved by the beginning of a fiscal year. Technically, the budget goes to zero (except perhaps for salaries), and the government might have to shut down. Concurrent resolutions to temporarily extend the current year's budget, the now normal procedure in the United States, have not been used in Mexico.

Proposals for Reform. During the 57th Legislature (1997–2000), the opposition parties united to report out of committee eight bills that moved the date of submission of the budget to September 15. (Table 2.14 summarizes these bills as well as several that were introduced in the 58th Legislature.) This reform would have given the Chamber of Deputies three months to review the budget bill. The amendment to Article 74 failed to gain approval by the necessary two-thirds vote: the roll call was 193 in favor (PAN, PRD, PT, and PVEM votes) and 175 against (PRI votes).

A consensus of the Commission for the Study of State Reform proposed setting September 15 as the date for submission of the budget.[61] However, the first four proposals introduced in the 58th Legislature set the date of submission as October 15, which would allow the Chamber of Deputies two months to review the budget legislation. These bills, sponsored by deputies from the PRD, the PAN, and the PRI, demonstrated a consensus within the legislative branch. On April 5, 2001, the executive branch introduced a bill in the Chamber of Deputies that proposed the same submission date. Two other bills moved the current submission date up five days—to December 10—in inaugural years. The president's bill was especially generous in this regard; it also set the submission date as October 15, even in inaugural years, assuming coordination between the outgoing president and the president-elect, and allowed the incoming president to make modifications to the budget until December 3.

However, the rest of the bill submitted by the executive branch was so radical (as described in the section discussing the president's veto powers) that the deputies began to react negatively. The next three bills (two from the PRD and one from the PRI) that modified the submission date in regular years set September 15, a month earlier than the date set by the prior consensus. In the spring session of 2002, all three major parties sent bills to modify the date of submission. The PAN and the PRI proposed October 15, and the PRD suggested October 1.[62] The consensus was moving back to October.

During the last week of the spring 2002 legislative session, the PAN came up with a radical proposal that called for sending preliminary macroeconomic parameters to the Chamber of Deputies by April 30 and the formal budget proposal on September 2—the day after the state of the union address and the second day of the fall session of Congress. According to the proposal, however, the Chamber of Deputies would still have only one month to approve the legislation because of the provision that the current budget was to go into effect if the budget were not passed by October 31. Of course, the Chamber of Deputies could still approve the new budget before December 31, but the uncertainty would be ameliorated somewhat.

Something of a consensus bill—sponsored primarily by the lone deputy from Convergencia and signed by several deputies from the PRI, PAN, PRD, PVEM, and PT—was introduced in May 2002. This bill set September 15 as the submission date in both regular years and inaugural years, thereby permitting the new president to send modifications within five days of taking office. The Chamber of Deputies or its committees could request the presence of the cabinet ministers or the heads of the autonomous agencies to testify about their budget requests.

The PRD submitted a bill in the Senate that would move the submission date to April 1 and require the Budget Committee of the Chamber of Deputies to make a general report on the bill by June 1. Thereafter, each committee of the Chamber of Deputies would meet in conference with the corresponding committee of the Senate to issue a report on appropriations in the areas of their jurisdiction within 60 days.[63] Because these congressional committees closely correspond to individual ministries, each committee would be able to examine the budget and engage in oversight of its respective area in the executive branch. The Chamber of Deputies would then vote on the committee's recommendations separately and send the bill to the Senate for final consideration.[64]

Therefore, with the exception of the PAN and PRD bills, which place the submission date in the spring, the consensus date appears to lie somewhere between September 15 and October 15. The former date is reasonable and is somewhat more likely to be approved. Spring submissions would require major reforms in the way the Finance Ministry and the president assemble the budget, but this modification could remain as a long-term goal for comprehensive budget reform.

A similar consensus appeared to be emerging about the submission of the public accounts by the Finance Ministry. At different times, the PAN, PRI, and PRD proposed setting the date as April 10—two months earlier than the current rules require. Other proposals have set March 15, March 31, April 30, or May 10.[65] The most likely date for submission of the public accounts would appear to be April 10.

Only one bill—the reform sent by the executive branch in April 2001—addressed whether the Chamber of Deputies could modify the budget proposal. When the proposal was under consideration, the administration contended that there was a great deal of controversy over

Table 2.14
Bills Amending the Budget Process

Legislator	Chamber	Party	Date	(a)	(b)	(c)	(d)	(e)	Reversion Point
Gerardo Buganza Salmerón	Deputies	PAN	April 7, 1998	Sept. 15	Dec. 15	Mar. 31	NA	NA	Current year's revenue law or budget.
Mauricio Rossell Abitia	Deputies	PRI	Nov. 19, 1998	Sept. 15	Dec. 10	June 10	Yes	NA	Current year's budget.
Pablo Gómez Alvarez	Deputies	PRD	Apr. 29, 1999	Oct. 1	Dec. 15	May 10	No	NA	President's budget proposal.
María de la Luz Núñez Ramos[1]	Deputies	PRD	Feb. 2, 2000	Mar. 31	Mar. 31	June 10	NA	NA	Current year's budget.
Committee Report[2]	Deputies		Apr. 28, 2000	Sept. 15	Dec. 15	NA	NA	NA	Current year's budget.
Eric Eber Villanueva Mukul	Deputies	PRD	Oct. 12, 2000	Oct. 15	Dec. 10	Mar. 31	NA	NA	Current year's budget, special session called through Jan. 31.
Julio Castellanos Ramírez	Deputies	PAN	Oct. 17, 2000	Oct. 15	Dec. 15	Apr. 10	NA	NA	Current year's revenue law or budget.
Amador Rodríguez Lozano	Deputies	PRI	Mar. 27, 2001	Oct. 15	Dec. 10	June 10	Yes	NA	Current year's revenue law or budget.
Executive	Deputies	NA	Apr. 5, 2001	Oct. 15	Oct. 15	June 10	Line item	Line item	Current year's revenue law or budget, except for the veto of congressional amendments, for which the president's original bill is the reversion point; special session should be called by Jan. 2.

(continued next page)

General note: Column headings are as follows: (a) Submission date; (b) Submission date in inaugural years; (c) Submission date for public accounts; (d) Budget veto allowed; (e) Revue law veto allowed.

(Table 2.14, continued)

Legislator	Chamber	Party	Date	(a)	(b)	(c)	(d)	(e)	Reversion Point
Luis Miguel Barbosa Huerta	Deputies	PRD	Apr. 5, 2001	NA	NA	NA	No	No	
Luis Miguel Barbosa Huerta	Deputies	PRD	May 23, 2001	Sept. 15	Dec. 15	Jun. 10	No	No	Current year's revenue law and budget (joint bill); special session called for Jan. 2.
Juan Manuel Carreras López	Deputies	PRI	Nov. 29, 2001	Sept. 15	Sept. 15[3]	Mar. 15	NA	NA	
Eric Eber Villanueva Mukul[4]	Deputies	PRD	Dec. 4, 2001	Nov. 15	Dec. 15	NA	NA	NA	
Martí Batres Guadarrama[5]	Deputies	PRD	Dec. 14, 2001	NA	NA	NA	NA	NA	
Tomás Torres Mercado	Deputies	PRD	Mar. 19, 2002	Sept. 15	Dec. 10	Apr. 10	NA	NA	
Felipe Calderón Hinojosa	Deputies	PAN	Mar. 20, 2002	Oct. 15	Dec. 15	Apr. 10	NA	NA	
Raúl H. González Villalva	Deputies	PRI	Apr. 2, 2002	Oct. 15	Dec. 15	May 10	NA	NA	
Uuc-kib Espadas Ancona	Deputies	PRD	Apr. 4, 2002	Oct. 1	Nov. 15[6]	Apr. 10	NA	NA	
José María Núñez Murillo	Deputies	PAN	Apr. 24, 2002	Sept. 2	NA	Apr. 30	NA	NA	Budget must be approved by Oct. 31; otherwise, current year's revenue law or budget. (continued next page)

General note: Column headings are as follows: (a) Submission date; (b) Submission date in inaugural years; (c) Submission date for public accounts; (d) Budget veto allowed; (e) Revue law veto allowed.

(Table 2.14, continued)

Legislator	Chamber	Party	Date	(a)	(b)	(c)	(d)	(e)	Reversion Point
José Manuel del Río Virgen	Deputies	CD,[7] PRI, PAN, PRD, PVEM, and PT	May 22, 2002	Sept. 15	Sept. 15[8]	NA	NA	NA	
José Manuel del Río Virgen	Deputies	CD, PRI, PRD, and PVEM	July 3, 2002	NA	NA	NA	NA	NA	
Demetrio Sodi de la Tijera	Senate	PRD	July 10, 2002	Apr. 1[9]	Dec. 10	NA	No	NA	Current year's budget for three months or until new budget is approved.
Sen. Emilio Gamboa Patrón[10]	Deputies	PRI	Aug. 7, 2002	Sept. 15	Dec. 15	NA	Yes	NA	Current year's budget for three months or until new budget is approved.
Alberto Amador Leal	Deputies	PRI	Oct. 24, 2002	NA	NA	Apr. 10	NA	NA	
Jorge Berlín Montero	Deputies	PRI	Nov. 14, 2002	NA	NA	Apr. 20	NA	NA	
Gilberto del Real Ruedas	Deputies	PRD	Apr. 24, 2003	NA	NA	Mar. 31	NA	NA	
Luis Miguel Barbosa Huerta	Deputies	PRD	Apr. 29, 2003	NA	NA	NA	Yes	Yes	
Uuc-Kib Espadas Ancona	Deputies	PRD	May 28, 2003	NA	NA	Mar. 10	NA	NA	

(continued next page)

General note: Column headings are as follows: (a) Submission date; (b) Submission date in inaugural years; (c) Submission date for public accounts; (d) Budget veto allowed; (e) Revue law veto allowed.

(Table 2.14, continued)

Legislator	Chamber	Party	Date	(a)	(b)	(c)	(d)	(e)	Reversion Point
Raymundo Cárdenas Hernández	Senate	PRD	July 30, 2003	Sept. 1	Nov. 9	NA	Yes[11]	Yes	Budget must be approved by Dec. 15; otherwise, the current year's budget remains in force until the budget is approved.
Jorge Chávez Presa	Deputies	PRI	Aug 27, 2003	Nov. 15[12]	Dec. 5	Mar. 15	NA	NA	

General note: Column headings are as follows: (a) Submission date; (b) Submission date in inaugural years; (c) Submission date for public accounts; (d) Budget veto allowed; (e) Revue law veto allowed.

Notes on individual items: (1) Revenue law and budget proposed by an autonomous institute. (2) Failed passage by a vote of 193–175, with one abstention (two-thirds vote required) on April 29, 2000. (3) New president can send modifications by Dec. 1. (4) Modifications to incorporate the head of government. (5) Merely requires the budget to be approved by Dec. 31. (6) President takes office on Oct. 1. (7) Democratic Center (CD). (8) New president can send modifications by Dec. 5. (9) Budget Committee of the Chamber of Deputies would be required to submit a general report by June 1, then each committee of the chamber would have 60 days to report the bill with regard to particular spending in the areas of its jurisdiction. Each committee would meet in conference with the corresponding Senate committee. The Chamber of Deputies would vote on each of the committee reports separately, then send the entire bill to the Senate under regular rules of Article 72 of the Constitution. Only the Budget Committee would submit a report during inaugural years. (10) Bill presented in the Chamber of Deputies because it also involves revenue. (11) Budget and revenue laws may be vetoed by the head of government, not by the president. (12) Preliminary budget estimates must be submitted by Sept. 5.

whether the chamber could amend the budget, but the chief executive "generously" conceded this power to the deputies.

Congress has addressed the question of the presidential veto over the budget more often than other issues—both directly and indirectly. If the Senate is allowed to approve the budget, barring an express exception, the chief executive could veto the bill. One bill introduced in the 57th Legislature by Mauricio Rossell (PRI) proposed that change, as did another bill introduced by Amador Rodríguez Lozano (then a PRI member, now an independent) in the first year of the 58th Legislature. A bill introduced by Emilio Gamboa Patrón in the Chamber of Deputies in August 2002 called for giving the Senate approval power over the budget and specified a veto for the president, although the proposal limited the time allotted for a veto to only three days.[66] Another bill, presented by Pablo Gómez, the PRD floor leader, would have prohibited a veto of the budget.

The bill submitted by the executive branch on April 5, 2001, would give the president a line-item veto for both the revenue law and the budget; the president currently has only a package veto. In case of disagreement with part of a bill, the president would send the entire bill back to the chamber of origin along with objections. The chamber could either accept the president's suggestions (totally or partially) or reject the modifications (and maintain the original version) by a two-thirds vote. If the other chamber did the same, the bill would be returned to the president for publication as amended, or the veto would be overridden, and the president would have to publish the bill as originally passed.[67]

However, the administration's proposal would allow the president to veto any modifications that Congress made to the proposed budget. If the Chamber of Deputies failed to override the veto by a two-thirds vote (or, in the case of a veto of amendments to the revenue bill, if both chambers failed to override), the president could publish the bill with the original unamended text. This reform would essentially give the president decree powers over the budget and the revenue law, which could only be overcome by a two-thirds vote of Congress.[68]

Obviously, the parties in Congress were not pleased with the proposed legislation. On the same day that the president's bill was submitted, Luis Miguel Barbosa of the PRD introduced a bill that made no modifications to other budgetary procedures but expressly prohibited presidential vetoes of the budget and the revenue law. On May 23, the same deputy presented another, more comprehensive bill that moved the submission date to September 15 and also prohibited vetoes of the two pieces of legislation. In addition, the PRD's comprehensive budget reform, presented by Demetrio Sodi, would expressly prohibit a presidential veto of the budget while allowing the Senate to consider the bill.

The executive branch clearly overstepped its bounds with its proposal. Had the bill stated only that the president could veto the budget—or implicitly created a veto by allowing the Senate to approve the budget as well—then it would be likely that the final version of the budget reform would include some sort of veto. Several bills (as well as the CERE report) have proposed making the budget a matter for bicameral approval, so the veto would have emerged naturally. However, in reaction to this overreaching by the executive branch, the legislation that is being introduced is now tending toward denying a veto to the president even when the Senate is granted the authority to approve appropriations.

The 59th Legislature passed a partial budget reform in spring 2004. The committee report combined 24 different bills on the matter. The reform modifies Article 74 of the Constitution, moving the date of the submission of the budget to September 8 and requiring the Chamber of Deputies to approve the budget by November 15. The bill specifically granted the lower chamber the power to amend the budget but no presidential veto over the budget.

Nine different bills introduced in the last two legislatures have addressed the question of what happens if the budget and/or revenue law are not passed by January 1. The problem, referred to as the reversion point in U.S. political science, is known as *reconducción* of the budget in Mexican politics. Two bills, one each from the PAN and the PRI, taken up by the 57th Legislature set the current year's budget as the reversion point in case the budget were not approved on time. Another bill in the same legislature (presented by the PRD) disallowed a presidential veto but, to compensate, set the president's original proposal as the resolution of the issue in case the budget were not approved by the beginning of the year.

The CERE report proposed that the budget for the current year be extended in case the legislation for the upcoming fiscal year was not approved in time. In the 58th Legislature, proposals by all three major parties, plus the bill submitted by the executive branch, set the current year's budget as the reversion point. Often the revenue law is treated in a similar manner. In most cases, the Constitution would allow for some adjustments for inflation, interest payments, and so on—some more specific than others (the administration's bill was particularly explicit).

Prospects for Further Reform. The 2004 budget reform resolved the timing problem, but two major questions still exist:

- Should the president have the power to veto the budget?
- What will happen if the Chamber of Deputies imposes a budget that is completely unacceptable to the executive branch?

In addition, the problem of *reconducción* is pending. The most likely reform would allow the current budget to remain in force until the new budget is approved.

The whole question of *reconducción* is probably exaggerated. The 2002 budget was not approved until the morning of January 1, which was embarrassing perhaps but did not lead to a crisis. Seven budgets have been approved without government majorities, and the other five were approved on time—usually with little time to spare. There is something to be said for having a reversion point set at zero: neither the executive branch nor the legislative branch desires this outcome. This development creates a game of chicken, for which, as everyone knows, the collision is not a Nash equilibrium—someone usually gives in at the end, and sometimes a compromise position can be reached (as has been the case with the last seven budgets). If the reversion is set at the current year's budget, then one of the two actors may prefer the status quo to the proposal (or the amended proposal), thereby increasing the players' intransigence, which is exactly what the authors of these bills fear most.

CONCLUSION

The state reform project, so highly touted by Vicente Fox during the transitional period and in the first year of his presidency, appears to be withering. Congress has made many proposals, but it has approved few. With the passage of each month of the second half of the 59th

Legislature, it is less likely that major reforms will be enacted, as the parties concentrate more on electoral competition for the 2006 presidential elections and less on cooperation on a common project: achieving political reform.

Notes

[1] Comisión de Estudios para la Reforma del Estado (CERE), *Conclusiones y propuestas*, ed. Porfirio Muñoz Ledo (Mexico City: Universidad Nacional Autónoma de México, 2001).

[2] For a summary of the state reform proposals, see http://www.usmex .ucsd.edu/conferences/state_reform.pdf

[3] The data are mostly taken from the *Gaceta Parlamentaria* of each of the chambers of Congress; for the Chamber of Deputies, see http://gaceta.cddhcu .gob.mx/; for the Senate, see http://www.senado.gob/gaceta.

[4] For details, see Juan Molinar Horcasitas, *El tiempo de la legitimidad: Elecciones, autoritarismo y democracia en México* (Mexico City: Cal y Arena, 1991); Juan Molinar Horcasitas and Jeffrey A. Weldon, "Reforming Electoral Systems in Mexico," in *Mixed-Member Electoral Systems: The Best of Both Worlds?* ed. Matthew Soberg Shugart and Martin P. Wattenberg (New York: Oxford University Press, 2001), 209–230; Jeffrey A. Weldon, "The Consequences of Mexico's Mixed-Member Electoral System, 1988–1997," in Shugart and Wattenberg, *Mixed-Member Electoral Systems*, 447–476.

[5] Actually, eliminating the list deputies would not have made a difference. The PAN would have still lacked a majority in either chamber, especially in the Senate.

[6] The only subject that affects the parties more directly is party finance reform, for which they have proposed formulas that maximize their own benefit.

[7] If the PRI had hit the ceiling and had won most of the districts, then nearly all of the list seats assigned to candidates representing indigenous voters would automatically have gone to the opposition parties, regardless of the total PRI vote among indigenous voters. The PRD could have ended up with most of the indigenous representation in Congress.

[8] Preciado became the commissioner for immigration during the first year and a half of the Fox administration. This office is also concerned with migrant workers.

[9] CERE, *Conclusiones y propuestas*, 146.

[10] The PRI did just that in 1994. The rules at the time held the PRI to the ceiling of 300 seats, only 60 percent of the chamber.

[11] Technically it is not possible to guarantee perfect proportionality while keeping the number of seats per state fixed. This bill would require some minor tinkering for the formula to work.

[12] This formula would have caused havoc in the National Society Party, in which all three deputies and the top losing list candidates were members of the nonindigenous Riojas family.

[13] These proposals would require a minor coalition partner assigned the minimum threshold of the vote for registration purposes to also get at least the same percentage of the vote for financing purposes. The PRD exploited this loophole in 2000 to increase its financing while protecting the registration of its partners.

[14] The 200-seat ceiling was proposed for the electoral law; it is not in the Constitution, thus making the ceiling unconstitutional.

[15] For details, see Molinar Horcasitas and Weldon, "Reforming Electoral Systems in Mexico," in Shugart and Wattenberg, *Mixed-Member Electoral Systems*, 209–230.

[16] CERE, *Conclusiones y propuestas*, 146.

[17] In the 2000 election, the PRI won 47 seats in the Senate by plurality or first minority, while the PAN's coalition won 38 and the PRD's coalition won 11. Had the proportional representation list been eliminated for the 2000 election, the PRI would have been one seat shy of half of the chamber, but with a 1.5 percentage point vote deficit. On the other hand, the PRI won 16 states, compared to 14 for the PAN and 2 for the PRD, so the advantage for the PRI by pure plurality would be much less. The party benefits most by the first minority rule.

[18] Electing senators by slate instead of separately has a long history in Mexican electoral law. Also, since 1940, both senators in each state were elected in the same year (the year of the presidential election, not the midterm election). This rule was temporarily abandoned in 1991, when half the Senate was renewed. In 1997, these plurality senators were replaced by senators elected according to a national list.

[19] This formula would disqualify systems that artificially create majorities for the party that wins a plurality.

[20] *Tesis jurisprudencial* 69/1998, *Acción de inconstitucionalidad* 6/1998 (Mexico City: Suprema Corte de Justicia de la Nación, September 23, 1998).

[21] Actually, the problem is more serious in the forced overrepresentation of small parties at the state level. Often parties are automatically granted seats when they reach 1.5 or 2 percent, even though the natural quotas would not grant them seats until they reached somewhere between 5 and 8 percent of the vote. This system tends to take seats away from the parties that come in second

place or third place, overrepresenting the winning party and the small parties. That, of course, is the intent of these laws.

22 On the other hand, in Guanajuato, the number of list seats varies so that the number matches the best fit possible for the legislature, taking into account the districts won by the parties. If the division of seats assigned by single-member districts happens to be exactly proportional to the vote (unlikely, of course), no list seats would be assigned. This state has the most proportional system in the country, thanks in part to the variability in the number of list seats assigned.

23 CERE, *Conclusiones y propuestas,* 143. The alternative vote, used in Australia, requires that every voter rank all the candidates on the ballot. If a candidate wins an absolute majority of the first-place votes, he or she wins. Otherwise, the second-place votes of the candidate in last place are reallocated to determine if someone has an absolute majority. If not, then the next candidate with the fewest votes is eliminated, his or her votes are reallocated, and so on.

24 For details on the veto in Mexico, see Eric Magar and Jeffrey A. Weldon, "The Paradox of the Veto in Mexico, 1917–2001" (paper presented at the 60th Annual National Meeting of the Midwest Political Science Association, Chicago, April 25–28, 2002).

25 A pocket veto in the United States occurs when Congress sends a bill to the president within the last 10 days of a legislative session. If the president refuses to sign the legislation, it cannot become law because there is no chamber to which the bill can be returned. Congress cannot subsequently override this veto, because the president never sent it back for reconsideration.

26 CERE, *Conclusiones y propuestas,* 197.

27 For details on this bill, see Eric Magar and Jeffrey A. Weldon, "Un superveto para el Ejecutivo," *Reforma* (Mexico City), April 17, 2001, p. 6A (*Negocios* section).

28 The veto in the unicameral Constitution of 1857 could also be overridden by a majority vote. The two-thirds rule was reinstated along with the Senate late in the nineteenth century.

29 The bill does not specify what should happen if the second chamber delayed beyond this point.

30 CERE, *Conclusiones y propuestas,* 176.

31 See Jorge Carpizo, *El presidencialismo mexicano* (Mexico City: Siglo XXI, 1978); Luis Javier Garrido, "The Crisis of Presidencialismo," in *Mexico's Alternative Political Futures,* ed. Wayne A. Cornelius, Judith Gentleman, and Peter H. Smith (La Jolla: Center for U.S.-Mexican Studies, University of California at San Diego, 1989), 417–434.

[32] See Matthew Sobert Shugart and John M. Carey, *Presidents and Assemblies: Constitutional Design and Electoral Dynamics* (New York: Cambridge University Press, 1992), 148–166.

[33] See Jeffrey A. Weldon, "The Political Sources of *Presidencialismo* in Mexico," in *Presidentialism and Democracy in Latin America*, ed. Scott Mainwaring and Matthew Soberg Shugart (New York: Cambridge University Press, 1997), 225–258; and Luis Carlos Ugalde, *The Mexican Congress: Old Player, New Power* (Washington, D.C.: CSIS, 2000), 124–138.

[34] For the distinctions between premier-presidential and semipresidential systems, see Shugart and Carey, *Presidents and Assemblies*.

[35] CERE, *Conclusiones y propuestas*, 175.

[36] Some state governors recently have merely handed over the printed document, witnessed the opening of the legislature, and left.

[37] The question of the timing of the state of the union address has contaminated the debate on lengthening the spring term of Congress. Dissatisfaction with the lack of resolution on this issue was responsible for some of the nay votes and abstentions in the Chamber of Deputies when the latter came to a vote in December 2002.

[38] A similar bill, from the PRD in the summer of 2002, would prohibit any former president from working for any firm, foreign or domestic, which he had been responsible for regulating during his term. In other words, former presidents would be prohibited from any employment, except perhaps in academia.

[39] Another 32 are elected by a proportional representation list and can represent any state.

[40] The INEHRM forums recommended modifying Article 51 so that federal deputies are recognized as representatives of their districts. In fact, most deputies already act as if it were so, as they certainly should, but this symbolic amendment would end a lot of sterile debate over whether deputies should represent the whole nation or their districts.

[41] CERE, *Conclusiones y propuestas*, 192.

[42] The PRD has also presented bills that would allow the Congress to intervene in foreign-policy decisions, including giving instructions to the president and setting guidelines outside of which the president is forbidden to negotiate. The INEHRM forums also recommended giving the Supreme Court, upon the request of the president or a certain percentage of either chamber of Congress, the power to review the constitutionality of international treaties before their ratification.

[43] This is surprising, considering the debate on whether certain treaties have the same hierarchy as the Constitution (particularly treaties dealing with

human rights). If treaties are of the same level, then a two-thirds rule, identical to that used for constitutional amendments, should be implemented.

[44] The relatively large size allows for the representation of each of the 32 states (by either a senator or a deputy), although this is not required. This norm was more likely followed in the years in which only *priístas* (members of the PRI) were elected to the body.

[45] Essentially, these are private bills, required by Article 37 of the Constitution.

[46] It is surprising that the Constitution does not require a two-thirds vote to elect the members of the Permanent Committee. Otherwise, one chamber, without a partisan majority, may elect its members proportionally; but the other chamber, in which one party has a small majority, may send the whole delegation of that party and thus control the two-thirds of the whole committee necessary to call for a special session.

[47] CERE, *Conclusiones y propuestas*, 198.

[48] An interesting compromise would set September 1, which opens the legislative year, for a prospective speech by the president to present the legislative agenda (along with the parties) and January 15 for a speech that is a more subdued and retrospective report on the state of the union.

[49] On the other hand, it is usually considered as a means to prevent one chamber from dominating the other.

[50] For example, in both Baja California and in the federal Congress, if a bill is defeated, it cannot be introduced again in the same term. In Baja California, this means a maximum delay of four months. For the Batres bill, consideration of a defeated bill could be suspended for up to 12 months.

[51] For greater detail, see Benito Nacif, "The Mexican Chamber of Deputies: The Political Significance of Non-Consecutive Reelection" (Ph.D. diss., University of Oxford, 1995); Ugalde, *Mexican Congress*; Weldon, "Political Sources of *Presidencialismo*," in Mainwaring and Shugart, *Presidentialism and Democracy in Latin America*.

[52] Daniel Cosío Villegas, *El sistema político mexicano* (Mexico City: Joaquín Ortiz, 1973), 29.

[53] Emma Campos, "Un Congreso sin congresistas: la no-reelección consecutiva en el Poder Legislativo mexicano, 1934–1997," (undergraduate thesis, Instituto Tecnológico Autónomo de México, 1996), 55.

[54] Jeffrey A. Weldon, "El Congreso, las maquinarias políticas y el 'Maximato': Las reformas antireeleccionistas de 1933," in *El legislador a examen: el debate sobre la reelección legislativa en México*, ed. Fernando F. Dworak (Mexico City: Cámara de Diputados/Fondo de Cultura Económica, 2003), 33–53; and Jeffrey A. Weldon, "The Prohibition on Consecutive Reelection in the Mexican Congress," *Election Law Journal* 3, no. 3 (2004): 574–579.

[55] This claim is quite false and would undermine the legitimacy of most electoral systems in the world. Considering that, for most parties, the district candidates are equally imposed by the central party leadership, there is really no substantive difference between the two.

[56] For details, see Maite Careaga Tagüeña, "Reformas institucionales que fracasan: El caso de la reforma reeleccionista en el Congreso Mexicano, 1964–1965," unpublished undergraduate thesis, Instituto Tecnológico Autónomo de México, 1996.

[57] For details, see Gerónimo Gutiérrez, Alonso Lujambio, and Diego Valadés, *Proceso presupuestario y las relaciones entre los órganos del poder: El caso mexicano en perspectiva histórica y comparada* (Mexico City: Instituto de Investigaciones Jurídicas, Universidad Nacional Autónoma de México, 2001); Ugalde, *Mexican Congress*; Jeffrey A. Weldon, "The Legal and Partisan Framework of the Legislative Delegation of the Budget in Mexico" in *Legislative Politics in Latin America,* ed. Scott Morgenstern and Benito Nacif (New York: Cambridge University Press, 2002), 377–410.

[58] See Ignacio Burgoa, *Derecho constitucional mexicano*, 9th ed. (Mexico City: Porrúa, 1994), 692; Carpizo, *El presidencialismo mexicano*, 86–87; and Felipe Tena Ramírez, *Derecho constitucional mexicano*, 21st ed. (Mexico City: Porrúa, 1985), 263–267.

[59] See Magar and Weldon, "The Paradox of the Veto in Mexico" (see note 24).

[60] See Ugalde, *Mexican Congress*, 34–35.

[61] CERE, *Conclusiones y propuestas*, 197.

[62] The PRD bill set the submission date for the inaugural year at November 15, but the inauguration was moved to October 1.

[63] This would be similar to subcommittee action in the Appropriations committees of the U.S. Congress. However, note that the conference is *before* final passage and is not held to resolve differences between versions of the bills submitted by the two chambers.

[64] In the Mexican Congress, the vote for passage occurs first, then there are votes to amend or delete articles in the approved bill. There is no final floor vote for passage of the bill as amended. Because there would be more than 20 major proposals for amendments from the committees, this could cause major chaos, as the amendments in one area might increase spending without the corresponding modifications elsewhere. If Congress were to adopt these rules, it should also change the method of voting to allow for a final vote on passage of the bill as amended. See William B. Heller and Jeffrey A. Weldon, "Reglas de votación y la estabilidad en la Cámara de Diputados," in *El Congreso Mexicano después de la Alternancia,* ed. Luisa Béjar Algazi and Rosa

María Mirón Lince (Mexico City: Asociación Mexicana de Estudios Parlamentarios, Instituto de Investagaciones Legislativas del Senado de la República, 2003), 85–119.

[65] The bill submitted by the executive branch maintained the June 10 deadline.

[66] The short time limit is probably justifiable, considering the lack of time for the Congress to resolve any presidential vetoes before the fiscal year begins.

[67] This was how Fox's second veto was resolved. Two transitional articles in the Law for Administrative Accountability for Public Servants were contradictory in the eyes of the legal office at Los Pinos, so the bill was returned within the 10-day period with suggestions for amendment. The Chamber of Deputies, then the Senate, amended the bill in the exact terms, and the president eventually published the modified bill.

[68] For details and comparisons with other countries, see Magar and Weldon, "The Paradox of the Veto in Mexico" (see note 24).

THREE

THE JUDICIAL BRANCH OF THE
MEXICAN FEDERATION

José Ramón Cossío

On January 1, 1995, several constitutional reforms entered into effect,
giving new features and powers to the judicial branch of the Mexican
Federation.[1] Significant progress in that direction had been made previously, primarily by giving new budgetary status to the judiciary and
by adjusting the scope of the Supreme Court's jurisdiction vis-à-vis
the circuit courts.[2] These two modifications, however, were made
within the framework of what can be considered the traditional structure of the Mexican judiciary, so that, despite the significance of the
changes, they made only a limited contribution to the development of
the judicial branch. These reforms did, however, result in more digni-
fied working conditions and opened the door to a new kind of discourse, which was to prove highly relevant in the years that followed.

To achieve the earlier, 1988 reform—which merely delegated certain types of cases to the collegiate circuit courts—the discussion began to center around the idea of giving the Supreme Court of Justice
the form of a "constitutional court." This idea had significant promo-
tional value because it made it possible to build an alternative rationale to the one developed in the United States—a concept that had
been fundamental in the founding of the Mexican state after the revolution. According to that initial structure—to a large extent reflecting
Mexico's nineteenth-century constitutions (those of 1814, 1824, 1847,
and 1857)—and to the one in effect today, the federal judiciary consisted of district courts, single-judge circuit courts, and a Supreme
Court of Justice; these courts were responsible for hearing federal cases or *amparo* proceedings.[3]

Translated by Monique Fernández

In 1989, the idea remained the same, except that the legitimization of the Supreme Court's loss of powers to the collegiate courts was justified by the argument that the Court itself could no longer address issues of legality, because that would be contrary to its role as a "constitutional court." This change adopted the European concept of constitutional justice as set forth in the Austrian Constitution of 1920 and later reproduced in the constitutional texts of postwar Germany, Italy, and Spain. From that point on, reforms of the judiciary in general, and of the Supreme Court in particular, have followed that track, encountering some difficulties in terms of how the Supreme Court is understood and what duties it fulfills in interpreting the Constitution.

1994 REFORMS

The reforms enacted on December 31, 1994, were of an organic and procedural nature and applied to Articles 21, 55, 73, 76, 79, 89, 94–108, 110, 111, 116, 122, and 123.[4] The president submitted his bill to the Senate on December 5, 1994, and even though he did not lay out his supporting arguments explicitly and completely, he presented the proposal in the following terms:

> By virtue of the new powers that must be conferred upon the Supreme Court of Justice and also because of the assignment of administrative duties to a specialized agency, a *more complex and highly qualified Supreme Court is sought, whose members will continue to be persons with recognized professional prestige and high moral virtue* and will be engaged exclusively in the review and resolution of the most significant legal controversies that may arise in the country. [Emphasis added.][5]

The reform appears to have followed two general tracks: (1) the Court's new powers and the justices' new status, and (2) matters concerning the creation of the Council of the Federal Judiciary and the early retirement of the justices who were active until 1994.

The Supreme Court as a Constitutional Court

At the time of the 1994 reforms, it was clear that the new understanding of the Constitution and its application within a democratic system made it necessary to grant the Supreme Court other powers in addition to hearing *amparo* cases. The *amparo* process, in fact, had proved inadequate for preserving the supremacy of the Constitution, because it could be set in motion only as a response to the violation of a particular constitutional right and its impact was limited to discontinuing enforcement of the regulation challenged in the specific case under review. For this reason, if the reforms were designed to make the Supreme Court function as a constitutional court, it would be necessary to (1) grant the Court the power to determine the constitutionality of any act by a government authority, (2) allow government agencies to defend their jurisdictions, (3) make it possible for the Court to raise abstract questions of constitutionality, and (4) give the Court's decisions general rulemaking effect. These are the powers that both characterize the kind of constitutional court that Mexico was trying to create and allow courts to become guarantors of the democratic process.

President Ernesto Zedillo's approach to achieving these goals involved a gradual broadening of the assumptions on which constitutional controversies could be based and creating the idea of the constitutional challenge, termed "action of unconstitutionality."[6] In both cases, the aim was to address potential violations of constitutional tenets, allowing the Supreme Court to declare legislation invalid with nullifying effects, provided that the ruling was rendered by a minimum of eight justices. In this way, it was believed that the Court's proceedings as well as their results would approximate those that characterized constitutional courts.

Thus far, it is clear that the idea underlying the constitutional reforms of 1994 was, to a great extent, the feature that allowed Mexico's Supreme Court to be transformed into a constitutional court. The question to be answered is: How might that reform affect the interpretation of the Constitution?[7] Considering the Court an arbiter of constitutionality was not conceived as a final stage in the Court's development, but rather as a mechanism for conferring on the Constitution its full normative function. Giving it that normative function, in turn, awoke a consolidation of the rule of law and enabled the democratic regime to manifest itself in the Constitution.

After the 1988 reforms, and especially throughout the six-year term of President Carlos Salinas and the electoral campaign of 1994, it became increasingly obvious that Mexico was on its way to becoming a pluralistic and politically complex society, in which a substantial number of social and political conflicts could no longer be resolved by appealing to the Constitution. The political monopoly in Mexico was dismantled, followed by the constitutional monopoly, triggering a process that has been called the "battle for the Constitution"—that is, a process through which various social groups sought to have their claims formally codified, because this was the only way that they could gain political viability and meaning.[8] Progress toward plurality and the desire to give it legal form brought with it the need to find channels for that change, and this could be made possible only by first granting the Supreme Court a number of new powers and then by ensuring that these powers effectively guaranteed constitutional supremacy vis-à-vis all players and phenomena in the social arena.

The reforms should have altered Mexico's understanding of the Constitution in terms of not only the changes that were expected to follow from the 1988 reform but also, and perhaps more significantly, the fully normative role that the reforms gave to the Constitution. This shift should have been reflected in the decisions of the body in charge of constitutionality, in all other aspects of constitutional practice, and in the jurists' daily activities.

However, primarily because of the composition of the Court that was appointed in 1995, as well as the fear of initiating a genuine dialogue between society and the highest court in the land, this outcome did not come to pass. As a result, Mexico's understanding of the text of the Constitution did not change, as had been anticipated. The Constitution continues to be regarded as a list of statements that define the political terms of the Institutional Revolutionary Party's authoritarianism—an outdated document that needs to be substantially modified in order to achieve democratic consolidation—or even as an intermediate phase that will be outgrown after a constituent assembly is convened. Thus, the objective the reforms sought to achieve—presumably a new understanding of the Constitution—has failed to truly materialize.

Even more important is the fact that the view of constitutional theory that originally formed the basis of the new structure of the Supreme Court has permeated the Court's own criteria for resolving many of the most important matters it has addressed.[9] This view was powerful or pertinent enough to be manifest in the application of two different criteria: (1) determining the conduct of entities that had specific legislative responsibilities for every successive design of the highest court (those determined in 1988, 1994, 1996, and 1999); and (2) serving as a guiding principle on which Supreme Court decisions are based. What is relevant to this discussion is that the second criterion operates as the theory underlying the actions of the Supreme Court. In other words, what began as an attempt to grant the Court certain types of powers (or, perhaps, to remove its jurisdiction in issues of legality) has become the primary starting point for interpreting the Constitution. The problem arising in this case is that the possible interpretations of the Constitution have been reduced as a result of the Court's inability to generate a constitutional theory or to go beyond the assumption that the Constitution itself and its jurisdictional responsibilities can be guided by a body that represents itself as a "constitutional court."

An attempt to identify the functions and ramifications that are associated with this concept shows that one aspect of these functions refers to limiting or redefining the scope of the Constitution. To the extent that the Court has failed to produce an independent construct or determination of the Constitution—that is, to ascribe its own meaning to the text—it has applied the notion under discussion as a way to reconstruct the text of the Constitution without giving it a unified meaning. Ultimately, both outcomes are possible as a result of the Court's adoption of a determining role in how the Constitution operates—precisely because of the Court's status as a constitutional court—and therefore the Court can establish the meaning of constitutional precepts without the need to refer to the determinations contained in the text itself; in other words, the Court could now rely on established precedents for its interpretation of the law.

This approach can open the door to a phenomenon that can be called "judicial decisionism" (which is therefore one of its functions)—that is, the potential to arrive at a given legal interpretation based on the idea that one is qualified to do so. A second consequence that can be identified is that such self-assigned positions encourage judicial activism[10]—a situation in which the body in charge of constitutional matters is granted the authority to reinterpret the legal problem and its solution beyond the strict limits set by the issues raised by the parties involved, procedural restrictions, or common interpretations—simply because the possibility of acting at a higher level precludes all these limitations.[11]

It is obvious that reliance on the concept of a constitutional court as a constitutional theory has, first and foremost, resulted in impeding the development of a theory of the Constitution in the commonly accepted sense of the word. A constitutional theory would focus on the text itself, its political foundation, and the functions assigned by its drafters. The theory would lay out the underlying model of political control and establish the relationships between specific excerpts or concepts and the overall sense of the document.[12]

The lack of this kind of constitutional theory has also made it possible to maintain a fragmented vision of the Constitution,[13] allowing officials to arrive at partial and inconsistent solutions instead of coming up with standards and meanings and organizing them into a coherent whole. Ultimately, this fragmented view makes it feasible to judge constitutionality in a limited way and eventually to bias results in favor of countless actions by authorities. Using constitutional theory in this way has also permitted the use of varied and inconsistent criteria for interpreting the text, which, in the final analysis, allows the courts to resolve relatively similar cases in different ways. Thus, for example, when faced with facts and issues of constitutionality that are generally comparable to one another, the Court might render very different rulings simply because it has not established rules for interpreting the Constitution, much less a method for matching cases to the rules that are applicable.

Again, these variations would be avoidable if the Court had begun by establishing—even if only in general terms—its understanding of the Constitution and its tenets. Having done so, the Court would then be able to stipulate that, to satisfy that understanding, it must base its decisions on a certain line of constitutional interpretation (and not others); that is the only possible way the Court's rulings can conform to that understanding. In conclusion, it can be argued that the lack of a constitutional theory or its reduction to a purely technical application of the concept of constitutional courts has broadened the Supreme Court's discretionary latitude, which in turn has prevented the development of an autonomous understanding of the Constitution, the fundamental basis of rule of law in Mexico.

Council of the Federal Judiciary

The reasons that led to the modification of both the Supreme Court's purview and the jurisdictional rights of its members seem to have been founded on the idea of moving toward the creation of a constitutional court. The motives behind the creation of the Council of the Federal Judiciary, however, and the dissolution and full renovation of the Supreme Court seem to have had a temporary quality and a somewhat speculative justification. In mid-1994, Mexico's so-called judicial apparatus was facing a critical situation that resulted in the creation of an agency responsible for managing the judiciary (with the exception of the Supreme Court). This step was an attempt to put an end to problems stemming from the model for the appointment of judges and magistrates that had been in effect until 1994, when, because of the rapid growth of the lower- and mid-level courts, some judges even formed influential groups within the judiciary.[14]

The positions of certain judges within Mexico's judiciary, enormous confusion about the legal issues prevailing in mid-1994, and the dynamics of the 1994 presidential campaign all led to the conclusion that it had become necessary to reform the justice system, starting with Mexico's highest court.[15] President Zedillo's reform bill seemed to justify the conclusion that the country was experiencing a comprehensive "renovation" of its judicial system, which began with dissolving and reconstituting the Supreme Court and laying the foundation for rebuilding the judiciary on the basis of professional credentials and requirements—in other words, creating the concept of a "judicial career." The mere possibility of beginning from the highest level of a government branch seems to have been the starting point required to bring about a change at its roots—almost a rebirth—by altering the method and criteria used to select the individuals who would be responsible for imparting justice in Mexico.

The hypotheses used in an attempt to understand the 1994 reforms seem to become fully valid when one reviews the reports issued by Congress, particularly the Senate opinion, which exhibited a much higher level of technical quality and introduced various modifications to the president's bill. The Senate report began by stating that "modern Mexico's greatest need is to strengthen of the rule of law." The congressional reports were based on this idea, establishing the relationship of the rule of law to the concept of democracy and then concluding that only the Constitution could guarantee both elements and only the Supreme Court could be responsible for protecting the Constitution. This is the reason for considering the need to turn the Court into a "true" constitutional court.

1999 REFORMS

The reforms enacted on June 11, 1999, affected the provisions contained in Articles 94, 97, 100, and 107 of the Constitution.[16] The reasons that led to this reform seem to have originated—however remote the connection may seem—in a speech delivered by the president of the Supreme Court of Justice on March 21, 1999.[17] In that speech, he basically outlined the main elements of the shape the reform would eventually take.

Eight days after that speech, President Zedillo submitted his reform bill to the Senate and cited several reasons for his initiative. He began his presentation by assessing the achievements of the 1994 reforms and then pointed out the need to extend the results in several directions. He stated, first, that in order to strengthen the Supreme Court's status as a constitutional court, efforts had been made to expand its power to refer to collegiate courts those cases in which the Supreme Court itself generally "deemed that its intervention was unnecessary."[18] The reasoning behind granting the Supreme Court this "power of rejection" was based on the idea that the nation's highest court should not address issues that it had already analyzed in depth to the detriment of other important matters that needed prompt resolution.[19] The president expressed this argument in the following terms: "For this reason, it is essential that we allow the Supreme Court—as other nations do—to focus all its efforts on addressing and resolving new issues or those that have a high degree of importance and transcendence and therefore have an impact on the interpretation and application of the nation's legal order.[20]

The president's second set of arguments justified the modification of the Council of the Federal Judiciary. First, according to his statement, the 1994 reforms had resulted in the creation of a new agency and a system of jurisdictional oversight and accountability unlike the one in effect previously.[21] These measures made it possible to guarantee the independence and autonomy of judges and magistrates while they were performing their duties and to "free the Supreme Court from administrative duties in order to allow it to focus all its efforts on the exercise of its important task of monitoring constitutionality."[22]

Even though the president lauded the results of the 1994 reforms, his argument held that further revisions were needed. The rationale for this need was that, if the judiciary's mission is to resolve conflicts between parties and this function should be assigned only to the courts, it was inappropriate to assign the responsibility to an administrative body as well. The argument maintained that the Federal Judiciary Council had to be, exclusively, a technically and managerially independent body, whose resolutions were also autonomous. The composition of the Council—based on appointments made by the Supreme Court in plenary session and no longer by ballot vote—was justified on the basis of the Court's ability to identify individuals who had the experience and skills required to fulfill the relevant administrative functions assigned to the Council.

In what was perhaps the most sensitive point of this part of the reform, the president's presentation specified that, in order to "harmonize organic relations between the Supreme Court and the Council," the Court was granted the power to develop and issue any resolutions it deemed necessary for the Council to function adequately.[23] The proposal even suggested that the powers to be granted to the Court did not limit the Federal Judiciary Council's own authority to issue the resolutions that it deemed relevant, which is an interesting point, because the bill also established that the Supreme Court in plenary session could revoke general resolutions issued by the Council of the Federal Judiciary, and the reform included this provision.

The president's bill was referred to the Senate's Committees on Constitutional Issues, Justice, and Legislative Studies (Comisiones Unidas de Puntos Constitucionales, de Justicia y de Estudios Legislativos) for comment. The most notable parts of this document—in an exercise intended to give the impression that it was dialectical—stated that, in light of the positive results of the 1994 reforms, it was important to continue in the same direction. In assessing the Supreme Court's new powers, the Senate—with a tremendous degree of technical inaccuracy—asserted that the power to reject a case was inspired by the U.S.

Supreme Court's use of the writ of certiorari, a claim that is obviously false. The Mexican Court has been granted express and rigid powers, but petitioning the U.S. Supreme Court is a benefit that only the U.S. judicial system provides.[24] Nevertheless, the Senate's opinion echoed the president's reasons for the reform and maintained that the power to be granted to the Supreme Court would allow it to focus its deliberations on rulings that would contribute to the improvement of the administration of justice in Mexico.

The Senate's reasons for supporting the modifications to the Federal Judiciary Council, as stated in the Senate report, began by quantifying the Council's core activities and describing them as successful. These sweeping statements were made with absolutely no qualifications, leaving the impression that it would seem contradictory to reform a body that was able to elicit nothing but praise for its achievements. The Senate's report provided only a list of justifications for the reform, pointing out that the modification would not make the Federal Judiciary Council subordinate to the Supreme Court, but rather would merely create a more precisely delineated distribution of powers between the two institutions.[25]

Having examined the fundamental characteristics of the 1999 reforms and the various reasons given by Congress, it is important to put the reform in context. The primary justification given for reforming the judiciary was that the modifications represented, in effect, a continuation or deepening of the 1994 reforms. This reason must be considered from two perspectives, given that its main thrust was twofold.

The rationale for reform of the Supreme Court was based on the fact that, since 1988, many in Mexico had joined the chorus repeating that the Court needed to be reformed in order to succeed in organizing it as a "true" constitutional court. No one seemed to know exactly what form this structure should take: whether the Supreme Court should be a European-style constitutional court, a homegrown creation, or something that resembled the U.S. Supreme Court. Apparently, the real question was how to use this rationale as a way to give any change the appearance of a progressive reform, thus lending it an air of legitimacy. The most recent reforms to the purview of Mexico's Supreme Court (1994 and 1999) succeeded only in adding one jurisdictional modification to the status quo that had been in place basically since 1950, which would allow the Court to reject certain cases and refer them to the collegiate courts. The fact is that neither the president's initiative nor the congressional committee reports have included any kind of analysis of the actual number of legal matters that reach the Court and are resolved there. On the contrary, the only statements generated were arguments to the effect that an attempt to make the Court resemble a constitutional court more closely than it did at the time required the Supreme Court to preside over fewer cases than it had previously.

The circularity of the argument is remarkable, and it is alarming that in a system in which judicial institutions are assigned specific powers, the issue of the Court's rejection of certain cases was dealt with in that way and for the reasons given. It is interesting to note that, although the model of a constitutional court generally is the European one, with the latest reforms, which were intended to make the Supreme Court approximate a true constitutional court, Mexico ended up turning instead to the solution used in the United States: the writ of certiorari.

The line of reasoning for the second major reform—dealing with the Council of the Federal Judiciary—turned out to be more complex because of the need to simultaneously claim success for the 1994 reforms and to justify the changes proposed in 1999. Thus, the presentation of the bill before Congress and the two congressional committee reports invariably began with a reference to the success of the earlier reforms and the Council's satisfactory operation, only to point out later the need to continue advancing in the same "spirit" or "direction." The first relevant issue here is that the changes were justified based on a seemingly harmless logic—that the changes involved only a fine-tuning of the distribution of powers between the Federal Judiciary Council and the Supreme Court. In reality, the reform did not propose any fine-tuning but, rather, the subordination of the Council to the Supreme Court en banc.

Once in effect, this reform affected the Supreme Court's relationship with the Council because of five provisions that gave the Court the power to

- designate four of the Federal Judiciary Council's seven members;
- propose the general resolutions the Council should enact;

- revoke the general resolutions passed by the Council;

- revoke a substantial portion of the individual decisions passed by the Council through administrative reviews; and

- try cases involving violations of individual guarantees by the Council through an *amparo* proceeding if the Court decided not to abide by the views expressed in the report of the Committees on Governance and Constitutional Issues and Justice of the Chamber of Deputies (*Comisiones Unidas de Gobernación y Puntos Constitucionales y de Justicia*).

Obviously, these provisions constituted much more than a mere fine-tuning of the functions for which the government's two judicial institutions were responsible.

In general, the 1999 reforms meant a return to some of the conditions that had prevailed in 1994, which, at the time, had led to the dissolution of the current, so-called highest court of the republic. The Supreme Court indicated that it planned to start gauging public and expert opinion on the question of whether the results associated with *amparo* verdicts (that is, the Otero formula, according to which these judicial rulings are applicable only to the winning party) should be retained. In addition, several Supreme Court justices have maintained that the Court should have the power to introduce legislation dealing with issues related to the way justice is rendered. It should be noted that adding these two powers to the Court's already extensive domain that resulted from the 1994 reforms would make the Court's position extremely powerful and—more important—its actions not subject to any type of control. In the future, Mexico's polity should avoid going along with the justices' proposals on the summary assumption that they are necessary for the creation of a "true" constitutional court, because too much accumulated power—and especially claims to it—can cause a constitutional system of checks and balances to become dysfunctional.

One of the most significant consequences of the 1999 reforms became evident when the Council of the Federal Judiciary was modified, a change that made the Council itself subordinate, to a considerable degree, to the Supreme Court of Justice en banc and to its president. The Organic Law of the Judicial Branch of the Federation, published in the official proceedings of Congress, *Diario Oficial*, on May 26,

1995, laid out the general principles and requirements for a career in the judiciary—the *carrera judicial*—establishing that principles of excellence, professionalism, objectivity, impartiality, independence, and seniority should be used as general measures of accomplishment.[26] Magistrates and judges would be selected through merit competitions based on these principles.[27] Since the time of those first appointments, a nomination system has gradually been developed and perfected and includes the following features:

- Questions have been created to test a candidate's knowledge along a large number of dimensions.
- The test has been refined in terms of the types of cases presented for the candidates to resolve.
- Experience has been gained in developing oral examinations.
- The Institute of the Federal Judiciary is providing training to those who aspire to a position in the judiciary.
- Guides have been developed for the competitive examinations.
- The necessary regulatory framework has been put in place to provide the proper support for every phase of each agency's individual merit competitions.

Through Resolution 21/1999, as published in the August 23, 1999, *Diario Oficial*, a plenary session of the Council of the Federal Judiciary voted unanimously to lay the foundation for the selection of district judges by means of a competition.[28] Using the guidelines listed above as a starting point, the Council established the principles for nominations for district judgeships.[29]

The Federal Judiciary Council's approach totally disregarded not only the constitutional assumptions associated with the concept of a judicial career but also the assumptions that were specifically reflected in the Organic Law of the Judicial Branch of the Federation. Despite the law's explicit refererence to the fact that all nominations would be based on competitive examinations—either internal or open—the judicial appointments resulting from Resolution 21/1999 were the result of nominations made directly by the Council of the Federal Judiciary. Similarly, even though the law provides for competitions consisting of a series of test phases—for example, questionnaires, test cases, an oral examination, and an evaluation based on criteria such as seniority, experience, or education—in the case of the Resolution 21/1999 appointments, only the evaluation criteria (seniority, experience, and education) were considered. All other phases of the test, which were a necessary part of a competitive examination or contest based on evaluation of expertise, were totally excluded from consideration.

The actual nature of the merit competitions used for judicial nominations brings to light a number of issues and—even at the risk of sounding speculative—it is useful to point these out. The first issue is the possibility of generating significant regulatory exceptions. One of the characteristics of modern law is that the legislative process is explained, at least legally, in its own terms—that is, the regulations enacted can refer to other rules, and the reasons given for establishing them can similarly be considered finished products in and of themselves because of the relevant legal assumptions on which the regulations were based. This requirement, however, was not satisfied in the case of Resolution 21/1999, because it does not seem possible to infer the rationale for rulemaking from the reasons given.

Another characteristic of modern legal systems is that, except for a handful of cases, legislation includes provisions to allow certain government agencies to review other agencies' decisions—first in terms of their legality and ultimately in terms of their constitutionality. This feature is not present in the case of judicial appointments made under Resolution 21/1999, however, because the conditions under which the merit competition was held would have made it difficult for an affected party to request an administrative review. In addition, parties who bring a case before a judge who was nominated on the basis of procedures that did not conform to the guidelines will have to deal with the issue of *incompetencia de origen* (judgment of illegitimacy of local authorities who had not been nominated in accordance with regulations).

The second issue that should be noted is that the merit competitions had the potential to create a situation in which the Federal Judiciary Council became subordinate to the Supreme Court. Few voices were raised to draw attention to this possibility when the judicial reforms of 1999 were passed, even though, given the origin of the reforms, this development seemed very likely.

PENDING REFORMS AND FORESEEABLE DEVELOPMENT OF MEXICO'S JUDICIARY

The judicial branch is one of the main topics of discussion surrounding the government's political agenda—not only because the judiciary is a branch of the federal government, which is sufficient reason in itself, but also because of the type of functions that various agencies that make up the judicial branch are mandated to carry out. A cursory examination of the judiciary created by the Constitution of 1917 demonstrates that the constitutional assembly sought to grant this branch the power to monitor the legality of the actions undertaken by government institutions and to take over some processes that were within the federal government's jurisdiction. Today, however, in addition to those functions, federal judicial institutions have broad responsibilities, such as controlling the constitutionality of laws and reviewing any new activities involving the Mexican state and its inhabitants. Therefore, as Mexico's society moves toward greater complexity and plurality and becomes more litigious as a result, solutions to the social conflicts affecting the majority of the population will be defined by the country's federal judicial agencies.

First, the Supreme Court has the authority to directly review the constitutionality of any laws that are enacted and international agreements that the government signs. In doing so, the Court can also review actions by federal, state, local, and municipal authorities according to a single criterion—interpretation of the Constitution as a whole—not just the individual rights it guarantees. The Supreme Court is thus in a position to intervene in political decisionmaking or, one could say, to permanently affect political arrangements or practices. Based on the Court's interpretation of constitutional precepts, the Supreme Court can determine the terms under which public power may be exercised and can intervene in cases in which it may not be exercised.

In addition to intervening in political conflicts, the federal courts make the final determination on the contents of a substantial portion of federal or local legislation. By means of direct *amparo* judgments, the collegiate courts determine whether interpretations of federal or local legislation by the respective courts are correct; and if they are incorrect, these courts can establish how the legislation is to be under-stood. Finally, the district courts and the single-judge circuit courts are in charge of hearing, among other cases, criminal cases involving fed-eral crimes such as drug trafficking—a crime that compromises both the security of the state and the public health of its citizens.

In the past, the judicial branch was viewed primarily as a set of in-stitutions designed to protect constitutional guarantees as well as the individuals who have those rights. Today, the judicial branch should also be recognized for its significant role in ultimately defining the rules of the game as they apply to the law as well as to society. Modify-ing several institutions that have such important functions will affect the balance of power in the government—that is, the distribution of the potential for exercising political power at all levels of government, as the examples discussed below demonstrate.

First of all, given the composition of the modern Supreme Court, whose 11 members determine the meaning of constitutional precepts and thereby also establish the possibility of the existence (that is, the validity) of the rest of the laws within the system, it is important to have a detailed understanding of each nominee for a seat on the Court. For this reason, the introduction of the three nominees by the presi-dent to the Senate and the nominees' appearance before that body must be done with an awareness of the significance of the nomination.

Second, it is necessary to consider the way relations between the various branches of government at the federal and local level are af-fected by granting these new powers to the federal courts. To date, guided by the notion that all the powers assigned to federal entities other than the executive branch will contribute to the exercise of de-mocracy, policymakers often have broadened the Supreme Court's ju-risdictional functions without considering the impact on the consolidation of constitutional order in Mexico. In any case, the dis-cussion of reform of the federal judiciary should take into account the general historical context of its transformation and focus on the issues covered in the conclusion of this chapter.[30]

Characteristics of the Supreme Court of Justice

An analysis of the jurisdiction of the Supreme Court and its position in the structure of the federal judiciary as a whole leads to the conclusion that the Court was based on two distinct jurisdictional models or conceptions that seem contradictory: (1) the Supreme Court is still at the head of the government's judicial branch and therefore, in principle, it should be in charge of unifying legal positions within the judiciary itself; and (2) the Supreme Court does not fulfill those functions because of the perception that it should address constitutional issues exclusively. An extraordinary peculiarity of Mexico's judicial system is that, under the pretext of trying to strengthen the Court's authority to interpret the Constitution, the Supreme Court's primacy within the judicial branch has been weakened.

Several solutions have been proposed for resolving this anomaly. One approach is to establish a higher-level body to conduct reviews within the judicial branch; this body would address certain types of rulings issued by the collegiate circuit courts, thereby unifying the policy on matters of legality. Another proposed solution involves creating a constitutional court that is independent of the judiciary and assigning this court specific functions related to constitutional issues. In view of these approaches—or even other solutions that may be proposed—it makes sense to ask: What is the most appropriate role for the Supreme Court of Justice, and what are the most appropriate functions that should be assumed by either the Supreme Court or the body in charge of ensuring the constitutionality of the nation's laws, international agreements, and government regulations?

Scope of the Judiciary's Rulings

A topic related to the nature of the Supreme Court is the question of the proper scope of application for the rulings in *amparo* cases, constitutional controversies, and what have been termed actions of unconstitutionality. *Amparo* judgments are governed by the so-called Otero formula, which provides that these judicial rulings are applicable only to the winning party. This approach to *amparo* rulings has been questioned for some time and for various reasons, including the following:

- The judgments have been blamed for producing inequities in applicable laws.
- Remedies for cases involving unconstitutional acts benefit only individuals who have higher incomes because of the expense that *amparo* proceedings entail.

- It makes no sense to preserve legislation whose constitutionality has already been questioned.

The solution proposed for addressing these complaints is to grant rulings of unconstitutionality nullifying effects so that they cannot be used as a precedent for future rulings—whether this occurs after a single judgment or through the accumulation of rulings that have the same effect.

The problem with judgments involving constitutional controversies and actions of unconstitutionality lies in the fact that, even when the possibility of declaring the unconstitutionality of challenged general legislation was established, that possibility was restricted because of the minimum of eight votes required for the ruling to pass. Particularly in the case of constitutional controversies, the rulings appeared to have been granted nullifying effects when they really continued to relate only to the parties involved in the case. To overcome those limitations, it has been pointed out that it is necessary to reduce the voting quorum required for a declaration of the unconstitutionality of a law or questionable action. To deal with legal controversies, the proposed solution is to generally nullify any federal legislation that has been declared unconstitutional.

In addition to the technical aspects of cases and to matters that are strictly related to the law, a prominent part of the discussion of rulings of unconstitutionality is the issue of the political ramifications of expanding the scope of these judgments. The decision to expand the scope of these judgments affects the system of distribution of power and, in particular, reinforces the position of the Supreme Court vis-à-vis other federal or local government agencies. It has been suggested that it is not advisable to grant new powers to an agency that does not have democratic origins, or that it is not advisable to do so at a time when the country's democratic institutions are still evolving. For this reason, the decision on the scope of resolutions issued in constitutionality proceedings is a matter that affects the form of government, the system of the distribution of power, and the role of the institutions charged with administering justice in Mexico's democratic system. Therefore, in light of successive reform proposals it is necessary to ask: What is the proper scope of decisions issued in cases involving constitutionality heard by the nation's Supreme Court of Justice and, in the case of *amparo* proceedings, heard by other bodies within the judicial branch?

Rotation of the Members of the Supreme Court of Justice

The judicial reforms of 1994 established a new staggered system of rotation of the terms of Supreme Court members: two justices were to retire from their posts in 2003, regardless of whether the departure was voluntary or forced.[31] At that time, the president and the Senate were required to nominate at least 2 members to serve on the Supreme Court, which consists of a total of 11 members. The members must be selected with care because of the significance of the Court's rulings on the issue of constitutionality and, above all, because of the transcendental nature of the Court's decisions that entail developing assumptions about the legal validity of social, political, and economic activities in the country. Therefore, it is necessary to ascertain that those who serve on the Supreme Court not only know the law of the land but also demonstrate awareness of the country's current situation and the degree of involvement and specific functions required from the Court at the time as well as an understanding of the Constitution and the scope that should be attributed to it when resolving the matters that are brought before the Court. Thus, the issue of selecting justices goes far beyond simple assessment of a candidate's level of honesty or legal expertise—simply because today the Supreme Court must address issues of overwhelming complexity and must serve as an arbiter in social conflicts as well. These demands raise another question: What qualifications are required for those individuals who aspire to be appointed to Mexico's Supreme Court of Justice?

Judicial Federalism

One dimension of the process of change that Mexico is experiencing is an increase in the number of states and municipalities requesting expanded jurisdiction. Of these, one of the most notable and compelling requests involves limiting the scope of direct *amparo* judgments.[32] By virtue of their authority to review final judgments issued by any entity with state-level jurisdiction, the collegiate courts, in effect, determine the meaning of legislation within the local legal system that may be cited in a trial. Thus, in a way, the collegiate courts represent a higher jurisdictional level in those states.

In addition to federalist motives for seeking the elimination of direct *amparo* proceedings, there are other reasons that follow the same line of thinking: (1) the enormous burden of work these matters represent for the judiciary, and (2) the delay that resolving these issues represents for the individual bringing the case, because rulings issued by the collegiate courts return to the bodies that originally issued them up to four times. Some of the reasons cited for preserving direct *amparo* verdicts have a long history, with the most significant reason summarized and highlighted as the lack of confidence in local judiciaries because of the perception that the local judges do not have the necessary qualifications, resources, or degree of influence to exert on local political officials.

Regardless of the origin of or justification for direct *amparo* proceedings, they have become the object of debate and challenges by local authorities. Among the proposals under consideration are some that deem it necessary to completely eliminate the possibility of challenging any final resolution issued by local courts. Other proposals recommend limiting the possible grounds for challenges, primarily through restrictions on the assumptions based on Article 14 of the Constitution.

Aside from the procedural considerations, the issue of eliminating (or preserving) direct *amparo* verdicts has significant repercussions for the structure of the federal judicial system and the terms under which justice is imparted to individuals. In the first case, local judges would immediately recover the authority to settle cases and to preclude the right to appeal them as well as to fully interpret state laws. In terms of social consequences, the parties' cases would be tried by local judges, and there would be no possibility of intervention by federal authorities. Issues would be resolved within a limited sphere and by people who are themselves part of the local political system. The question here is the following: Is it or is it not necessary in the end to preserve *amparo* judgments with respect to local judges' decisions, and if so, in what form should they be preserved?

Characteristics of the Council of the Federal Judiciary

Currently the Council of the Federal Judiciary as a body is subordinate to the Supreme Court to such an extreme degree that the council can be considered just another administrative agency of Mexico's Supreme Court of Justice. Given the Council of the Federal Judiciary's responsibility to appoint, train, and discipline judicial officials (including judges and magistrates) and to allocate resources to the jurisdictional bodies, the council's function continues to be extremely relevant for the adequate operation and control of the judiciary. Thus, it makes sense to ask: Will the concept of the Council of the Federal Judiciary be retained and, if so, what authority and structure will the Council of the Federal Judiciary have? Also, what should be the relationship between the council and the Supreme Court?

The Power to Submit Legislative Initiatives

According to some justices and members of the judiciary, one of the major issues that has yet to be resolved is the matter of granting the Supreme Court the power to submit legislative initiatives to Congress. Various possible solutions have been proposed thus far, and they have emanated from different agencies or jurists, including, of course, the Supreme Court justices themselves.[33] The arguments presented are very similar in all the cases that have been proposed. For example, a proposal that a group of National Action Party deputies submitted in December 1997 suggested adding some language to Article 71 of the Constitution, empowering the Supreme Court of Justice to propose laws or decrees "on matters within the jurisdiction of the judicial branch of the federation." Although the following discussion refers to this specific bill, it should be made clear that the reasons given for this proposal are similar to others commonly presented on the issue, and therefore the analysis here can be generalized to a certain extent.

The deputies' reasons for proposing additional language fall into three categories. The first is the belief that the Supreme Court is the body that is competent to submit legislative proposals because of its expertise in certain areas. However, this argument ignores the distribution of responsibilities established in the Constitution since 1994. Today's Supreme Court has jurisdiction over cases of last resort in which there is a claim that general legislation (*amparo* trials, constitutional controversies, and actions of unconstitutionality) is unconstitutional—primarily in the case of the resolution of contradictory interpretations and the investigative powers stipulated in Article 97 of the Constitution. In contrast, the Council of the Federal Judiciary is responsible for all issues related to the administration and oversight of the judicial branch, with the exception of the Supreme Court and the

Federal Electoral Tribunal. In light of this division of authority, the question arises: On what basis should the Supreme Court be considered the entity that is best suited to the task of submitting bills on matters that are within the jurisdiction of the judiciary?

The second reason for adding this language to the Constitution was based on the argument that granting such powers to the Supreme Court does not pose a danger, even if the Court were to eventually find itself in a situation in which it were compelled to review the constitutionality of laws resulting from bills introduced by the Court itself, given that in various cases the Court has modified its legal rulings and allowed its interpretation criteria to evolve. Thus, some think that the Court is unimpeded in exercising its functions of constitutional control, even with respect to general provisions arising from the Court's own autonomous initiatives; the opinion relies on the frequent renewal of the Court's members and the resulting innovation in opinions and judgments. Proponents of the idea attempted to support the deputies' proposal by appealing to the notion of empirical knowledge, shifts in judgment, and the rotation of the members of the Court. The problem with this argument is that it is not supported by empirical data.[34]

The third argument rests on a series of examples from comparative law and Mexican local legislation. However, there are two major problems with the examples drawn from other countries' legal systems: (1) in some cases, examples drawn from other legal systems have no real bearing on the subject to which a bill refers, and (2) the examples ignore the fact that a constitutional court is one thing and the judiciary is another, and in Mexico, the Supreme Court exercises the functions of both of these types of bodies. As for the examples drawn from local legislation, suffice it to say that there are no objections to granting the judiciary the power to introduce bills of law at the local level for the simple reason that the Court's agencies will never be able to pass judgment on the constitutionality of legislation that results from bills that the Court has introduced.

The bill spawned by the National Action Party's proposal to add relevant language to the Constitution seems to have been motivated by a desire to strengthen the institutions of the state so that they can act as a counterbalance to the excessive power of the executive branch. Determining whether the transition can actually be achieved in this way is a separate issue, but it seems necessary to recognize that Mexico's constitutional system includes institutions that already serve certain functions. Therefore, before assigning new ones, it is important to consider how the proposed new functions would affect the ones that already exist. In any case, there is no reason to believe that weakening the executive branch would necessarily be accompanied by more powers granted to the Supreme Court of Justice.

Allocation of a Fixed Percentage of the Federation's Expenditures Budget

One last matter to be discussed is the idea of allocating a fixed percentage of the federal budget to the judiciary. The problem here is that this notion clashes with republican principles, because there seems to be no justification for requiring all federal institutions to appear before the Chamber of Deputies to negotiate and justify the budgetary percentages they hope will be allocated to them and, at the same time, placing a small number of courts in the exceptional position of not having to do so. Arguably, this provision would give the institutions of the judicial branch greater autonomy vis-à-vis other public institutions, but extreme care must be taken to avoid a situation that allows the judiciary to avoid all democratic controls, because the very nature of its formation makes it inherently exempt from them.

THE UNFINISHED STATE OF JUDICIAL REFORM: CONTEXT AND PERSPECTIVES

The idea of the unfinished state of judicial reform in Mexico is an essential part of the subject itself; in other words, judicial reform cannot ever be considered complete. Why? Different kinds of social conflicts are resolved through the justice system; in a legal system that has its origins in Roman law, these conflicts are reflected with some precision in statutes. Therefore, for the organs of this system to be able to deal with the conflicts before them, statutes must be renewed constantly. Thus, creating new statutes or changing existing ones is predictable; examples include establishing new appointment procedures, making new subjects the object of judicial adjudication, simplifying and reducing the number of legal procedures, creating new procedural possibilities for remedies (such as class action suits), and establishing

accountability controls over judges. If the justice system remains un-
changed, a gap between social problems and legal remedies will be
generated. Sooner or later, this gap will lead to a crisis, even if it is
just a problem involving the legitimacy of the justice system.

If this initial and brief diagnosis is correct, a question arises: Within
the current context of the country, what should be understood by "judicial reform"? Furthermore, what reasons lead to the assertion that
the reform remains "unfinished"? If something is considered to be unfinished, it is still in progress; the process began at some point and has
a foreseeable end. Nevertheless, as has been stated, judicial reform is a
continuum. Therefore, it is necessary to consider the current reform as
a stage—a fragment of a whole that mutates constantly.

To adequately assess where Mexico finds itself in its efforts to enact judicial reform, it is important to identify the different stages in
the process and then determine the features of the one currently in
progress. Only then will it be possible to identify what is still pending
before the stage can be concluded. This endeavor is clearly beyond
the limits of this discussion; therefore, the analysis must take into account only the federal level of the justice system.[35] To understand the
distinction, it should be noted that the original text of the 1917 Constitution contained a reference to the federal justice system that was limited only to the federal judicial branch: the Supreme Court of Justice,
circuit and unitary courts, and district courts, which are organized in
an organic structure similar to the federal justice system in the United
States.

The process of federal judicial reform in Mexico can be divided into
three stages. The broad rationalization of the justice system—not the
diversity of particular changes—will characterize these stages and determine the order in which they will take place.

The first stage coincided with the creation of the administrative
courts—initially the establishment of boards of conciliation and arbitration (*juntas de conciliación y arbitraje*),[36] followed by the Federal
Tax Court (Tribunal Fiscal de la Federación), and years later by the
Federal Court of Conciliation and Arbitration (Tribunal Federal de
Conciliación y Arbitraje). The leading idea behind this stage was to
create judicial-administrative organs outside the federal judicial
branch and within the sphere of the Federal Public Administration
and to give these organs the power to solve, in the order cited above,

legal conflicts between workers and their employers, taxpayers and the government's taxation agency, and bureaucrats and the state in the role of employer.[37]

The second stage can be identified with the problem of docket over-flow that afflicted the federal judicial branch just a few years after the 1917 Constitution was implemented. This stage temporarily over-lapped with the first stage, and it was characterized by an increase in the membership of the Supreme Court from 11 to 26 justices, the es-tablishment of the circuit courts, and the substantial modification of the Court's jurisdictional rights, thus leaving the Supreme Court in charge of certain functions and delegating the rest to the newly created circuit courts. The large number of pending resolutions was attribut-able to the Supreme Court's power to review practically every decision reached not only by federal courts and tribunals (mentioned in the first stage) but also by the states and the Federal District as well as most resolutions related to a whole range of legal issues (civil, criminal, commerce, tax, labor, and so forth). Far from modifying the organic and jurisdictional structure of the judicial system to make it more ra-tional and efficient, this model created new organs to manage an ever-increasing number of cases and modified the Court's jurisdictional functions in order to avoid the problem of the Supreme Court's accu-mulating a large number of unsolved cases (which, in the early 1950s totaled 30,000).

The third stage of federal judicial reform in Mexico was linked tem-porarily and structurally to the conclusion of the second stage and is characterized, first and foremost, by the transformation of the Su-preme Court from the highest tribunal within the country's judicial branch to a body empowered to resolve problems related almost exclu-sively to the enforcement and interpretation of the federal Constitu-tion. This objective required several modifications, including giving the circuit courts the power to resolve legal issues not directly related to the Constitution and transferring the Supreme Court's administra-tive responsibilities to the Council of the Federal Judiciary.[38] The final modification needed was the creation of new procedures to allow oth-er authorities at the same level of government to directly contest the constitutionality of general norms and actions of federal, state, and municipal officials *(controversias constitucionales)* or to enable congressional minorities to contest the constitutionality of the decisions taken by the majority (*acciones de inconstitucionalidad*).

From the point of view of this author, this last stage of judicial reform has been concluded. Since 1951, enough amendments to the Constitution have been passed to give Mexico's Supreme Court the character of a constitutional court, making it a unique combination of the U.S. and European models. This stage could be developed further by introducing certain modifications that would strengthen the model that Mexico has chosen. These changes include reinforcing the Council of the Federal Judiciary and creating a federal court of appeals, following, in some respects, an idea that Chief Justice Warren Burger propounded in the United States in the 1970s.[39]

It is within this context—the conclusion and consolidation of the final stage of judicial reform—that the unfinished state of judicial reform must be understood. Almost everyone believes that Mexico's justice system is undergoing a problematic period, and there is consensus that reforms are necessary. However, there has been no agreement about what aspects need to be reformed and how the reforms should be undertaken. On the one hand, the system is at a point where the previous stages have been concluded; on the other hand, it is not possible to imagine what changes are needed to solve the country's most pressing problems.

This paradox has various roots, only some of which can be addressed here. For one, the diagnosis may be wrong. If the malady is not identified correctly, a remedy cannot be devised. Second, even if the problems are known, the solutions may not be clear. If this second possibility is accurate, it seems important to acknowledge that the system has been insisting that the solutions can be achieved by means of partial and minor modifications rather than by deep structural changes. A third possibility is that the system might be trying to devise a large number of partial solutions, and their diversity and the potential contradiction between them is generating more problems rather than solving existing ones.

Considering these alternatives, it seems that Mexico's judicial system is facing a combination of factors that have an impact on future reforms. On the one hand, the problems that afflict the system have been diagnosed incorrectly: for example, the assumption that the

power of review of practically all decisions made by the country's judicial organs must be eliminated because of the amount of cases that
have accumulated on a court's docket and not because of the distortions this generates in the federal system. On the other hand, continuing with the same example, another problem arises from the
perception that completely eliminating this form of judicial review
would go against the structure of the Mexican legal system and, therefore, the most convenient solution is to introduce only minor adjustments. Hence, this approach results in knowingly not solving the
fundamental problem.

The only way out of this stagnant situation is to provoke a national
debate on the topic, discuss the problems that plague the judicial system, and develop the most viable solutions, thereby producing a new
stage of judicial reform. For the discussions to lead to a conclusion it is
important to avoid arguing for the best abstract technical solution and
instead to guide the discussions along functional criteria, concentrating on each of the integral parts of the system. The perceived end points
that each of the particular reforms is expected to achieve must be determined and then integrated as part of a master plan to be developed over
a period of time through a combination of statutory amendments and
implementation of policies.

In August 2003, the Supreme Court initiated a consultation process
that was directed toward different sectors of Mexican society and designed to expound their own diagnosis of the problems facing Mexico's justice system and possible solutions to them. By August 2004,
4,800 proposals had been received from judges, barristers, public servants, academics and nongovernmental organizations. All these proposals have now been classified, and several groups of experts will start
sorting through the information and analyzing it. At the conclusion of
this process, a master plan will be elaborated in order to determine
what features need to be reformed and how and when the reforms
should be enacted. A second group of experts—in collaboration with
the country's political actors—will then prepare a set of proposals to
present to the government for approval.

These steps will enable the members of the Supreme Court to work
with Mexico's legal profession and political actors and to assume a
fundamental role in the fourth stage of the process of ongoing reform

of the judicial system. By undertaking this task, we hope to create a better system of justice for the Mexican people in the twenty-first century.

Notes

[1] The discussion of the judiciary reforms refers to the Supreme Court, the collegiate and single-judge circuit courts, and the Council of the Federal Judiciary. This chapter does not deal with the Federal Electoral Tribunal, which was placed within the judicial branch as a result of the changes to the first paragraph of Article 94 of the Constitution made in 1996. The justification for the distinction lies in the fact that the Federal Electoral Tribunal's special status authorizes separate and independent treatment.

[2] The change affecting the budget, which began to be implemented in 1998, consisted of increasing the judiciary's budget and matching the salaries of members of the judiciary to the standard within the federal government (see José Ramón Cossío, *Jurisdicción Federal y Carrera Judicial en México* [Mexico City: Universidad Nacional Autónoma de México, 1996]). The second change meant that, starting in 1988, the Supreme Court, as a court of appeals, would hear cases that challenged the constitutionality of general legislation, including state constitutions, federal and local laws, international agreements, and federal and state regulations. The Court would no longer address the proper enforcement of the laws by local and federal courts of last resort. On this last aspect, see H. Fix Zamudio and José Ramón Cossío, *El Poder Judicial en el Ordenamiento Mexicano* (Mexico City: Fondo de Cultura Económica, 1996).

[3] *Amparo* cases consist of a process by which collegiate circuit courts review the final resolution of a case issued by any entity with state-level jurisdiction. In this case, all the *amparo* cases were sent to the Supreme Court for review, and the Court interpreted the constitutional and legal precepts for the entire country, albeit with individual results. As a result of the growing problem of pending matters accumulating in the Court, the major issue to be resolved was internal, because it was related to the operational conditions of the judicial institutions caused by that backlog. This was the reason for several reforms enacted between 1951 and 1989, which focused on the collegiate circuit courts (see José Ramón Cossío, *La Teoría Constitucional de la Suprema Corte de Justicia* [Mexico City: Fontamara, 2002].

[4] The organic reforms consisted of the following changes: (1) Justices were barred from becoming deputies or senators unless they had withdrawn from their posts two years before the election (Article 55). (2) Justices were to be appointed by a two-thirds majority vote in the Senate from the group of three individuals nominated by the executive branch (Articles 76, 89, 95, and 96). (3) The Council of the Federal Judiciary was created as one of the agencies

mandated to fulfill judicial functions (Article 94). (4) The number of Supreme Court members was reduced from 21 justices to 11 (Article 94). (5) The term of justices was set at 15 years with no possibility of reappointment; prior to the expiration of their term, justices could only be removed pursuant to a congressional determination that the individual acted in violation of federal law or the Constitution, as stipulated in Title IV of the Constitution, and they would be entitled to a pension upon the conclusion of their term (Article 94). (6) Selection requirements were modified (Article 95). (7) The terms and conditions for the appointment of the president of the Supreme Court were established (Article 97). (8) The conditions were established for replacing justices in cases of temporary or permanent vacancies, and for granting leaves of absence. (Articles 98 and 99). (9) A framework was established for constituting the Council of the Federal Judiciary as the body in charge of the administration and oversight of the judiciary, with the exception of the Supreme Court, and established the definition of and criteria for the judicial career (Articles 94 and 100). (10) Individuals who had previously served as justices, magistrates, or judges were prohibited from serving as lawyers, employers, or representatives in litigation before the institutions of the judiciary (Article 101). (11) The removal of all the members of the Supreme Court was ordered for the purpose of reconstituting the Court through the processes that were to result from the reform (Article 2, provisional).

The following procedural and jurisdictional reforms are relevant to this discussion: (1) The Court was empowered to issue general resolutions for referring to the collegiate courts those matters for which the Court had already set a legal precedent (Article 94). (2) *Amparo* proceedings were determined to be relevant in the case of actions by federal authorities (Article 103). (3) Constitutional controversies and unconstitutional acts were defined (Articles 104 and 105). (4) Greater specificity was provided about certain assumptions on the subject of *amparo* procedures, such as the power of attraction (the Court's authority, on its own initiative or at the request of a collegiate circuit court, or the attorney general of Mexico, to take from lower federal courts any *amparo* case that merits special attention because of its overriding importance); suspension (the act or law that is challenged does not have effects for the aggrieved party while the *amparo* procedure is settled); contradictory theses (when two Supreme Court resolutions contradict each other, any Supreme Court justice or the attorney general may request the Court to rule on which will prevail); and the enforcement of *amparo* rulings (a resolution only has effects for the aggrieved party, unless the court concludes the same in five consecutive judgments) (Article 107).

[5] *Compilation VIII: Federal and Federal District Law.* CD-ROM. Suprema Corte de Justicia de la Nación, Mexico City, 2003.

[6] Constitutional controversies involve three types of disputes (all included in Section 1 of Article 105): (1) disputes between different legal *orders* on the question of the constitutionality or legality of general or specific legislation (subparagraphs a, b, d, e, f, and g); (2) disputes between the *bodies* of different legal orders for the same reasons and types of legislation (subparagraphs c and j); and (3) disputes between *bodies* of the same legal order with regard to the constitutionality of that entity's general or individual legislation (subparagraphs h, i, and k). Acts of unconstitutionality are the proceedings used by factions within Congress or local legislatures, the office of the federal attorney general, or the leadership of the political parties (with respect to electoral laws) to challenge the general legislation issued by the legislative bodies themselves (see José Ramón Cossío, "El Artículo 105 Constitucional" and "Similitudes y Diferencias entre las Controversias Constitucionales y las Acciones de Inconstitucionalidad," in José Ramón Cossío, *Constitución, Tribunales y Democracia* [Mexico City: Themis, 1998], 3–25, 27–38).

[7] The question was posed in hypothetical terms, because issues related to constitutional practice have not yet been addressed.

[8] On this subject see José Ramón Cossío, "Régimen Democrático e Interpretación Constitucional en México," in Cossío, *Constitución, Tribunales y Democracia*, 143–183.

[9] Among these matters were plenary Resolutions 5/1999, 6/1999, and 10/2000, which the Supreme Court used to refer to collegiate courts certain cases that the Constitution expressly assigned to the Court's jurisdiction; Constitutional Controversy 31/1997, through which a border conflict between the municipalities of Cuernavaca and Temixco, in the state of Morelos, was resolved; Consultation 698/2000-PL by the president of the federal judiciary, who was also the president of the Supreme Court, in which he sought a ruling of unconstitutionality for a legal precept; and Constitutional Controversy 22/2001, through which the regulatory framework of the electricity sector was declared unconstitutional, because, in the Court's view, it exceeded the provisions contained in the Constitution and the law. For the first three cases, see Cossío, *La Teoría Constitucional de la Suprema Corte de Justicia*, particularly the last section in chapter 2; on the latter issue, see José Ramón Cossío and Josefina Cortés, "La Inconstitucionalidad del Reglamento de Energía Eléctrica (y las inconsistencias de la sentencia que la declara)," *Este País*, no. 136 (July 2002).

[10] Among many other works on this topic, an interesting discussion is found in Edmund Hewar, introduction to *Lord Mansfield* (London: Barry Rose, 1979).

[11] Although it is true that, in most cases, these elements are, in fact, taken into account in the resolutions issued, the same reasoning allows one to argue that there is no reason for labeling them as the outcome of judicial activism.

[12] José Ramón Cossío, "La Teoría Constitucional Moderna (Leciones para México)," *Metapolítica 4* (July–September 2000): 102–127.

[13] Cass Sunstein, *One Case at a Time: Judicial Minimalism on the Supreme Court* (Cambridge: Harvard University Press, 1999).

[14] For a description of this model and its operation, see Cossío, *Jurisdicción Federal y Carrera Judicial,* 61–74.

[15] President Zedillo commented as follows: "The bill being submitted for your [the Senate's] consideration seeks to lay the constitutional groundwork for beginning a process of strengthening a new system of justice and security in the country. Later, the bills of law are to be introduced successively to ensure the comprehensive reform that society has been demanding." *Compilation VIII: Federal and Federal District Law.* CD-ROM.

[16] The reforms encompassed a variety of features, which are better addressed separately and in summary form. The first reform affecting Article 94 provided that judicial power would be exercised by the Supreme Court, the collegiate and single-judge circuit courts, and the district courts—not by the Council of the Federal Judiciary, as was the case previously. No longer the depository of part of the judicial function, the Federal Judiciary Council remained in charge of the administration, oversight, and discipline of the judiciary, with the exception of the Supreme Court. The second reform of Article 94 entailed assigning the Supreme Court, in plenary session, the power to pass (and enforce) those general resolutions that would allow it to refer to the collegiate courts those cases that the Court deemed would result in "improved delivery of justice." The reform of Article 97 meant that judges' and magistrates' complaints about matters of constitutionality should be heard by the Supreme Court and no longer by the Council of the Federal Judiciary, as established by the 1994 reform. Specific reforms of Article 97 in 1999 included the following changes: (1) The first part dealt with the concept of the Council (in connection with the new provisions in reformed Article 94), establishing that it "will be an agency of the judicial branch of the federation with independence in technical and managerial aspects as well as in the passage of its resolutions." (2) The reform considered the way the Council was constituted. In the past, the three members of the Council had been selected by ballot vote from among the district judges and the magistrates of the collegiate and single-judge circuit courts; the reform established that the three members had to be appointed by the Supreme Court en banc from among judges and magistrates in general. (3) The reform established the requirements for candidates for Council membership: each candidate (except the candidate for president of the Council) was required to fulfill the standards for professional and administrative skills, honesty, and honor in the conduct of their activities (in the past this was required only for those appointed by the president and the Senate); in addition, individuals appointed by the Court were to be recognized

members of the judicial field. (4) Even though the power to pass general resolutions still resided in the Federal Judiciary Council, the Supreme Court could
now request the issuance of those resolutions it deemed necessary for the
proper exercise of its judicial function. (5) The reform granted the Supreme
Court the power to review and, when appropriate, to revoke resolutions
passed by the Council, as long as eight votes had been cast in favor of doing so.
(6) The reform established that resolutions issued by the collegiate courts on
the subject of direct *amparo* cases would not include the option of review "unless the issue being decided was the unconstitutionality of a law or a direct interpretation was being made of a precept of the Constitution when the
resolution, in the opinion of the Supreme Court of Justice and in accordance
with general resolutions, involves establishing an important and overriding
criterion."

[17] See Stephen Zamora and José Ramón Cossío, et al., *Mexican Law* (New
York: Oxford University Press, 2004), especially chap 6, "The Judicial System."

[18] The only example given as to when such an intervention may prove unnecessary (bearing in mind that the Court already had the power to refer matters on which a precedent had already been set) was a case in which there was
a well-defined opinion but no precedent.

[19] It is easy to recognize the confusion that exists about the proper jurisdiction of a body devoted to constitutionality issues and the problem of managing the backlog of cases that body faces.

[20] The text of the bill indicates that granting that power to the Supreme
Court is accompanied by the need to modify subparagraph 9 of Article 107 of
the Constitution, because this would allow the Court to address only those
matters whose significance requires intervention by the country's highest institution responsible for imparting justice. *Compilation VIII: Federal and Federal District Law.* CD-ROM.

[21] Before the 1994 reforms, the administration of the judiciary resided in
the Supreme Court en banc, its president, and the Governance and Administration Committee (see José Ramón Cossío, *Las Atribuciones no Jurisdicciona-
les de la Suprema Corte de Justicia de la Nación* [Mexico City: Editorial Miguel
Angel Porrúa, 1992]).

[22] *Compilation VIII: Federal and Federal District Law.* CD-ROM.

[23] The amended text of the reform of Article 100 established that the Court
could request the Council to provide only those resolutions that the Court
considered necessary for the proper functioning of the judiciary. This change
was introduced in the opinions issued by the relevant commissions of the
Senate.

[24] For a brief outline, see H. J. Abraham, *The Judicial Process*, 6th ed. (New
York: Oxford University Press, 1993), 174–179.

[25] In its report, the Senate introduced a number of modifications to the president's bill: (1) The president's proposal indicated that the main functions of the Council should be mentioned in Article 94, whereas the Senate preferred to include them under Article 100. (2) The president proposed that the Court's power to refer cases should apply to matters within its jurisdiction, but the Senate proposed that this power should apply to those matters in which the referral could be justified in the interests of more appropriate delivery of justice. (3) The president proposed that the Council of the Federal Judiciary should be made up of seven members (the president of the Supreme Court plus two members selected by the Court, two selected by the Senate, and two by the president of the republic), whereas the Senate proposed that, in addition to the president of the Court, the appointments should include three members selected by the Court, two by the Senate, and one by the president of the republic. (4) The Senate's report also modified the president's proposal in terms of the scope of application of resolutions passed by the Supreme Court en banc regarding the Council by making it possible for the Court only to propose resolutions, not issue them. (5) The president's bill was also modified to require that the cases to which subparagraph 9 of Article 107 refers be based on general resolutions.

The report issued by the Committees on Governance and Constitutional Issues and Justice of the Chamber of Deputies (Comisiones Unidas de Gobernación y Puntos Constitucionales y de Justicia de la Cámara de Diputados) expressed views similar to those of the Senate; therefore these are not listed here. It should be noted, however, that the basic intent of the Chamber of Deputies' report was to provide justifications for the modifications that the Senate introduced to the president's bill. There are two particularly important aspects of the lower house's report: (1) the report submitted to the Chamber of Deputies, in its role as a permanent constituent body, indicated that the Supreme Court's power to request or revoke general resolutions would be considered an exception, and (2) the report indicated that the only way to review the Federal Judiciary Council's resolutions would be through a process of administrative review and not, as the Supreme Court had held previously, through an *amparo* proceeding.

[26] Similarly, the law established that appointment and promotions of judges and magistrates would be based on "internal competitive" examinations and "open competitive" examinations. According to the law, the internal competitive examination for the position of district judge is open to judicial officials below the level of judges, such as secretaries of the Supreme Court and of mid-level and lower courts; the open competitive examination is open to individuals who satisfy all the legal requirements and are not serving in the judiciary at the time of their candidacy. The most interesting feature is that access to the competition is available only through established channels, and regard-

less of the form the competition takes, it requires the completion of very specific stages. These seven stages are the same for both types of competitions and consist of the following: (1) publication of an announcement giving specific entry requirements; (2) completion of a questionnaire by candidates; (3) selection of five individuals for each available position based on their qualifications; (4) selected candidates' resolution of the legal cases that are assigned to them; (5) administration of an oral public examination covering "all kinds of issues related to the functions of ... a district judge"; (6) assignment of scores on the basis of seniority within the judiciary, performance, and academic degrees attained in addition to continuing education and specialized courses; and (7) issuance of a report of the competition containing the names of the successful candidates and identifying the selection method used. Once the winners have been announced by way of a "regular" appointment process, objections may be raised by requesting an "administrative review" to be conducted by "any of the persons who participated" in the process. The Supreme Court is the competent body to conduct such a review, and the outcome of a decision favorable to the complainant is perceived as a declaration that the initial decision was invalid. Thereafter the Council of the Federal Judiciary must issue a new resolution, making it understood that this nullification would not result in the invalidation of the decisions made by the official in question. Because of the exceptional nature of both this proceeding and the institution, the Supreme Court itself has held that it is the only entity with the jurisdiction to determine whether or not it is competent to hear the case (see *Semanario Judicial de la Federación y su Gaceta*, 9th period, vol. 5 [Mexico City, March 1997], 259–260).

[27] Two exceptions occurred in August and September 1995, when the previous Council of the Federal Judiciary, citing the recent publication of the law and the lack of the necessary systems for the competitions, issued two resolutions (Resolutions 5/1995 and 7/1995) regarding appointments of magistrates and judges through the merit system.

[28] The part of the deliberations that is relevant here are the two reasons given for the competition: (1) that "at the present time there is an urgent need to appoint 40 district judges in order to fill the positions that will open up in various jurisdictional agencies as a result of the Fourth Internal Competitive Examination for the Appointment of Circuit Magistrates, as well as those generated through assignment changes"; and (2) that "the Council of the Federal Judiciary's efforts to enforce the law notwithstanding, because the administration of competitive exams to which the Organic Law of the Judicial Branch of the Federation refers would take longer than the length of time that positions potentially becoming available in the jurisdictional bodies can prudently be kept vacant, and with a view to complying with Article 17 of the Constitution, there is an extremely urgent need to appoint district judges in

order to avoid a backlog of work within the jurisdictional function and a delay in the delivery of justice." Consejo de la Judicatura Federal, *Semanario Judicial de la Federación y su Gaceta*, 9a, August 1999, 895.

[29] These guidelines included the following four points: (1) Individuals under consideration could be secretaries of the Supreme Court or persons who, having held such a post previously, were currently serving in other capacities within the judiciary. (2) Candidates were required to submit curriculum vitae, copies of certain documents, and an essay explaining their reasons for seeking to participate in the competition. (3) The Council expected the Commission on Judicial Careers to recommend selected candidates to the Council. (4) The selection criteria would be based on the candidate's performance as a Supreme Court secretary or in another relevant position within the judiciary, seniority in that post and in the judiciary, the number of posts held in the judiciary, academic credentials, and existing need for that individual's particular services. In accordance with Resolution 21/1999, on August 23, 1999, the official announcement of the competition was published in the official register, *Diario Oficial*, which on September 7 also published the list of 40 candidates who, in the Council's opinion, had fulfilled the requirements and met the criteria necessary for appointment as district judges.

[30] These issues are also covered in P. Muñoz Ledo, ed., *Comisión de Estudios para la Reforma del Estado: Conclusiones y Propuestas* (Mexico City: Universidad Nacional Autónoma de México, 2001); see also José Ramón Cossío and M. Sarre, "Procuración e Impartición de Justicia en las Campañas Electorales del 2000," in *México 2000: Alternancia y Transición a la Democracia*, ed. L. Salazar (Mexico City: Cal y Arena, 2001), 252–263.

[31] This system of succession in which justices are replaced every two years in a staggered rotation is subject to changes under certain circumstances, as was the case recently with the passing of Minister Humberto Román Palacios. In accordance with the Constitution, the Mexican Senate designated Minister Sergio Valls Hernández to replace the late minister. See Zamora and Cossío, *Mexican Law*, 205–206.

[32] Procedurally, there are two types of *amparos*: the direct or judicial *amparo*, which is used in cases where judicial procedures at the federal, local, or jurisdictional level are violated; and the indirect *amparo*, which is used in cases of general violations of the Constitution (i.e., not necessarily judicial in nature). Ibid., 266–272.

[33] See Minister Juventino Castro, *La Posible Facultad del Poder Judicial para Iniciar Leyes* (Mexico City: Suprema Corte de Justicia de la Nación, 1999).

[34] Although it is certainly true that the members of the Supreme Court have changed their judicial opinions, this has not occurred as frequently as it would appear. The Court's jurisprudence has changed in the context of broad-

er social and political changes but has not led to a scenario in which the Court decides to declare the unconstitutionality of legislation that the Court itself first introduced. In addition, the criticism that the justices are rotated too frequently has no basis in fact. Before the 1994 reform, when the causes for removal that are valid today did not exist, the average tenure was 15 years; today, the reform has provided for a specific 15-year term for Supreme Court justices. Finally, taking into account that achieving a pattern of rotations requires replacing the justices currently in office two at a time every three years starting in 2003, a majority that is different from the proportion created by the 1994 reform will not be established in the Court until 2009.

[35] José Ramón Cossío, *Bosquejos Constitucionales* (Mexico: Editorial Porrúa, 2004), 386.

[36] See Zamora and Cossío, *Mexican Law,* 430–434.

[37] Years later, three more organs with the same characteristics would be created: the Council for the Protection of Minors, the Electoral Tribunal, and the Agrarian Tribunals.

[38] See Zamora and Cossío, *Mexican Law,* 197–199.

[39] José Ramón Cossío, *La Teoría constitucional de la Suprema Corte de Justicia* (Mexico City: Fontamara, 2002), 141.

FOUR

MEXICO'S ECONOMY: ARE FURTHER REFORMS NECESSARY?

Jonathan Heath

The Mexican economy grew at an annual average rate of 6.28 percent between 1941 and 1981, a period referred to as Mexico's golden years. The entire period was characterized by an import substitution policy framework, with a special emphasis on building an industrial base. The first 18 years of this period were typified by growth accompanied by inflation, mainly as a result of constant external shocks. The 1960s, however, were stable, and the absence of international turbulence helped Mexico achieve a remarkable level of economic stability, which Antonio Ortiz Mena, the finance minister from 1958 to 1970, later christened the period of "stabilized development."[1] Regardless of whether the government implemented correct economic policies, this is the only period in Mexican history when external debt levels were insignificant[2]—indicating a correlation with a high rate of growth that proves difficult to ignore. The lesson seems to be that low debt ratios are another necessary—but insufficient—condition for sustained growth.

Nevertheless, economists have subsequently shown that the 1960s induced structural weaknesses into Mexico's economy. The government's protectionist policies caused inefficiency in production, lack of competitiveness, and an allocation of resources that was far from optimal. In 1963, Raymond Vernon wrote about what he called the dilemma of economic development in Mexico.[3] He predicted that, if the government did not carry out substantial changes in economic policy geared toward opening up the economy and making better use of market forces, the economy would eventually stagnate and create dangerous social consequences. The dilemma was created by the existence of political opposition to any type of change, which itself could give rise to an even greater danger.

According to Vernon, one way out of this dilemma was external borrowing. Because Mexico had prepaid all its external obligations that had resulted from the Suarez-Lamont negotiations[4] conducted in 1942, public external debt was near zero at the beginning of the 1960s. The problem with this option, Vernon argued, was that it had its limits and could not be an adequate strategy for long-term sustained growth.

The predicament that Vernon foretold was delayed for more than a decade, because the government resorted to external borrowing and achieved high economic growth rates throughout most of the next three presidential terms. In the 1960s, however, industrialization was characterized by hidden inefficiencies, high rates of return, monopolistic and oligopolistic markets, and a slow but steady diminution of public finances. As a result, many firms were created and maintained in these economic conditions that otherwise would never have survived in a true market-driven environment. The problem was one of structural weaknesses in the economy in the sense that policies did not lead to a problem in the short term, but would clearly impede growth in the longer term.

Not only did political opposition stop Mexico from implementing the necessary corrections, but the inefficiencies increased because of measures taken by two consecutive populist governments—those headed by Luis Echeverría Alvarez (1970–1976) and José López Portillo (1976–1982). These administrations discarded fiscal prudence and induced expansionist monetary policies as a way to foster economic growth. By the early 1980s, the structural weaknesses of the economy had begun to manifest themselves, and the country was plagued by substantial fiscal and external disequilibrium. The economy crashed in 1982, with the government virtually bankrupt and unable to meet its foreign financial obligations. As a result, economic growth averaged near zero throughout the decade of the 1980s.

Major structural reform was painfully necessary, and by that time the economy was surrounded by high levels of instability. High inflation, lack of foreign exchange, and large fiscal deficits forced the government to adopt a sustained depreciation policy that only aggravated reform efforts and created vicious cycles. In spite of fiscal retrenchment, initial privatization of certain sectors, and early attempts at trade liberalization, in 1987 the government's deficit was hovering at about 16 percent of the gross domestic product (GDP)—almost the same level observed five years earlier.

Almost 20 years later, the dilemma that Vernon had foreseen for Mexico sprang forth with a vengeance. Not only did Mexico lose a decade of economic growth, but the social consequences that Vernon predicted appeared and became a force in themselves. The incumbent Institutional Revolutionary Party (PRI) had to resort to the most fraudulent elections in Mexican history in order to hang on to its almost 60 years of power and to overcome not only strong political opposition but also widespread discontent over the lack of economic progress.

The elected president in 1988, Carlos Salinas, had to implement difficult and unpopular structural reforms and had to deliver relatively quick results if he wanted to legitimize his presidency. As a result, he put into practice a shock treatment as a way to stabilize the economy and then carried through a decisive reform program. Within his first year in office, Salinas renegotiated Mexico's external debt under the so-called Brady Plan, picked up the pace of privatization, started an all-inclusive deregulation program, and announced his intention to negotiate a free-trade agreement with the United States.

Proceeds from privatization were used to reduce the fiscal deficit, and within three years, Mexico was bordering on having a balanced budget. The rate of inflation dropped significantly, along with domestic interest rates, helping to diminish the cost of debt service. Vicious cycles were converted into virtuous cycles, because lower deficits required lower expenditures for debt service and led to a decline in the rate of inflation. For the first time in seven years, positive expectations created voluntary capital inflows. Foreign exchange reserves increased, the economy stabilized, and economic growth resurfaced.

President Salinas broadly followed the reforms set forth in the "Washington Consensus," a term coined by John Williamson in 1989.[5] The original list of recommendations consisted of the 10 reforms listed below, and definite progress was made in implementing most of them:

1. The huge fiscal deficit that Salinas had inherited was eliminated, and Mexico achieved a fiscal surplus between 1991 and 1993.

2. The priorities for public expenditures were reordered, with indiscriminate subsidies and high interest payments giving way to funding for basic health, education, and poverty reduction programs.

3. A moderate tax reform was carried out, resulting in an increase in the tax base and a reduction in the top income tax rate.

4. The financial sector was privatized, interest rates were liberalized and left to market determination, and financial reforms were introduced.

5. A transition toward a more flexible exchange rate regime was introduced, by gradually increasing the Central Bank's target zone.[6]

6. Trade liberalization was pursued actively, culminating in the enactment of the North American Free Trade Agreement (NAFTA).

7. A new foreign direct investment law was introduced, effectively eliminating discretionary measures and its previous protectionist bias.

8. Privatization was actively pursued in several sectors, including the telephone monopoly, banks, airlines, and almost all other enterprises, with the only two notable exceptions being the state-owned Petróleos Mexicanos (Pemex) oil company and state-owned electrical power plants managed by the Federal Electricity Commission (CFE) and Luz y Fuerza del Centro.

9. Deregulation was pursued actively, focusing on easing barriers to entry into the market and reducing red tape.

10. Strengthening property rights was the only reform that was arguably ignored or at least postponed.

Almost 30 years earlier, Raymond Vernon had warned that political opposition would emerge if Mexico carried out reforms designed to allow market forces to operate properly. This outcome was the result of the bureaucratic structures that gave the PRI discretion in protecting industries and the enormous profits many *priístas* (members of the PRI party) made in the process. Although the system was inefficient, it benefited political leaders, who continually used and abused their power for economic gain and political control. Bureaucracy and regulation not only were a means to an end in terms of making many political leaders rich but also gave the PRI the ability to control political appointments and nominations.[7] As a result of all these factors, Vernon's prophecy came true.

Even though Salinas's reforms affected the traditional bases of political and economic control in Mexico's political system, the changes did not eliminate all the mechanisms of control, and many measures were not carried out to their ultimate end. Many of the reforms were inconclusive and required a second round of measures designed to reinforce the original objectives. For example, even though the deficit was reduced and fiscal discipline is considered a necessary mainstay for economic stability, low levels of revenues prevented the government from carrying out the investment required to improve the country's infrastructure, broaden educational coverage, enhance health care facilities, and develop comprehensive poverty programs. Salinas's tax reform was insufficient, and Mexico still remains dangerously dependent on oil revenues. Finally, nonbudgeted items have created a precariously large gap between the narrowly defined public deficit and the total public-sector borrowing requirements.

Despite the privatization and subsequent liberalization of Mexico's financial sector, the banking crisis of 1995 virtually eliminated the ability and incentives to grant credits to the country's private sector. Not only did the weakness of property rights become much more apparent, but the need to implement comprehensive reforms in this area could no longer be postponed. Between December 1994 and April 2002, real direct credit that commercial banks gave to the private sector dropped by more than 77 percent. As a result, as of 2003, the World Bank ranked Mexico 106th in the world in terms of private-sector credit as a percentage of GDP—a ranking that places Mexico alongside most African countries and below Eastern European countries despite the fact that Mexico has the 13th largest economy in the world.[8]

Many have criticized the Washington Consensus, considering it a set of neoliberal policies imposed on hapless countries by Washington-based financial institutions and leading these governments into crisis and misery. Although there is still a push for furthering these reforms and for what many call the second wave of reforms (which consist mostly of institutional strengthening), the "damaged brand name" of the Washington Consensus has given rise to a significant level of political antagonism.[9] The opposition to further reforms or even to the conclusion of previous reforms has come from what is perceived to be an outright failure of the recommendations made by the Washington Consensus and from what has been coined the "reform fatigue syndrome."

Whether it is fatigue, failure, or both, the first step toward assessing the need to reinforce the reform process is to understand why the results have been disappointing thus far. Is the Washington Consensus based on a neoliberal ideology? If so, is this bad? Did the Washington Consensus fail, or was it just ill applied? The answers to these questions are important, because they will help determine if further reforms are worth pursuing or if another road altogether should be explored.

It should be recalled that, when John Williamson first put forward his list of 10 reforms as a summary of the measures that most people in Washington believed Latin American countries ought to be undertaking, the original intention had been to make a "list of policy prescriptions that would command general assent in the Washington of George H. W. Bush shortly after Ronald Reagan had left office."[10] The proposal was a list of reforms that, at the time, almost everyone would have agreed had to be carried out. Williamson emphasizes that the purpose of the conference where the list was first presented was to persuade Washington that Latin America was engaged in serious reform measures.[11] The Washington Consensus was never meant as a policy agenda or a set of recommendations; rather, it was a list of what was already under way. In this sense, the Washington Consensus can hardly be considered a list of policies that were "imposed" on Latin American countries.

Nevertheless, governments made a basic error in the way they interpreted the Washington Consensus and took it for much more than was originally intended. The proposal was adopted as an ideology in its own right and basically construed as an all-inclusive list of everything that had to be done for a country to become a member of the "First World." Many governments accepted the illusion that immediate sustained growth would follow if they carried out the reforms on the list. These governments were never told how to carry out the reforms or that the list consisted of necessary—but far from sufficient—conditions. Most countries ended up applying different versions and levels of the reforms, but at the same time, they implemented additional policies that either neutralized these efforts or at least diluted them.

Mexico was a case in point. Even though Salinas achieved a small fiscal surplus in 1993, he also approved a change in the definition of public finances by allowing "financial intermediation" to be excluded from the final balance. This item had been less than 1 percent of GDP until then and primarily represented financing that agencies like the World Bank granted to the private sector. The government's logic back then was to question why a guarantee should be considered part of its deficit. However, the following year, expenses related to financial intermediation jumped to almost 4 percent of GDP, leading to most of the financial instability that characterized 1994 and serving as the precursor to the peso crisis of 1995. Fiscal discipline had been one of the main pillars of the Salinas reforms, but it was not cemented as an irreversible objective.

Since 1994, fiscal discipline has been portrayed as a trademark of the Mexican government. For example, Ernesto Zedillo managed to maintain a fiscal deficit of 0.7 percent of GDP throughout his six years in office. But again, the definition of fiscal deficit remains at the core of the problem. By excluding the cost of the bank bailout program and other similar items and by deferring the cost of investment programs, the deficit as officially defined is not an accurate indicator of the government's "true" fiscal balance. Vicente Fox introduced a new measure, labeled the "public-sector borrowing requirement," that includes most of the missing budget items. The new numbers show that the narrowly defined deficit averaged 0.7 percent of GDP during the Zedillo administration, but the all-inclusive deficit, the public-sector borrowing requirement, averaged 5.2 percent of GDP.

Salinas carried out a tax reform that increased the tax base and reduced the top income tax rate and, as a result, revenues from taxes increased. Nevertheless, the government continued to rely on oil exports, which kept revenues highly dependent on the price of oil. The overall tax system remained highly complicated because of the large number of exemptions, which not only preserved the incidence of tax evasion but also continued to provide incentives for a growing informal economy. More than a decade later, the need to enact a tax reform remains on the government's agenda, and Mexico has one of Latin America's lowest tax intakes.

Another error in the government's interpretation of the Washington Consensus was that the list of reforms was simply a very generic enunciation of principles and not a detailed guideline on how to carry out each measure. For example, the financial sector was liberalized and banks were privatized with no consideration given to the transition problems that could arise from the sudden and substantial rise in bank credit to the private sector. At the same time, the significant reduction in the federal deficit and privatization of the banks resulted in a huge increase in liquidity that banks had to channel to the private sector quickly despite their lack of both experience and skills at managing credit risk. Consequently, businesses could not efficiently absorb the new credit flows and nonperforming assets increased quickly, leading to the banking crises of 1995.

Nothing was ever said about how banks should be privatized. An authoritarian government with a tradition of corruption cannot be expected to handle the privatization of almost 1,000 enterprises without glitches, graft, and favoritism. Ten years later, after those who originally bought the banks had lost their entire capital, a different set of stockholders owns almost all of Mexico's banks. A large number of privatized firms ended up as nonperforming assets owned by the governmental corporation in charge of rescuing banks during the crisis.

Because the recommendations of the Washington Consensus were broad-based, incomplete, and not accompanied by an instruction book, most reforms were curtailed, neglected, or neutralized by contradictory policies. Given the crash of Mexico's economy in 1995, barely six years after the beginning of the serious phase of the reform process, it is easy to see why most of the finger-pointing was aimed at those who had led the reform process. What was left was not just reform fatigue syndrome but a much stronger fear of carrying out further reforms that might have more of the same consequences.

As John Williamson and Moisés Naím have argued, in spite of the harsh criticism of the Washington Consensus as a set of neoliberal policies imposed on hapless countries, the basic recommendations do not imply that they are based on a radical right-wing ideology. Ideas such as the privatization of education, social security, or health services are nowhere to be found. The proposal never suggested that tax reform should include a sharp reduction in taxes or that the government should minimize its participation in areas involving helping the poor or improving income distribution. For example, the original list included a reordering of the priorities for public expenditures so that the government could increase its attention to lower-income families.

If the original list did not include specific measures to improve income distribution and reduce poverty, it was because priorities at that time were different. Mexico, like the rest of Latin America, was emerging from a decade marked by no growth and one that was also plagued by high inflation, instability, debt overload, and basic macroeconomic disequilibrium. As a result, the consensus was that most Latin American countries needed to implement serious structural reforms in order to stabilize their economies and to correct the damage imposed by the populist regimes of the 1970s. Most also agreed that this outcome could be achieved through macroeconomic discipline and a better use of markets. The consensus, however, stopped there.

After the peso crisis of 1995, priority had to be placed again on economic stabilization and crisis management. Although the banking sector faced the possibility of a systemic meltdown, the rest of the economy was much less affected than was initially apparent. After a deep recession lasting six months, economic activity bounced back sharply and then grew at an average rate of more than 5 percent over the next five years. It is doubtful that this could have happened without President Salinas's initial reform efforts.

Nevertheless, political opposition grew, and Mexico went through another transition—this time from authoritarianism to democracy. In the process, Mexico again learned that democracy is far from perfect and in many cases makes changes even more difficult. Zedillo lost his party's majority in Congress in 1997 and, as a result, failed to achieve many important changes during the second half of his term. After winning the presidency in 2000, Vicente Fox, whose successful campaign had focused on change, has also failed to gain congressional support for his initiatives. Even though Fox won the election with 42.5 percent of the vote (versus 36.1 percent for the PRI's Francisco Labastida), voters delivered Fox's party, the National Action Party (PAN), only 41.4 percent of the seats in the Chamber of Deputies (compared with 41.8 percent for the PRI). What resulted was a population confused by the notion of further reforms, political parties more interested in their own agendas, and an inexperienced government with a notorious lack of ideas about how to pursue what is seen as reforms needed to achieve sustained growth.

The effect of the Salinas reforms is hard to assess, given the many positive and negative results. On the positive side, fiscal discipline reduced the public deficit, helped stabilize the economy, paved the way for reducing foreign debt, and contributed to lowering interest rates. As a result of trade liberalization, Mexico was able to generate its own foreign exchange, to increase productivity in the manufacturing sector, to introduce an important engine of growth, to promote job creation in the *maquiladora* sector, to open oligopolistic markets to competition, to lower prices for many consumer products, and to help keep inflation in check. Privatization contributed to the reduction of public debt, eliminated many inefficient enterprises, opened up markets to trade, and attracted foreign direct investment.

On the negative side, privatization can be blamed in part for its role in the banking crisis; the measure also failed to break up the telephone monopoly. The airline industry ended up creating a system that combined a monopoly with a duopoly that caused the cost of domestic air travel to be far more expensive than the cost of international travel. Even though the government continually posts progress reports on deregulation, the perception is that almost nothing has been done; starting a business still entails an endless number of requirements and time. Tax reforms have produced, at most, partial results: slightly lower tax rates but a system that is still far from competitive compared with the ones in many other countries. Moreover, the tax system remains extremely complex and keeps changing year after year. Trade liberalization failed to create jobs in the non-*maquiladora* manufacturing sector and faces heavy opposition from organized agricultural groups. Liberalization of the financial sector not only led to a major banking crisis but also failed to significantly reduce the cost of intermediation by commercial banks. In fact, in 2002, real credit granted to the private sector was equivalent to the level that was in place in 1985, when banks were owned by the state and faced up to 100 percent marginal reserve requirements in order to finance the federal deficit. Foreign direct investment has failed to grow significantly over the past years because of the growing perception that the Mexican economy lacks competitiveness.

Many of these negative points were caused by incomplete reforms and could have been corrected through further measures. However, formulating a complete list of required reforms would be nothing short of utopia if the exercise failed to consider the political reality. Many political parties are deeply opposed to the current reform agenda for a number of reasons:

- It is politically convenient to expose the negative aspects of past reforms and campaign on the notion that these were neoliberal policies imposed on Mexico from abroad.

- The negative aspects of past reforms and the lack of concrete results cloud the overall balance, convincing many that past reforms hindered the economy more than they helped it.

- The current political system favors the opposition parties' efforts to block any type of reform or progress that would benefit the current administration.

- Most of the reforms represent major blows to certain groups and organizations that have powerful lobbying abilities within Congress.

- Some of the reforms contain clauses that are not very popular and leave the impression that they would create additional burdens on the lower classes (in the case of fiscal reforms) or eliminate earned privileges for the working class (in the case of labor reforms).

FOX'S STRUCTURAL REFORM AGENDA

Vicente Fox's very clever 2000 presidential campaign was aimed at capturing votes from a discontented population that was fed up with Mexico's recurrent financial crises and extremely corrupt political system. His main promises can be summed up in one word: *change.* Fox promised to change just about everything that could be seen as wrong from the previous 71-year rule of the PRI. Obviously, change means reform, and Fox based his entire strategic plan for his six years in office on implementing major economic and political reforms that would build a foundation for sustained growth, significant job creation, stronger institutions, and less corruption.

By law, the incoming president is required to publish a National Development Plan within the first six months of assuming office. In May 2001, Vicente Fox released his six-year plan, which outlined five broad-based objectives for "economic growth with quality":

- to maintain macroeconomic responsibility,
- to increase and extend competitiveness,

- to ensure more equitable economic development,
- to promote balance in economic development of all regions, and
- to create conditions for sustainable development.

Given that these objectives are generic and broad-based, in mid-2001 the government announced its National Program for Financing Development (Pronafide), which goes into greater detail about how the government plans to pursue these objectives and includes a broader outline of the administration's goals for economic policy. In this document, the government states that achieving its employment goals requires a higher and sustained rate of economic growth and a major effort in terms of investment. The Pronafide outlines five basic strategies designed to lead to a permanent increase in financial resources for productive investment by creating incentives for domestic private and public savings and implementing key structural reforms. The strategies include the following:

- implementing structural reforms,
- increasing public savings,
- promoting private savings,
- using external savings only as a complement to domestic savings, and
- strengthening the financial system and transforming development banks.

The first strategy not only deals with structural reform but also gives the government's overall approach to achieving its goals a key role in the process. The approval of structural reforms is expected to provide the legal and economic environment needed to increase competitiveness, to reduce the size (and necessity) of the informal financial sector, and to encourage solid gains in both human and physical capital. At the same time, structural reform would increase the resources allocated to investment and thus increase prospects for economic growth and job creation. In sum, the Pronafide contemplates implementing reforms in 10 key areas—four dealing with economic issues and the remainder with Mexico's political, social, and judicial systems:

1. *Public finances:* These reforms are aimed at broadening the revenue base in order to allow a significant reordering of expenditures and reduce dependence on oil exports.

2. *Labor:* These reforms are designed to promote a new labor culture that would strengthen job creation, induce competitiveness, and increase workers' development opportunities.

3. *Energy:* These reforms are expected to attract participation by the private sector and to increase administrative efficiency, leading to improved services at more competitive prices.

4. *Private finances:* These reforms are intended to encourage domestic savings, provide a legal framework that would allow for the reactivation of banking activity, and strengthen the financial sector's role in promoting economic development.

5. *Education:* These reforms are aimed at establishing a flexible and decentralized educational system that would raise the quality of education and also reduce social inequality.

6. *State reform:* The objective of these reforms is to reach a federal pact among states and municipalities that will enhance the abilities of each level of government to tailor programs to the population's needs and to distribute both resources and obligations more efficiently.

7. *Federal budget:* These reforms are intended to modernize budgetary planning in order to increase transparency and efficiency, provide certainty, avoid paralysis, and establish ground rules for the treatment of public finances.

8. *Judicial system:* These reforms deal with ways to reduce corruption, enhance transparency, strengthen the rule of law, and guarantee a more efficient administration of justice.

9. *Pensions and social security:* The aim of these reforms is to prepare a more modern and self-sustaining pension system for government workers, provide better health care services, and improve coordination within appropriate qualified institutions.

10. *Telecommunications:* The goal of these reforms is to increase and improve competition, attract investment, and provide access to the benefits derived from globalization.

The four fiscal reforms were expected to have an impact along several lines. The administration anticipated that the reforms focused on public finances would (1) minimize competition with the private sector for scarce resources, thereby lowering the cost of funding; (2) decrease the volatility of public revenues by making the government less dependent on oil exports and also limit the impact of external shocks; (3) condense the size of the informal financial sector, thus allowing more workers to benefit from social security and pension programs; (4) moderate distortions in the tax system from excessive exemptions and generate a more competitive environment; and (5) strengthen the government's capacity to provide basic necessities to a growing population.

The reforms dealing with labor were expected (1) to establish a more flexible regulatory framework that would promote job creation and lead to better salaries; (2) to create more job training programs and a new labor culture based on productivity and competitiveness; (3) to promote further transparency among employers, workers, and government; and (4) to promote greater correlation between wages and productivity.

The reforms in the energy sector—electrical energy in particular—were expected (1) to provide more competitive prices and services and limit the waste of resources; (2) to decrease public funding for the energy sector in order to increase resources for education, health care, and infrastructure improvements; and (3) to guarantee sufficient energy reserves that would prevent interruptions in energy production.

In the area of private finances, the government expected the reforms (1) to promote more domestic savings and financial deepening; (2) to increase financial options available to firms in a more competitive environment; (3) to improve efficiency of allocating scarce financial resources; and (4) to generate more efficient operational systems.

These structural reforms not only play a key role in Fox's strategic plan but also are considered the basis for achieving higher economic growth rates and offering the possibility of reaching other objectives. To emphasize this role, the Pronafide provides two macroeconomic scenarios for the last four years of Fox's administration: the outcome with and without approval of these reforms. The first scenario is labeled the "macroeconomic framework with structural reform." This scenario anticipates an accumulated growth rate of 26.6 percent between 2003 and 2006, which implies an average growth of 6.1 percent per year, reaching 7 percent in 2006. The second possibility is labeled the "inertial" scenario and projects an accumulated economic growth rate of about 16 percent—a difference of 9.2 percent by the end of Fox's term. The average rate of growth would be limited to 3.8 percent, a difference of 2.2 percent per year. In other words, the government estimates that the timely completion of the proposed reforms would provide Mexico with an additional annual growth of 2.2 percent and would reach an additional 2.8 percent by 2006. The gap between the two scenarios implies, among other things, the creation of an additional 1.5 million jobs in the formal sector.

Even though it can be assumed that these scenarios were constructed on solid grounds, the administration has already had two major setbacks. First, with the exception of the financial sector, all other reforms were notably absent from the 2000–2003 legislative agenda, indicating that Mexico should be much closer to the inertial scenario in terms of growth and other macroeconomic objectives. The second setback consists of a bleaker external environment than the one that was assessed originally. The government assumed that the U.S. economy would grow by at least 3 percent in 2003 and then at an average annual rate of 3.5 percent throughout the rest of Fox's administration. Not only has the rate of growth in the United States been much lower than expected, but also the core of the less dynamic setting is concentrated in a lackluster industrial sector, which has a greater impact on Mexico's economy. As a result, Mexico experienced a recession that lasted 36 months and was by far the longest in the country's recent history.[12]

The government had projected a growth rate of 1.7 percent and 3.5 percent (under the inertial scenario) for 2002 and 2003, respectively. However, the recession resulted in GDP growth of only 0.9 and 0.7 percent in 2002 and 2003, respectively. This places cumulative economic growth in 2002 and 2003 at 1.6 percent, instead of the 6.7 percent projected under the scenario that posited the completion of reforms. Thus, as of 2003, the economy was already 5 percentage points below the government's original projections; 1.5 percentage points are attributable to the lack of reforms and 3 percentage points to the recession. Nevertheless, the recession is a temporary setback brought about by a normal business cycle, whereas the lack of reforms is causing more permanent damage and is a consequence of the absence of a political consensus in favor of reforms.

ARE THE PROPOSED REFORMS THE RIGHT ONES
FOR THE COUNTRY?

Vicente Fox realized the need for structural reform and based his administration's strategy on this understanding. But, are the proposed reforms the right ones for the country? Are any reforms missing? Two different attempts have been made over the past years to come up with a new list of desired reforms for Latin America. The first was an attempt by heads of state to come up with a new common policy agenda in what became known as the "Monterrey Consensus"; the second was a study headed by Nancy Birdsall and Augusto de la Torre and published under the title *Washington Contentious*.[13]

The Monterrey Consensus involves broad policy recommendations and cooperation agreements between developing and developed countries in their pursuit of economic growth, poverty eradication, and sustainable development. Having met in Monterrey, Mexico, from March 18 to 22, 2002, at the invitation of Vicente Fox, Mexican government officials played a key role in formulating these recommendations and thus ensuring their consistency with Fox's agenda for structural reform.

The original Washington Consensus did not deal with issues of social equity. Instead, it focused primarily on recommendations that would ensure stability and enhance efficiency in a region that was dominated at that time by overindebted countries plagued by inflation and a tremendous misallocation of resources resulting from excessive intervention by the state. At that time, equity and poverty reduction were simply not the primary issues for consideration. On the other hand, *Washington Contentious* proposed 10 (plus 1) policy tools from which a "new and overriding objective emerges: to reduce poverty and improve equity without sacrificing growth."[14] Unlike the original Washington Consensus, however, the authors of *Washington Contentious* emphasized that there was no consensus about their recommendations; hence they used the word "contentious" in their title.

Regardless of whether the list lacked a consensus, the overall objective was consistent with Fox's vision of implementing a more humane model for Mexico's economic development. Therefore, it is worth examining the recommendations in order to determine if Fox's list of reforms is incomplete, at least by this account, and if some additional policy recommendations are needed. The following list compares the

10 recommendations included in the *Washington Contentious* with Fox's proposed reforms:

1. *Imposing rule-based fiscal discipline:* This reform takes the Washington Consensus recommendation of fiscal discipline one step further toward a healthy budget that is grounded in transparent rules and procedures. This policy is consistent with Fox's proposed budget reform.

2. *Smoothing out economic booms and busts:* This translates into the implementation of countercyclical fiscal and monetary policies. During the 2000–2003 recession, the Fox administration was blamed for carrying out a pro-cyclical monetary policy and failing to increase the budget deficit. However, whether or not monetary policy was actually restrictive is a debatable point, given that interest rates reached historical lows and the monetary base grew by almost 10 percent annually in real terms. On the fiscal side, until a balanced budget is achieved on average over time, there is very little room for a countercyclical policy. Nevertheless, one can argue that Fox's fiscal reform includes measures to expand the revenue base in order to contemplate eventual countercyclical policies.

3. *Creating social safety nets that trigger automatically:* Although Fox's reforms do not address additional social safety nets that are automatically triggered during economic slumps, there has been a significant increase in public spending that specifically includes subsidies to help families keep their children in school.

4. *Finding schools for the poor:* Fox's educational reform addresses the centralization issue and the recommended expansion of Internet access.

5. *Taxing the rich and spending more on the rest:* One of the central ideas of Fox's fiscal reform is to close tax loopholes and reduce the incidence of tax evasion, as considered in this recommendation. Eliminating consumption taxes, however, is not addressed, because this measure is likely to reduce revenues. Fox's tax reform proposals for 2002 and 2004 (which were rejected) included extending the value-added tax to food and medicine, which could arguably increase the tax burden on the poor. Fox's proposals do not consider higher taxes for the rich, but a more broad-based tax system that would raise revenues in order to spend "more on the rest."

6. *Giving small business a chance*: Fox's financial and judicial reforms address the issue of providing better access to financial services, and Fox has directed significant efforts designed to help small businesses.

7. *Protecting workers' rights*: The labor reform proposed by Fox specifically addresses making unions more independent and democratic and replacing inflexible rules that discourage job mobility and growth.

8. *Dealing openly with discrimination*: One of the few reforms that Fox has been able to approve involves a constitutional amendment that deals with discrimination.

9. *Repairing land markets*: Even though it can be argued that this recommendation is dealt with indirectly through a more aggressive housing program, it is probably the only policy recommendation that Fox has not addressed specifically. In fact, it could be argued that his administration has faced major setbacks in the area of property rights.

10. *Consumer-driven public services*: This policy recommends placing the poor and other low-income consumers at the heart of a new culture of service delivery. The Fox administration has placed great emphasis on increasing social programs geared toward this segment of the population.

This brief examination of the proposals contained in *Washington Contentious* shows that Fox's reform agenda is mostly consistent with international recommendations and includes the same objectives that are considered necessary for equitable growth, eradication of poverty, and promotion of competitiveness.

The administration's proposals for economic reforms—those that deal specifically with financial, electricity, fiscal, and labor reforms—are considered the backbone of Fox's strategy. Therefore, it is helpful to discuss what exactly these reforms entail.

Financial Reform

The only reform that has been approved thus far in Fox's administration is the financial reform, which consists of 10 separate sets of laws:

1. *The Law of Credit Institutions and the Law Regulating Financial Organizations*: The objectives are to channel a larger proportion

of domestic saving through the financial system, to encourage longer-term savings, to strengthen the government's regulatory and supervisory roles, to promote transparency and competition, and to enhance corporate governance in financial institutions. The law introduces mechanisms that help identify risks based on capitalization levels, furthers regulation on related lending, introduces requirements for independent board members, and extends the list of authorized services that banks can provide.

2. *Laws Governing Insurance Companies*: The objectives of these laws are to strengthen the institutional and regulatory frameworks in line with international standards, increase efficiency, bring the judicial framework in line with that of the financial sector, and develop better practices related to corporate governance. The changes in the laws involve improvement in the corporate structure of insurance institutions, establishment of a judicial framework that allows a proper dispersion of risk through reinsurance, uniform requirements for authorization of different insurance policies, and new capabilities for issuing debt.

3. *The Law of Savings and Popular Credit and the Organic Law of the Bank of National Savings*: These laws aim to strengthen the institutional framework for low-income savings and credit schemes and to increase market access for low-income families and small businesses. The Law of Savings and Popular Credit creates a new state-run bank (the Bank of National Savings) designed to provide savings and credit services to low-income families and businesses that do not have access to traditional banking services. The Organic Law of the Bank of National Savings not only regulates the activities and operations of popular savings and loans institutions but also offers job training and access to consultants.

4. *The Law for Auxiliary Organizations and Credit Activities:* The objectives of this legislation are to define the legal framework for auxiliary credit organizations and foreign exchange institutions and also to establish procedures that enable the detection of money-laundering activities.

5. *The Organic Law for the Federal Mortgage Society*: This law creates a state-run mortgage institution in order to increase the housing supply for workers. This new institution is designed to promote construction and acquisition of housing, to allow the creation of a

secondary market for mortgages, and to increase available credit mechanisms for low-income families.

6. *The Law Regulating Corporations That Collect Credit Information*: This law regulates credit bureaus and establishes transparency rules for these types of corporations. The law provides a legal framework and defines basic concepts related to the use of the borrower's credit history.

7. *The Law Related to Mutual Funds*: This law is designed to promote the growth and development of mutual funds, to provide operational transparency, to avoid conflicts of interest, and to grant access to a larger range of savings options for the small investor.

8. *Laws Related to the Stock Market Law and the National Banking Commission*: The objectives of these laws include modernizing brokerage firms, bringing stock market requirements in line with international standards, providing the market with further transparency and efficiency, establishing basic rights for minority stockholders, improving corporate governance of the stock market, and promoting the use of stock offerings.

9. *Laws Governing Development Banks*: This set of laws reduces excessive regulation, improves corporate governance, establishes administrative autonomy, and sets a requirement for further transparency as well as capital requirements for all development banks.

10. *Laws Promoting and Strengthening Lending by Banks*: This legislation is designed to strengthen the legal framework for secured credit transactions and to improve the execution procedures related to trusts, security trusts, non-possessory pledges, and other credit transactions that involve commercial and mortgage loans. Amendments were introduced to seven laws that are aimed at reducing the cost of transactions and expanding options for securing credit transactions and promoting competition. These reforms complement various improvements introduced three years earlier, which were aimed at improving credit guarantees and reestablishing bank credit.

After the banking crisis of 1995, it became clear that the entire financial system needed a new regulatory and legal framework based on transparency, reinforced property rights, and a stronger supervisory structure. Although the set of new laws passed by Congress between 2001 and 2003 can be considered an integral reform of the financial system, the legislation cannot be considered separate from the efforts carried out during the last years of the previous administration. Nevertheless, in order to reactivate bank credit, the banking system needed much stronger guarantees that would minimize nonperforming assets and impede the conditions that could give rise to a future crisis.

Real direct credit from commercial banks to the nonfinancial private sector peaked in December 1994, when the devaluation of the peso triggered a deep recession, rekindled inflation, and caused interest rates to soar. As a direct result of the banking crisis and its repercussions, the credit market dried up and fell continuously for 88 months. Between December 1994 and April 2002, real credit declined by an accumulated total of 77.2 percent. After hitting bottom in April 2002, credit started to grow for the first time in more than seven years, but then began registering negative growth rates again by mid-2003. While a recovery finally seemed to be taking place in 2004, it was focused on consumer and housing credit, with a persistent and notable absence in direct business credit.

Even though low interest rates and an improved legal framework historically favor renewed economic growth, the recession dictated a very slow recovery. Nonetheless, it is difficult to foresee a sustained level of future economic growth without a functional banking system. This reform is a key factor in establishing the necessary conditions that will enable new credit flows into the economy as economic activity picks up the pace in the near future. Fortunately, this is the one area on which all political parties have agreed and, hence, have approved the necessary reforms.

Electricity Reform

Congress has discussed different versions of electricity reform for nearly a decade without reaching any kind of consensus. The debate has left the economic issues behind and has entered the realm of pure politics, thus losing the focus on issues that truly matter. In January 1999, Ernesto Zedillo, Mexico's last PRI president, first introduced a proposal for a major reform, which was rejected primarily by PAN, the leading opposition party. Two years later, Vicente Fox, the first PAN president, introduced a similar bill, which the leading opposition party, this time the PRI, rejected. This turn of events is probably the best example of the current political problems Mexico faces as it experiments with its new democracy. This section will address some of the basic questions that have persisted throughout the debate.

Will the gap between supply and demand for electric energy increase? The original reasoning behind Ernesto Zedillo's proposal in 1999 was that the modernization of Mexico's electrical power sector required a vast sum of investments over the next 10 years in order to ensure the necessary growth in the supply needed to meet the country's demand. Given increasing budget constraints, the federal government was not capable of financing all the efforts along these lines; thus, the only recourse was to open up the sector to private investment.

The opponents to Zedillo's reform, however, argued that private investment was not necessary. The lack of resources to invest in basic electricity infrastructure projects is a consequence of the financial structure of the state-owned electric company, the Federal Electricity Commission, or CFE, which has little say over the use of its own resources. The federal government milks the CFE through high taxes, transfers, and rights, leaving it without the funds required for investments. The CFE is then forced to turn to the government for new investments, which means competing with all other federal needs. The solution is to grant the CFE complete financial autonomy and to treat the CFE from a tax perspective exactly the same way that an ordinary private company is treated. This way, the CFE would be self-sufficient and able to make all its future investments on its own.

Zedillo's original strategy was to paint a scenario of selective power blackouts and a continued increase in the cost of electricity as the gap between supply and demand continued to grow. Increased demand was projected over the next 10 years in order to illustrate the growing need for investment in electricity generation. The amount projected was so large that it led to the almost immediate conclusion that it would be nearly impossible for the government to channel enough financial resources to the CFE.

The opposition responded by questioning the projections and accusing the government of running a campaign of intimidation designed to justify privatizing the CFE. Since then, so many projections of the demand for electricity have emerged—together with calculations of financial needs—that no one knows which estimates to believe.

Nevertheless, it is not necessary to have firm projections to substantiate logic, which indicates that demand will continue to grow at the same pace as, or faster than, it has been growing in the past. At the same time, however, there is no reason to believe that supply will fail to grow at the pace required to meet users' demands. Investment outlays will be made, because the federal government will never allow electrical power to become scarce and thereby create a major bottleneck for economic growth.

This argument leads to an initial conclusion: There will be no lack of supply in electrical energy in the future, and all necessary investments will be made to ensure future supply. What is not known, however, is where the financial resources will come from. The federal government is facing growing budgetary constraints that imply a significant opportunity cost for each peso spent. Exactly what is the opportunity cost? The government has a limited supply of resources and needs to pay wages to public employees, including teachers and health care providers, and at the same time it needs to build and maintain schools and hospitals, improve security, and fulfill a growing number of obligations. Every peso spent can potentially be considered for an alternative project. The opportunity cost is precisely the amount that is not spent on other needs because of the increasing requirements for investment in the electricity sector.

What are the options for channeling resources into electricity generation? Ernesto Zedillo argued that 87 percent of programmable government expenditures were previously committed to specific projects, leaving very little flexibility for deciding where to allocate new investments. In spite of his constant criticism of inefficient public spending throughout his presidential campaign, once he took office Vicente Fox found this percentage to be above 90 percent. If the trend of growing government commitments is extrapolated, it is clear that the maneuvering room will continue to dwindle over time. And no matter how much effort the government puts forth in saving money, the trend appears to be irreversible.

All governments face budget constraints that time and again have proven impossible to ignore. When facing chronic deficits, the ongoing problem is how to finance government programs. Mexico's recurring crises have all originated in abuse of the federal budget deficit. Experiences in other countries and at other times all end up with the same conclusion: a government cannot spend beyond its revenues indefinitely.

In the past, Mexican governments have used public debt in a recurrent fashion. Domestic debt has caused inflation and instability to the extent of impeding economic growth. Foreign debt has caused problems with Mexico's balance of payments, which led to the devaluation crises. The lesson that has been repeated constantly throughout history is that the country faces significant losses as a result of excessive debt. Fortunately, Mexico has reduced foreign debt levels to sustainable levels. As of December 2003, public external debt as a percentage of GDP was approximately 12.5 percent—much lower than the 60.6 percent that Mexico faced in 1986. Over the last 10 years, Mexico has gone from a severely indebted country by World Bank standards to a less indebted country. This shift has allowed the government to maintain both stability and control over its balance of payments in order to avoid future crises.

The current problem lies in Mexico's domestic debt, which not only has remained at relatively high levels but also has been growing year after year with chronically high public-sector borrowing requirements (PSBR). According to the traditional definition of public debt, the federal deficit was projected at 0.3 percent of GDP for 2004, but this figure does not constitute a true indicator of the condition of public finances. As a result, Mexico's Finance Ministry produces another measure—PSBR—which is estimated at almost 3 percent for the same year. While this definition is broader, it still does not include state and local governments' deficits or contingent liabilities from pension programs.

An additional problem lies in the government's dependence on nonrecurring revenues—that is, sources of future financing that are not reliable—for financing the public deficit. At the same time, the current revenue stream depends heavily on income from oil exports, which fluctuates from year to year and is a volatile, imprecise source of revenue that complicates financial planning.

Public finances in Mexico are in a precarious state, and at some unforeseeable moment this situation could coincide with declining oil revenues resulting from low international prices or dwindling oil reserves. The immediate effect is upward pressure on interest rates, which not only causes a fall in productive investment and increases the cost of living but also implies an increase in federal revenues that must be used to service the debt. As the government's financial requirements rise, private investment is crowded out.

This state of affairs leads to a second conclusion: The government must find alternative ways to increase its budgetary restraint while simultaneously reducing present debt levels. This can be achieved through a fiscal reform that increases revenues and reduces the incidence of tax evasion. Another option is to reduce nonpriority spending and a decline in transfers to the private sector, as long as the government can still maintain the public welfare. This is precisely the most important argument for involving private investment in the electricity sector. It is not an issue of indiscriminately opening up the sector to private investment, because the government maintains its responsibility to provide electrical energy to the entire population, including low-income households. The government can allow this sector to open up to private investment in an intelligent way, one that still ensures the protection of the nation's interests.

Is privatization necessary? Given the scarcity of resources, the government needs the support provided by private investment to carry out public programs. However, this need by itself is not enough to signal the need for privatization. The issue goes beyond purely economic reasoning and has failed to achieve a consensus because of the ideological reasoning to which it has been subjected. Therefore, it is important to address the political context of privatization.

On the one hand, right-wing neoliberal dogma states that productive operations must be privatized. The central argument is that the private sector, which must respond to supply and demand, will always make better use of scarce resources and allocate them more efficiently. Therefore, according to this argument, privatization becomes the only means to an end and is also compatible with a higher level of welfare. The counterargument to the neoliberalists' position is that privatization cannot be an automatic response to all economic problems. Certain natural monopolies—such as public lighting, the national army, and public security, to name a few—function better under state control. In addition, society prefers to have the government be responsible for certain social needs—for example, reduction of poverty, delivery of public health services, and the development of the national infrastructure—because one cannot expect the private sector to address these issues. As a result, privatization cannot and should not be an end in itself, but simply a means, among many others, to reach a specific objective, like providing social welfare. Thus, this argument holds that when the government chooses to privatize, it must have very clear objectives in mind.

On the other hand, left-wing ideology, which is just as dogmatic and narrowly focused as the position of the extreme right, holds the view that privatization must be avoided at any cost, because profit mentality inevitably leads to higher prices and neglect of the common good. Just as neoliberalists propose privatization as an end in itself, the left proposes avoiding privatization as a basic principle. The counter-argument to the left-wing position is that, if the state operates a business that can just as easily be run by the private sector, the government's bureaucratic structure will cause the enterprise to become bloated and confuse its priorities with actions that are not in the public interest. Although government intervention is sometimes necessary, undue interference with market forces usually causes more problems than it solves.

These two extreme positions commit the same error: They both confuse the means with the end. It seems illogical to have a debate on electricity reform with each side predisposed to acceptance or rejection of privatization. Privatization should be viewed as a means that can sometimes work very well in terms of certain objectives, but one that should be avoided in other cases. What should really matter is the final objective. Will privatization help guarantee sufficient electricity for the country's needs? Will it promote higher economic growth without distortions in equity? There are no obvious answers to these questions.

A more modern, center-left perspective is starting to emerge in Mexico, where the issue is no longer seen in ideological terms. The fall of the Berlin Wall and the disintegration of the Soviet bloc were catalyzing elements for the world's left. A new left, more pragmatic and less dogmatic (like Europe's third wave), has emerged, and its adherents accept certain concepts that until recently belonged only to the right. Today the importance of sound public finances, the autonomy of monetary authorities, and a more widespread use of market forces (still within the realm of the public interest) are basic elements of the positions of many Socialist parties throughout the world. The extremes are being abandoned and a new left-of-center position—one that respects market forces while cautioning against their indiscriminate use—is emerging.

Nevertheless, contradictions between private thinking and public discourse remain. For example, Cuauhtémoc Cárdenas, the moral leader of the Democratic Revolutionary Party (PRD), has reiterated his opposition to reform of the electricity sector that includes opening it up to private investment. However, in a private interview, Cárdenas maintained that

> privatization should be seen simply as one more political and economic scheme within a larger range of options to satisfy problems. If something works well, no matter in whose hands it is operating, we should leave it alone. If something fails to work properly, we should analyze it and then make a decision. Private investment is a natural complement to public investment, which should be promoted when we need to amplify investment. The sale of electric installations, however, will not increase the capacity to generate electricity. We can justify opening up the sector to private investment in order to increase capacity, as a complement to the existing stock. But it would be an error to sell something that is working fine in the hands of the government.[15]

The issue of privatization is highly controversial. History has shown that, for better or worse, difficult times have resulted in expropriations of certain industries. In 1938, Mexico's oil industry was nationalized as a response to clear foreign abuses. In 1962, the electricity sector was nationalized more for practical reasons than for any other reason. In 1982, the banking sector was nationalized for reasons that were rather unclear. Privatizations came in waves starting in the mid-1980s as the core of a new development strategy for the country. Even though privatization has its logic, deals were carried out in the early 1990s that involved suspicious operations and many of these transactions ended up flagrant failures. The major arrangements were with commercial banks, and less than four years after the deals were consummated, they quickly ended in a systemic crisis and led to a massive increase in the public debt. As a result, society began to question the sale of public assets and to demand greater transparency in government operations.

The Mexican experience demonstrates that before an industry is privatized, the need for such a measure and any existing alternatives must be thoroughly examined. The final objective of the electricity reform is to increase installed capacity without hindering the public sector's borrowing requirements. The privatization of the CFE by itself will not increase generation capacity. In fact, a legitimate doubt exists whether a privatized CFE would be interested in expanding the national transmission grid, especially in rural areas and marginalized regions of the country. It hardly seems profitable to expand electricity to the remaining 5 percent of the population currently living in darkness.

There seems to be no convincing argument that justifies the privatization of the CFE at any cost. Nevertheless, regardless of the final outcome, it seems logical for the CFE to have control over its own management through administrative and financial autonomy in order to prevent its resources from being used to finance the government's budget deficit. The CFE is not an inefficient company and it does not need to be one just because it is in the government's hands.

This realization leads to a third conclusion: Privatization per se does not seem to be completely justified in light of past experience. Privatization by itself does not guarantee that the final objectives will be met, and it could also lead to social and political problems. Privatization is not the only means available for channeling resources to meet investment needs.

What is the difference between opening up the electricity sector to private investment and privatization? Given the country's experiences, it is clear that Mexican society does not favor privatization; that is, the people oppose privatizing either because they consider it a fad or because it is idiosyncratic to technocratic ideology. However, Mexico should avoid the other extreme, that of avoiding opening up certain industries to private investment simply because it could end up in privatization. Congress must be pragmatic and base its decisions in terms of what is needed to promote competition, reduce prices, and obtain resources for further investments.

If private investment is a natural complement to—not a substitute for—public investment, there should be no impediment to fostering this policy. Opening up the electricity sector to private investment in order to expand generation capacity should not be a threat to the CFE, but a complement to existing capacity. There is no convincing argument for avoiding private investment as long as the CFE remains in state hands and continues to guarantee access and unfettered use of the national transmission grid.

Why does opposition to opening up the sector to private investment exist? The main arguments are that this step will eventually lead to privatization, that it will increase fees for electricity, and that the state will lose control over the market. But even with private investment involved in the generation of electricity, the government's reform proposal states that the CFE would still guarantee supply to rural areas and less attractive regions within the country and would ensure the generation, transmission, and supply of all the electric power that is needed for public use. Mexico's Energy Commission would determine long-term prices in order to avoid fluctuations and would avoid the short-term conflicts that arise between buyers and sellers. Private investment would be limited to providing scarce financial resources and aimed primarily at large-scale users within the private sector—the consumers primarily responsible for intraday volatility in consumption.

This line of thinking leads to a fourth conclusion: Both government and society would win by opening up the electricity sector to private investment. The key to electricity reform does not lie in who the owner might be, but in proper regulation of the sector. The problem is that the marginal cost of producing electricity varies widely over time, forcing producers to confront capacity constraints. As a result, most countries have opted to regulate prices and thereby avoid having the retail price reflect cost variations. Opening up the sector to private investment does not mean that the government will stop regulating, supervising, and determining the rules of the game.

Is modification of the Constitution necessary? Article 27 of the Mexican Constitution states that the generation, transmission, conversion, distribution, and supply of electrical energy for the purpose of providing a public service is the exclusive responsibility of the government. The Constitution also states that the government cannot grant the private sector concessions to carry out any of these activities. Mexico's Supreme Court has ruled that this provision means that the generation of electricity for self-consumption and the sale of any excess to the national transmission grid (permitted by a law passed in 1992) are unconstitutional.

The court's ruling indicates that the Constitution must be modified in order to allow private investment for the generation of electricity. It is not necessary, however, to eliminate the exclusive function of the state but, rather, only to specify that this exclusivity is limited to the provision of public services, which include maintenance of the national transmission grid. It is also necessary to clarify the government's role in regulating the market in order to ensure that private investment is limited to power generation. To avoid discussion of eventual privatization, an article could be included in the Constitution that specifies that the CFE remains a state-run company.

Thus, a fifth conclusion can be made: It would be prudent to modify the Constitution to permit private investment for the generation of electricity and to grant legal certification of investments made by the private sector since 1992. Care should be taken to arrive at a precise constitutional interpretation that maintains the role of the state as the entity responsible for providing electrical power as a public service and for regulating the electricity sector.

Can the proposed reform ensure better service and lower prices? Public opinion polls indicate that people are opposed to the privatization of the electricity sector because they fear higher prices. However, opening up the sector to private investment—in contrast to privatization—does not mean that the current scheme of price fixing needs to be changed. Prices would still be regulated by the Energy Commission, which would be in charge of setting competitive prices, even according to international standards.

In the ongoing debate, one side argues that prices will increase if private firms distribute electrical power, whereas the other side holds that privatization would guarantee lower prices. The problem is that the discussion involves myths and confusion surrounding the cause and effect of the different variables involved. The price of service is not determined by who the owner would be but by various other factors that are independent of whether the ownership is in the private sector or the public sector.

Electricity markets are difficult to regulate and restructure compared with most markets that have served as examples of deregulation, such as airlines, transportation systems, highways, gasoline, and banking. Demand for electricity is harder to predict and is not sensitive to short-term price fluctuations. Supply faces constraints during peak hours, and maintaining inventories is extremely costly. Therefore, if supply and demand are used exclusively to determine prices without restrictions, prices would be characterized by excessive short-term volatility, indicating that prices could increase or could decrease just as easily.

Most countries have two options for limiting price fluctuations. The first involves having a market regulated by the government or by an independent commission. In this case, an average price is established that uses profits to compensate for losses over time. The other option, which is similar to and not excluded by the first, involves establishing long-term contracts between buyers and sellers.

These considerations lead to a sixth conclusion: An important part of electricity reform is the regulation of the market and creation of appropriate mechanisms for this purpose. Privatization is unnecessary as long as the market is open to private investment. Deregulation should be avoided and supervisory roles must be maintained and strengthened in order to guarantee good service and accessible prices.

Is the experience of other countries relevant? Many analysts have looked to other countries for experiences that can apply to a particular economy. Most studies, however, are biased toward the results that analysts want to find. Some studies show success stories with privatization, whereas others point to successful electricity sectors under state control. The conclusion seems to be that privatization is not a necessary condition for success, but neither is a state-controlled electrical industry. Therefore, it is dogmatic to insist on privatization as the only solution for Mexico's electricity sector. By the same token, however, insisting on avoiding privatization at all costs is just as narrow a view.

For every country that has a successful private industry, there is another one that has encountered problems. Similarly, every thriving state-owned sector can be matched with another problematic case. Positive results are not highly correlated with ownership, which, above all, appears to be irrelevant. Regulation and supervision, however, play highly important roles even without regard to the dichotomy between the private and public sectors.

Thus, it is possible to arrive at a seventh conclusion: International experiences are not that relevant for determining whether private or public ownership is preferable. Experiences are too broad and inconclusive to form a basis for a definite recommendation. It should be noted that Fox's proposal does not call for privatization, but only for opening up the sector to private investment for generation of electrical power. This reform seems to be a well-balanced proposal that would attract additional investment without hindering public finances and at the same time leaving the ownership issue intact.

After more than four years of intense discussion, the PRI and the PRD rejected Fox's proposal. The PRI's support for and opinions of the reforms vary, but Senator Manuel Bartlett (a member of the PRI and the former governor of Puebla, minister of education, minister of government, and presidential pre-candidate) took up a personal campaign to prevent the reform from being approved. Given that this reform originated in the Senate, which is not up for election until 2006, it is unlikely that the proposal will be given further consideration in the second half of Fox's term. Many expected a new bill sponsored by the PRI with the support of the PRD to be debated; this bill would have only granted the CFE more autonomy. Even this much lighter version of an energy reform is all but dead today. Nevertheless, financial pressure arising from the condition of Mexico's public finances will continue to mount, and it is highly likely that the issue will be re-addressed after 2006.

Fiscal Reform

Almost every study of Mexico's public finances starts by singling out the fact that tax revenues as a percentage of Mexico's GDP are among the lowest not only in Latin America but also in the world. Some may argue that this is not by itself a negative factor, given that taxes create a burden on society and crowd out productive investment. Mexico's low tax base is not, however, a product of a carefully planned strategy or relatively low tax rates, but a result of a highly complex system that has more exceptions than rules, a high incidence of tax evasion, and a large informal financial sector.

At the same time, oil exports account for 15–20 percent of Mexico's total revenues, depending on the international price per barrel. This dependence on oil exports causes volatility and a continuous need for budget adjustments when oil prices are lower than anticipated. The gasoline tax represents an additional 15 percent of revenues, bringing Mexico's dependence on oil-related revenue to more than 30 percent.

Mexico's public deficit stood at 16.1 percent of GDP in 1987, prior to President Carlos Salinas's reform efforts that started in 1988. Salinas was able to reduce the deficit gradually, achieving a budget surplus of 2 percent of GDP in 1991. After maintaining a surplus for three years (1991–1993), a balanced budget was reported in 1994, the last year of the Salinas administration. Although the fiscal retrenchment efforts during the Salinas years were definitely impressive, the government toyed with different definitions for calculating the deficit. For example, in 1992 the Finance Ministry reported three different numbers: a surplus of 3.5 percent of GDP for the overall balance; a 0.5 percent surplus, which excluded nonrecurring income from privatization; and a 1.6 percent surplus, which excluded nonrecurring income and financial intermediation. The following year, the government dropped the concept of financial intermediation altogether and reported a surplus of 1 percent of GDP in 1993 and a balanced budget in 1994. If financial intermediation had been included in the figure reported in 1994, the government would have registered a deficit of approximately 4 percent.

The budget deficit increased sharply during President Ernesto Zedillo's administration as a result of the reform of the pension system and the bank bailout programs. Although Zedillo can be credited with enforcing fiscal discipline, the expanded definition of the deficit—the public-sector borrowing requirement—indicates that the average deficit during Zedillo's administration was 5.2 percent of GDP. Despite an additional effort introduced by Fox during his first year in office, PSBR still reached 3.73 percent of GDP in 2001. As a result, another fiscal reform was necessary if only to reduce PSBR and guarantee future economic stability.

Fox promised to increase tax revenues by up to 6.5 percent of GDP within the first four years of his administration. The resources were to be used to finance key programs in education (3 percent of GDP), health (1 percent), poverty (1 percent), and industrial policy (1 percent). At the same time, Fox proposed to balance the budget by 2004 and to achieve a surplus of 0.5 percent of GDP by 2005. The primary goals of his proposal were to simplify and homogenize the tax structure in order to reduce the incidence of tax evasion from an estimated 35 percent to 20 percent of the tax base. Estimated revenue from these measures was expected to reach 4 percent of GDP in three years. Modernization of tax administration and adjustments in the process of tax collection were considered sufficient to lower the incidence of tax evasion by an estimated 35 percent. These measures were expected to bring in an additional 2 percent of GDP in tax revenue over four years.

A great deal of the discussion at the time focused on how to incorporate social equity and poverty reduction issues into a fiscal reform proposal. The left and left-of-center wanted to use income policy, together with public spending, to incorporate a more progressive tax structure that would tax the rich and help the poor in order to achieve equitable income distribution. The government, however, estimated that public spending by itself would be much more effective if poverty alleviation programs and other equity-based policies were implemented. The administration believed that reform should be aimed at increasing tax revenues as much as possible without hindering private investment incentives in order to have more income to spend. This approach would require using more consumption-based taxes, which are considered regressive in nature. The government argued, however, that the regressive impact on lower-income families could be more than offset by spending programs that were properly focused.

As a result, the government came out with its fiscal reform proposal in March 2001—called the "new distributive public finances"—aimed at maintaining healthy finances, promoting an equity-based reorientation of public spending, and reducing dependence on oil revenues. At the same time, the proposal addressed the need to reduce the incidence of tax evasion, to avoid crowding out private investment, and to increase the total intake from taxes in order to finance additional programs.

The core of the proposal was to eliminate exceptions to the value-added tax (VAT), which included unifying the tax rate across all regions and for all goods and services. In theory, the value-added tax is the easiest to administer and promotes compliance, as long as there are no exceptions or exemptions. In practice, the VAT has multiple exceptions, exemptions, and rates, and these vary from region to region. The government estimated that it could increase tax revenues and simplify the process by having a single VAT rate with no exceptions. To compensate lower-income families for the imposition of a higher value-added tax, which affected them primarily as a result of applying the VAT to food and medicine, the government proposed providing a subsidy through income tax payments and an increase in poverty reduction programs. Nevertheless, the PRI and the PRD opposed any tax at all on food and medicine, a position that turned out to be the biggest stumbling block and the main reason for the reforms being rejected.

The approved 2002 budget included only a few of the provisions addressed in Fox's original reform proposal. To compensate for the lower income that resulted from a rejection of the VAT proposal, Congress introduced a luxury tax and special taxes on specific goods. Nevertheless, actual revenue fell far short of projected income, and the attempted reform was considered a complete failure. In theory, some measures were introduced to simplify procedures, but the consensus among business owners is that Mexico's tax system today is much more complex than it was just a few years ago. Some of these issues were raised again in the 2003 and 2004 budget proposals, but all were readily rejected by Congress. As a result, fiscal reform is still a pending issue on Fox's agenda.

Prior to the 2003 budget approval process, the government tried to negotiate another attempt at fiscal reform but failed to arrive at anything close to a consensus even for a minimum of changes. The Finance Ministry then decided to wait until after midterm elections in July 2003 to restart negotiations with a newly elected Chamber of Deputies, having found it almost impossible to negotiate with the outgoing Congress. The federal government, however, found that the newly elected Congress for the 2003–2006 term was even further away from any type of a consensus on the issue than its predecessors had been.

Even though all parties have stated that they were willing to negotiate and work at approving a fiscal reform within the last couple of years of Fox's administration, it seems very unlikely that Congress will reach an agreement that meets Fox's objectives. This means that Fox will be forced to finish the second half of his term without the additional revenue the government needs and still dependent on oil revenues. As a result, potential GDP growth will remain below 4.5 percent, needed investment for maintaining and improving the infrastructure will be limited, and resources for expanded education, health care, and poverty reduction programs will not be available.

Labor Reform

Mexico's labor laws, which are considered to be extremely rigid, contain many socialistic provisions that some believe overprotect the worker. Therefore, government officials have targeted labor reform for many years. Carlos Salinas was the first president to try to change several provisions in the law, but he quickly learned that organized labor was unwilling to budge on these issues. Ernesto Zedillo readdressed the issue again, also without success, with union leaders taking a tough stance against what they perceived to be a movement to weaken workers' rights. Nevertheless, the World Bank, the International Monetary Fund, and the International Labor Organization have all insisted that Mexico needs to inject large doses of flexibility into its labor markets.

The real appreciation of the peso between 1999 and 2002 introduced an additional sense of urgency to find ways to increase overall competitiveness in the economy. Between 1996 and 2001, average dollar costs for a unit of labor in the manufacturing sector increased by 53.9 percent, sharply eroding Mexico's labor advantage. Nevertheless, the government learned that exchange-rate policy is not the way to ensure competitiveness, given that the policy reduces purchasing power, causing inflationary pressures, and is also difficult to maintain over time. Therefore, the government must enact reforms in current labor laws that will ensure continued productivity gains, reduce hidden costs, and introduce much needed flexibility to help labor adjust to different circumstances.

Of all the pending reforms, the most difficult one has always been related to labor, given the deep divisions between business and union leaders in terms of what can and should be changed. Nevertheless, the Labor Ministry began talks in early 2001 with an open mind and a renewed hope that some consensus could be achieved. The strategy was to avoid discussing the more sensitive issues at first and to concentrate, instead, on areas in which some sort of change was feasible for both sides. After a year of almost daily talks, the government thought it had enough points of agreement to muster together what it called the first wave of reforms in Mexico's labor laws.

In spite of the difficulties involved, the Labor Ministry was overly optimistic that this first wave would be approved, because the approach to this reform was quite different from the one adopted for the fiscal and electricity reforms. The government made it clear from the outset that it had no prior recommendations or a specific agenda on the table, but that both business and labor leaders would decide what issues would be negotiated. The government saw its role as a simple mediator, bringing labor and business representatives to sit down together. Another reason for the optimism was that, from the very beginning, the negotiations involved PRI legislators who were also labor leaders. Moreover, these leaders were members not only of Congress but also of the congressional committee that oversees labor issues. The government believed that this strategy would help any agreements reached in these talks to be easily approved by the congressional committee, with a high chance of final approval by the entire floor of the lower house. Given that the negotiations involved a PAN government and PRI labor leaders, the administration thought that the reform would have the support of both parties, and thus enough for approval.

The Labor Ministry's strategy included leaving the media out of discussions in order to minimize the politicization of the issues under discussion, something that had severely damaged the effort to pass fiscal reform. The second consideration was to explicitly avoid the recommendations made by the International Monetary Fund and the World Bank, or at least the exact wording used in their reports. For example, the word "flexibility" was completely avoided in stating one objective of the reform, given that the term was identified with demonized words like "privatization" and "globalization." Instead, the Labor Ministry emphasized "rationalization" of labor markets, a well-accepted term that had no political stigma attached.

The government's third consideration in the effort to pass labor reform was to avoid the more controversial aspects that could have dominated the agenda and blocked progress on other issues. This strategy meant carrying out labor reform in various steps (or waves), instead of a one-time, all-inclusive approach. The Labor Ministry initially targeted fall 2002 for the first wave of agreements and 2004 for a second wave. The first attempt was finally submitted to Congress toward the end of 2002 but never even reached the floor. In spite of careful planning and a change in strategy, the issues proved to be much more delicate than anticipated, and legislators preferred to postpone any serious discussion until after midterm elections in July 2003.

The first wave of labor reforms included measures that were designed to

- ensure and increase transparency and accountability in unions,

- reinforce antidiscriminatory measures,

- recognize particular circumstances involving small- and medium-sized firms,

- eliminate bureaucratic steps,

- strengthen the liberty, independence, and governance of unions,

- provide job training and productivity enhancement, and

- establish new contractual possibilities.

Because unions' current voting practices are extremely vulnerable to manipulation, the labor reform proposed public registration of unions that would eliminate "paper" unions and inject transparency into the voting process. The proposal called for universal secret voting on neutral grounds that would minimize intimidation tactics. Firms with fewer than 20 employees would be exempt from the legal requirements for registration. Unions would be able to negotiate specific dates for holidays—for example, moving them to the nearest Friday or Monday. Layoffs and temporary work suspensions would be recognized through more precise wording in the law—for example, stating that collective contracts complement the Federal Labor Law—and the law would recognize the legality of work suspension agreements stipulated in contracts.

What was not included or changed in the first wave of labor reform? The business sector has long argued for the elimination of the profit-sharing scheme currently required by law. Businesses have also asked for a reduction in the legal compensation required when a worker is dismissed or laid off. Labor leaders have asked for unemployment insurance or compensation. However, from the outset of negotiations, the parties agreed that these issues would not be subject to discussion in these early rounds.

Another item in the labor law that will not be changed is the one related to hourly wages. Even though the law recognizes part-time employment, wages cannot be paid on the basis of the number of hours worked. Thus, if a person is hired for five hours a day, the employer must pay for five hours of work, even if the employee put in fewer hours. However, the reform includes the possibility of accumulating working days without a break in order to have longer periods away from work. For example, a person would be able to work 10 straight days without a break and then have 4 or 5 days off. This practice already occurs regularly in many sectors but is not currently legal.

THE REFORM AGENDA: WHAT HAPPENS NEXT ?

Vicente Fox based the entire strategy for his six-year term on the approval of his reform package. Of his list of 10 reforms, only one—financial reform—was approved during his first three years in office. The president now faces the second half of his term without most of the reforms on which he had depended. Therefore, it is very likely that Fox will be unable to meet his goals for economic growth and employment. The results of the 2003 midterm elections were not promising, with the president's party, the PAN, losing 53 of its 207 congressional seats.

During the 2000–2003 legislative sessions, the PRI had 209 seats in the Chamber of Deputies, as opposed to the PAN's 207 seats. In 2003–2006, however, the PRI will have 223 seats against the PAN's 154. Instead of a difference of two possible votes, the government will now have to try to negotiate unpopular reforms facing a deficit of 69 votes in Congress. The difference is even greater if the PRD allies itself with the PRI against the government's proposed reforms, something that was apparent throughout 2004 and is likely to continue. The PRI–PRD coalition increases the total number of all opposition parties' votes from 261 to 319, which means that the bloc has a 165-vote advantage compared to the 54-vote difference in the previous Congress. This alignment points to a very difficult uphill battle, at best.

If any of the administration's reforms are approved, they will be deeply influenced by the PRI's agenda. Thus, the electricity reform would probably exclude opening up the sector to private investment; any tax reform is bound to retain the exemption of food and medicine from the value-added tax (a primary reason that Fox's 2003 proposal was rejected); and the labor reform will most likely be very incomplete, limited to most of what was negotiated in the first wave.

This outlook leaves Fox no alternative but to try to change as much as he can without the support of new legislation. Deregulation efforts will need to be enhanced, and the government will need to increase its efforts to reduce nonpriority expenditures. Nevertheless, it is doubtful that potential GDP growth can be increased significantly, which means that Fox will surely fall short of most of his objectives.

The good news is that Mexico has risen to the top of the list of emerging market countries and has achieved a sharp reduction in the perceived level of risk associated with the Mexican economy. The government has made significant improvements in its external debt ratios, price stability, and fiscal discipline. As a result, a new economic crisis is not likely to arise any time soon. Thus, Mexico will not be taking any steps backward, as it has done so often in the past. The bad news is that Mexico does not appear to be moving forward either. Progress is projected to be remarkably slow in the upcoming years if there is no support for completing President Fox's reform agenda.

Notes

[1] Antonio Ortiz Mena labeled this period the "*desarrollo estabilizador*" and promoted the idea that conservative fiscal and monetary policies had provided the framework for growth accompanied by stability. The previous period of growth accompanied by inflation (1946–1958) had been the result of expansionary policies. Recent research into this period, however, shows that economic policy was more conservative in the 1950s than it was in the 1960s; the difference was the presence of external shocks during the 1950s (see Enrique Cárdenas, *La Política Económica en México, 1950–1994*, Fideicomiso Historia de las Américas, *Serie Hacienda* [Mexico City: El Colegio de México y Fondo de Cultura Económica, 1996]).

[2] Mexico was born as a republic in 1823 with external debt problems. As a result of renegotiating past debts, in 1942 external debt obligations were virtually eliminated in the famous Suárez-Lamont Agreement (see Jan Bazant, *Historia de la Deuda Exterior de México, 1823–1946* [Mexico City: El Colegio de México, Centro de Estudios Históricos, 1968]).

[3] See Raymond Vernon, *El Dilema del Desarrollo Económico de México* (Mexico City: Editorial Diana, 1966).

[4] Eduardo Suarez, Mexico's finance minister, and Thomas Lamont, the president of the Banking Steering Committee, agreed to forgive almost 90 percent of Mexico's debt, while the remaining 10 percent was to be paid in 30 years with a 20-year grace period.

[5] John Williamson, "What Washington Means by Policy Reform," in *Latin American Adjustment: How Much Has Happened?* ed. John Williamson (Washington, D.C.: Institute for International Economics, 1990). See also John Williamson, "Did the Washington Consensus Fail?" (presentation at the Center for Strategic and International Studies, Washington, D.C., November 6, 2002).

[6] While Salinas was blamed for maintaining a noncompetitive exchange rate, the rate remained at the bottom of the target zone throughout most of his administration, proof that the real appreciation was a result of capital flows. The problem of the exchange-rate regime was more a lack of flexibility than anything else.

[7] For a personal account of his reform efforts and what items were missing, see Carlos Salinas, *Mexico: The Policy and Politics of Modernization* (Mexico City: Plaza y Janes, 2002).

[8] Departamento de Análisis de REFORMA, *Reforma* (Mexico City), April 2003.

[9] See Moisés Naím, "Washington Consensus or Confusion," *Foreign Policy* (Spring 2000), and Moisés Naím, "Washington Consensus: A Damaged Brand," *Financial Times*, October 28, 2002.

[10] See Williamson, "Did the Washington Consensus Fail?"

[11] See Williamson, "What Washington Means by Policy Reform."

[12] If the Composite Index of Coincidental Indicators, produced by the Instituto Nacional de Estadística, Geografía e Informática, is used as the best mirror of the Mexican business cycle, the recession started in October 2000 and ended in September 2003. See www.inegi.gob.mx/bdine/bancos.htm.

[13] Nancy Birdsall and Augusto De la Torre, *Washington Contentious* (Washington, D.C.: Carnegie Endowment for International Peace, 2001).

[14] The "plus one" refers to an international policy recommendation to reduce rich-country protectionism, as opposed to the other 10 domestic policies.

[15] Private interview conducted by the author on April 3, 2000.

FIVE

CIVIL-MILITARY RELATIONS AND SECURITY POLICY IN MEXICO

Oscar Rocha

A study of civil-military relations in democratic Mexico brings to the forefront a troubling duality: recognition of the unique institutional strengths that the Mexican military represents to society, on the one hand, and a consequently surprising lack of knowledge and understanding among civilian and political society about the Mexican armed forces, on the other. In simpler terms, the military has become uncomfortably indispensable. The resulting tension in the civil-military relationship is compounded by profound changes in the Mexican political system that have effectively done away with the predictability that ruled the relationship before, and by the fact that no consistent and deliberate effort is being made in the political and policy realm to define new mechanisms and arrangements that correspond to the current circumstances. "Reform" is thus more an accidental result of daily interaction than a concerted policy directive.

The central proposition in this chapter is that in trying to modernize the civil-military interface in Mexico, it would be useless and counterproductive to focus only on the superficial expressions of civilian control of the military, as has been the focus in the rest of Latin America, given the political role that the military has had in many of the region's countries. Rather, the current dilemma demands the much more substantive process of making civilian authorities and society in Mexico take on the responsibility of co-ownership of defense and security policy with the military, so that the armed forces are able to perform effectively as an essential asset of a democratic state and so that politicians, civil society, and civilian institutions can feel that they have in the military a reliable and responsive institutional partner.

This chapter departs from the usual analytical treatment of the Mexican military in that it is a belated acknowledgement of the need to broaden the discussion beyond the limited confines of political science dogma regarding civil-military studies in Latin America,[1] with its holy grail of enforcing civilian control over the military and preventing the military's intervention in political affairs.[2] Instead, the analysis seeks to incorporate a public policy perspective that gives defense and security issues a voice in explaining the motivations and concerns of the professional military and its relations with civilians. This perspective not only is necessary to better understand how civilians and the military interact; it is the cornerstone of any reasonable attempt to positively influence *how* they interact. It is not difficult to argue that the relationship between civilians and the military in Mexico, from the perspective of both democratic control and security policy effectiveness, can be improved only through the construction of a dialogue in which both parties can communicate their priorities and views while recognizing each other as stakeholders in a common goal. This approach will not, in and of itself, eliminate friction and controversy, as civilians and the military have significantly different perspectives on policy, politics, and values, but it will make these phenomena more manageable.

Before contrasting these two sides of the equation—democratic control and security policy effectiveness—it is necessary to identify the main issues that affect them both, starting with Mexico's current dilemmas.

MEXICO AT THE CROSSROADS, AGAIN

At the dawn of the new century, with all its post–September 11 undertones, Mexico finds itself at an important crossroads. The country has the thirteenth-largest economy in the world, is the United States' second-largest trading partner, has more than 100 million inhabitants, and finds itself positioned for strong and stable development in the coming decades. Mexico certainly has the potential to achieve its domestic and international goals. However, as is the case with many other developing countries, Mexico has to deal simultaneously with a wide array of public policy demands. The polity has learned to discuss and reach general consensus on fairly complex economic policy choices, particularly those related to economic stability, among them setting low inflation targets, operating within budget constraints, and opening up the country's markets to trade. There is also widespread agreement with regard to the electoral criteria for the distribution of political power and a working system to achieve this in a way that the population can depend on in the future.

The Mexican polity has dealt much less effectively, however, with three broad security demands: the population's expectations of democratic governance, economic globalization, and international cooperation on security matters—all of which could seriously jeopardize Mexico's development and are seldom given the attention they deserve. The Mexican armed forces play a decisive role in each of these areas.

Political accountability has been on the rise in the past decade in Mexico, as voters have learned to voice their complaints and punish elected officials who fail to meet their expectations. In the recent past, the electorate seems to have found few issues to be more relevant than law enforcement and public security. Yet the political system has failed to deliver substantive results in these areas. It is not that politicians are oblivious to the significance of the issue. If someone were able to deliver tangible results in making Mexicans safer, the political opportunities would be enormous. The problem seems to lie in the lack of managerial expertise among civilian public figures, the dismal state of the police forces with which authorities must work, and the interconnectedness of a wide array of challenges that weaken isolated reforms and demand a much more comprehensive and consistent overhaul of the law and its enforcement. Furthermore, democratic accountability will remain a hollow concept as long as such an important area of public policy is not fully under the control of democratically elected authorities and impunity gets mixed up with corruption and general mismanagement. Given the failure of civilian politicians to deliver results, it is no surprise that the military has been sucked in to fill this void.

When it comes to globalization, few would still believe that its benefits can be reaped by countries that focus only on removing obstacles to economic activity and opening themselves up to international capital and investment flows. Economic development also requires human capital and a stable environment marked by trustworthy rule of law that, for the most part, are the result of a working polity and its institutional framework. That is why foreign investment flows toward certainty more than toward cheap sources of labor. The fact that Mexico's economy has supposedly been among the strongest in Latin America in recent years is circumstantial, given the woes that Argentina, Brazil, Venezuela, and Colombia have experienced.

Many structural inefficiencies are lurking in the Mexican economy, ready to impose their punishment in the struggle for international competitiveness. One relevant—but hard to measure—handicap is the cost that the crisis in Mexico's law-enforcement sector imposes on the economy, with the country's firms and business owners feeling compelled to take on many of the costs and risks associated with their own security. Similarly, Mexico's judicial system is still too much a source of uncertainty for the economic environment. For all the apparent success of Mexico's political and economic transformations, domestic insecurity and ambivalent attitudes about the rule of law have turned out to be the Achilles' heel that curtails the country's development as they interfere with the government's investment goals.

The international front is also becoming a major source of direct and indirect threats to Mexico's security, stability, and governance. Even though the reality does not yet appear to have sunk into the minds of Mexico's current policymakers, sharing a more than 3,000-kilometer land border with the United States—the country that was the site of the terrorist attacks on September 11, 2001, and the potential target of any consequences that might follow from the invasion of Iraq—has radically inserted Mexico into a vortex of insecurity for which it is materially and conceptually ill prepared.

A handful of potential threats illustrate the magnitude of the challenge Mexico faces. If security is more an exercise in prevention than in reaction, what would be the consequences of a smallpox bioterrorist attack in the United States that in no time would presumably reach the common border region and beyond, with the first responders and military personnel in one country having been vaccinated and those on the other side not? Similarly, what would happen if terrorists were able to hijack an airliner in Mexican air space? With no radar coverage in the northern two-thirds of the country and no fighter aircraft capable of intercepting a seized aircraft, the Mexican military would, in effect, be forced to relinquish defensive action to the United States Air Force.

If Mexico does not acknowledge the nature and level of these threats and acquire the capabilities and expertise to respond adequately, the country will only become a magnet for terrorists seeking to exploit its weaknesses and its proximity and level of integration with the United States. The consequences for the bilateral relationship if Mexico were used as a launching pad for a major terrorist attack against the United States would be devastating and irreversible, the North American Free Trade Agreement (NAFTA) notwithstanding. Similarly, a terrorist attack inside Mexican territory aimed at a popular resort, as occurred in Bali, for example, would devastate a significant economic sector and source of employment.

Mexico has a powerful handicap when it comes to addressing the consequences of international insecurity, and the country's recent history can explain this drawback. Countries like the United States and most of those in Europe that lived through the Cold War for a half-century, after emerging from an extraordinary conflict like World War II, learned and internalized at all levels a daily concern for security. Politicians in these countries spoke constantly of threats and the instruments that had to be acquired for national defense. The public was permanently aware of discussions about military policy; sizable budgets had to be devoted for the armed forces; and being part of the military at some point in life was an important and defining personal experience for the citizens of these countries.

On the other hand, during the Cold War, Mexico had a cozy geostrategic position—far removed from the front lines of the conflict. The absence of immediate threats to its own existence never created the conditions for the term "security" to become a household word. Civilians relegated any knowledge about military policy to the armed forces, and the Mexican military itself focused almost completely on issues relating to domestic stability and the armed forces' extensive role in rural law enforcement. Surprising as it may be to international analysts, not even the new security-dominated atmosphere that sprang from the September 11 attacks has been able to alter this pattern in Mexico. The extent of the difference between Mexico's historical experience and that of most other nations is what lies behind Mexico's lack of appreciation for the risks and threats that exist to its *own* security today, let alone the population's inability to understand the sense of vulnerability felt by people in other nations. It will take no small measure of strategic clarity and political leadership to reverse this trend and to narrow the gap between existing threats and the way they are currently misperceived.[3]

Aside from lacking a strategic vision about how it is affected by the international security environment, Mexico faces a set of challenges related to the physical resources of the only entity that is capable of effectively addressing all these broad security demands—that is, the state and its institutions. Now, more than it seemed just a few years back, the health and vitality of the state's infrastructure are a fundamental asset that a country like Mexico cannot do without.

Mexico is among a group of nations facing a crisis of identity as well as a crisis of performance. These states have not achieved the level of economic and institutional stability that would allow them to take their survival and position within the international arena for granted. Until recently, the forces of globalization had been undermining some of the main tenets of the concept of the nation-state, creating pressures for a more relaxed concept of sovereignty, a more limited scope of government actions, fostering regional autonomies within its territories, and greater conformance between national policies and internationally acceptable standards of behavior.

Facing this weakening of the state's traditional capabilities and jurisdictional scope, there is a growing wave of threats and challenges: drug trafficking, terrorism, organized crime, separatist movements, falling budgets, decaying infrastructure, social unrest, and growing populations. This group of states is fighting to validate their capability to provide their societies with security, stability, good governance, development, and some degree of equality. In the best of cases, the goal of these states is to become part of the developed world and to join the nations that have already solved most of these domestic challenges. In the worst-case scenario, these states are trying to avoid falling into the next category, that of failed states that exist primarily on paper and that simply coincide with territories marked by lawlessness and anarchy.

Meanwhile, the armed forces, the state's most traditional instrument, face their own dilemma. On the one hand, the downward trend in interstate conflict reduces the need for military forces and produces a peace dividend that leads to their downsizing. At the same time, the new threat environment and the weakness of other institutional forces, particularly law enforcement, pushes the military in countries like Mexico to assume new missions.

The change in the way the armed forces is used for nonmilitary missions has brought with it a gradual but important transformation of the structural conditions under which the military interacts with government and society. But this shift in missions has not been accompanied by a policy whose purpose is to harmonize them with the underlying set of agreements—both formal and informal—that regulate civil-military relations. This process of adaptation does not occur automatically or naturally; quite the contrary, it encounters profound resistance to change and can be successful only when strategic clarity is joined by a strong political will.

Democracy, for all its virtues, makes no guarantees regarding policy and institutional performance and provides no automatic correction to the troubling lack of attention given to the institutions themselves—particularly those within the executive branch—that carry most of the burden of policy implementation. In the case of Mexico, the historical development of the federal government has also produced strong asymmetries among agencies, and there is often a glaring mismatch between the missions that institutions are individually assigned and their organizational strength, legal support, political accountability, and funding.

Nevertheless, the existence and importance of the three broad security demands—expectations of democratic governance, economic globalization, and international cooperation on security matters—and the need to reconstitute an institutional capability to organize public policy in the security arena have, for the most part, not been able to trigger in Mexico the legislative, budgetary, and bureaucratic transformations that are required in the current global climate. These modifications have happened in other parts of the world in response to new threats to international security or for domestic reasons. But Mexico's current leadership does not seem able or willing to find the resources and the political commitment needed to make these changes, as other, seemingly more pressing, issues top the government's agenda. Reform has been limited to whatever each federal agency head wants and is able to do. In the case of the armed forces, there is also a reluctance to tinker with a capability that is continuously being asked to perform a wide array of missions.

This missed opportunity to reframe Mexico's security policy in light of the new international threat environment contrasts sharply with what has occurred in many other parts of the world. The institutional framework of nations of all stripes has found the terrorists' attacks on the United States to be a blessing in disguise. Nonstate actors have created such a sense of vulnerability that the global community is witnessing weaker states' willingness to reembrace the most classical form of the nation-state as the only conceivable human construct capable of organizing national defense and reestablishing the expected level of protection and international cooperation. At the same time, the stronger states' armed forces, law enforcement agencies, and intelligence services have been able to relegitimize their roles and budgets by focusing on their new mission: the war against terrorism.

Thus, in assessing the quality of governance in Mexico, a key question arises: How can the polity adjust its institutional framework to better respond to the changing set of challenges? This institutional outlook is perhaps the strongest reason for the Mexican military to become part of mainstream policy discussions. The military should be included not only for the changes that the armed forces themselves require but also—and even more important—for the organizational characteristics that they already possess and that propel them into all sorts of missions and responsibilities commonly associated elsewhere with civilian authorities.

THE PARADOX FACING THE MEXICAN MILITARY

To understand the position and the potential that the armed forces have with regard to shoring up the governance "rating" of the Mexican state, it is important to recognize that the Mexican military has long been caught in a paradox in which it is simultaneously needed but not wanted. Many in Mexico's political, economic, intellectual, and social elite—as well as most foreign analysts—consider the military an outdated and obsolete organization, with no true military capability to speak of or external threat to justify its existence, and also an institution that is enmeshed in human rights abuses and repression. European press accounts, for example, do not differentiate between the Mexican army's actions in Chiapas and the repression carried out in Central America in the 1980s. The underlying perception is that the

Mexican armed forces strive to keep themselves beyond the reach of accountability, that they lack the ability to cooperate with other institutions, and that they are the inheritors of an authoritarian era that would best be left behind. Even the military's budgets, which are modest by international standards, are seen as consuming valuable and scarce resources through obscure and unaccountable spending procedures. In a way, the military is thought of as the "uncomfortable" institution within Mexico's new democracy.

The first two years of Vicente Fox's administration were sprinkled with anecdotes that reflected this pervasive opinion. President Fox himself came into office saying that he would never put his own life at risk by accepting the protection of the Estado Mayor Presidencial (EMP), the military presidential security and logistics unit that has guarded all civilian presidents in Mexico. After September 11, 2001, in an interview with television broadcaster Larry King, President Fox expressed a very poor and dismissive opinion of the Mexican army's military capability. Several of his aides and even some cabinet members have publicly made derisive comments about the military—without any visible reprimand. One of Fox's campaign advisers, Adolfo Aguilar Zinser, was able to convince the president to create the position of national security adviser to serve as a coordinating clearinghouse for the government's security policy. Zinser left government a little more than a year later, when his office was eliminated, allegedly because of the military's refusal to have Zinser coordinate its activities.[4]

In addition, Mexico's once powerful foreign minister, Jorge Castañeda, tried to commit Mexico to a new level of participation with the international community that would include taking part in international peacekeeping operations. His effort proved unsuccessful, however, when General Gerado Clemente Vega García, the national defense minister, would not budge from his rejection of such an involvement.[5] In the end, the hard-fought campaign to earn a temporary seat on the United Nations Security Council is seen in some quarters as one of Mexico's worst possible diplomatic disasters. In the wake of September 11, Mexico had to confront the vote on the UN resolution dealing with Iraq as well as deliberations that irked the United States and seriously distanced the Fox and Bush administrations from each other. Furthermore, all votes cast by Mexico that have dealt with UN peacekeeping operations around the world have been tainted by the flimsy argument that by paying its budgetary contribution to the UN peacekeeping effort, Mexico contributes more than enough.

Not only do the political and economic elites feel increasingly estranged from the military, but the current political leadership has felt that as part of the democratic transition it is necessary to break some of the rules and conventions that used to regulate interaction between the civilian and military sectors, without assessing the functional contribution of these unwritten rules to the relationship and thus without replacing them with a new set of explicit rules.

The paradox is that, in the recent past, every Mexican president of varying political stripes and personal styles, including President Fox, has increasingly and repeatedly relied on the Mexican military as the only trustworthy institution they could count on for security, particularly for help in confronting the drug trafficking threat or in organizing and carrying out any credible law enforcement reform. No police force could have possibly arrested the seemingly untouchable Benjamín Arellano, the head of the Tijuana cartel, as army counternarcotics intelligence units did in early 2002. Similarly, the new Federal Preventive Police (PFP), which was created at the end of the Zedillo administration, would not currently be the spearhead of the Fox administration's law enforcement efforts if the PFP did not rely on its military police battalions and have most of its command and intelligence structure made up of navy and army officers. At the public perception level, in recent years, whenever Mexican society at large has been polled about the Mexican military in comparison to other institutions involved with security matters, the military comes out on top in the public's perceptions of trustworthiness, reliability, and effectiveness.

Furthermore, in assessing these ambivalent views about the armed forces, it is important to realize that, in sharp contrast with the rest of Latin America, the military in Mexico is perhaps the most egalitarian institution in terms of social access and mobility today. No other professional leadership originates in a more broad and more diverse social base. Is it not a perplexing contradiction that, precisely during the years of a democratic transition at the political level, the authoritarian organization par excellence is providing almost the only means for upward mobility to Mexicans of any regional origin and income level, shaming a much broader set of political and educational institutions that progressively limit socioeconomic mobility to individuals who already have the means to support themselves?

As a side note, analysts have overlooked the general polarization within Mexican society that is being caused by increasingly limited social access to leadership positions in the political, professional, and intellectual arenas, a trend that will surely exacerbate the political tensions arising from income inequality. In the past, the consequences of this inequality were at least mitigated by the ability of young enterprising individuals to climb up the social, economic, and political ladders. With nowhere to go, many of these individuals are now providing the leadership for alternative expressions of power, converging in political confrontations that clash with democratic governance mechanisms.[6]

The diverging nature of elite recruitment is partly the reason that the armed forces have become even further removed from the civilian elite. The point is that ignorance of and absence of channels of communication have created a gap between the military leadership and the elites in Mexico that is far greater than the gap between the mid- and lower-income groups with respect to the armed forces. What happens when the cosmopolitan, globalized, and English-speaking elite that is trying to move Mexico into even greater integration with the United States has to interact with the military elite, which is a more accurate reflection of the Mexican population, both socially and behaviorally? Given the post–September 11 climate, what are the implications for policy formation and implementation of an integrated foreign and security policy when the purported strategists are becoming so alienated from the viewpoints of one of their main instruments?

Beyond identifying the paradox, it is important to examine how these two broad conflicting views of the Mexican military coexist and how they will influence the future. With the aftermath of the terrorist attacks compounded by the aftershocks of Mexico's transition to democracy, determining if Mexico has found a stable equilibrium or if the paradox itself can generate tensions that could ultimately hurt governance in Mexico will have significant implications for policymaking. It is worth asking not only what the military contributes to the governance of Mexico—whether viewed as a neutral instrument of the state or as a willful player with its own agenda—but also if the military's own interaction with other political and social actors could itself become a source of instability, or at least of ineffectiveness and lost opportunities. In this context, it is surprising how little discussion there is about how the Mexican armed forces should fit into the new political system and what their role in a post–September 11 world is or should be.

The leaders of the Mexican armed forces are caught up in this same ambivalence; they realize that they are products of a different era. Even though the leadership does not take democratic inquisitiveness lightly, much less encourage it, it is actively, though discreetly, seeking ways to fit into the new century better. The unusually public proceedings of the War Council that sentenced two army generals in 2002 on charges of drug trafficking, and later indicted them for the disappearance of political activists in the past, were an exercise in accountability, albeit controlled accountability, and responsiveness that had not taken place before. This unprecedented trial partly responds to President Fox's encouragement to the military to be more responsive and transparent and has set an important example, though it does not seem to signal a broader transformation in the way the military interacts with the media and deals with public opinion. In a similar vein, because of its own motivations driven by the navy's need to modernize its fleet, the leadership of the Mexican navy has gone out of its way to explain to Congress why the navy needs additional resources, thus putting these leaders in a position where they have had to reveal more information and detail than they ever needed to reveal before.

In their own way, and in their own coded language, the armed forces are signaling their acknowledgment of the need for change. But is the political system listening? Or are the signals getting lost in the background noise of the daily menu of rhetoric, squabbling, scandals, and accusations? The point is that the myriad expressions—either on the civilian or on the military side—that are related to civil-military relations and to security policy do not add up, either by process or by content, to a coherent dialogue that could lead to a reformulation of this important area of public policy.

ORIGINS AND DEVELOPMENT OF AN INSTITUTION

While it is not the purpose of this chapter to provide a detailed account of the historical development of the Mexican military, it is important to highlight some of the most salient events and issues of the last century that have made it what it is. The Mexican army, by far the most significant and largest of the three armed services, was born out of a cataclysmic event, the 1910 Revolution, which produced, among many other things, a complete upheaval of the existing institutional framework under which politics and the economy had been operating. General Porfirio Diaz, who was in power for three decades, did not rely on the military to support his dictatorship and was wary of a large standing army that would be expensive to maintain and risky to control. During the Diaz regime, the institutional use of violent, coercive means of social control was needed less than a Bismarckian ability to craft checks and balances among a wide range of regional strongmen, as well as among the investment interests of a diverse set of foreign capitals. Relative autonomy at the regional level allowed a measure of stability unheard of in Mexican history to that date, and social control and repression were mostly exerted by the *rurales*, a mounted police force.

That the diverse movements of small landowners and peasants who rebelled could build up a rival army and defeat the federal army on its own terms—that is, through a series of decisive conventional military battles, not a low-intensity guerrilla warfare seeking attrition—attests to the fact that the federal army was neither too large, nor too well equipped, nor too well trained. The success of the revolutionary movement also says a great deal about the leadership talent that was available for political mobilization in the country at that time and was funneled by the revolution into all those generals in their mid-30s who proved to be tactical geniuses and able leaders not of professional soldiers but of revolutionary contingents. It was from this pool of talent that the new Mexican state and army were born.

The victory of the revolutionary movements quickly led to their own infighting, and several decades passed before General Plutarco Elías Calles was able to develop and implement his formula for political stability: all ambitions and conflict were to be managed within a political party, along with the definitive extraction of the military as an institution from politics. But this last policy required transforming the motley crew of revolutionary bands that maintained a complex web of personal loyalties into a professional army. General Joaquin Amaro, the war and navy minister (the department combined the two functions at that time), accomplished this institutional transformation between 1925 and 1931, which was so central to the ability of the political system to perpetuate itself without the string of coups that prevailed in the rest of Latin America. In a relatively short time, Amaro was able to achieve this goal through one of the most energetic stages of institutional reorganization ever experienced by the Mexican government. To this day, the lasting effects of Amaro's reform are proof of how well it fit into the political requirements of the moment. The political stability and lack of political intervention by the military that set Mexico apart from the rest of Latin America for the rest of the century was attributable essentially to this little-recognized chapter of civil-military relations.

Interestingly, roughly until the 1980s, the Mexican army was a reflection of the political values and social mores of its time. The army was a source of stability and support for the political regime, and the absence of an external military threat removed any pressure for the army to become a leading source of innovation. It was, and still is, an army fully and permanently deployed throughout rural Mexico, often providing the only presence of a government authority in vast areas of the country. In the past two decades, however, the internal development of the armed forces has moved decisively toward making the officer corps substantially more professional. This effort was almost entirely the initiative of the military leadership at the time and had no particular encouragement from the civilian sector. Today, no other public institution takes such care to build up its own ranks with a combination of professional experience and educational requirements. That is why Mexico's armed forces clearly lead the way in providing leadership for law enforcement, for example.

The suppression of a student demonstration in 1968, which, according to most accounts, resulted in hundreds of deaths, will forever darken the history of civil-military relations in Mexico. Though the exact sequence of events and participants will probably never be known, the alleged manipulation of the student movement by powerful political figures, including then-minister of government Luis Echeverria, and the role of paramilitary units in triggering the initial shooting have gradually consolidated the perception within the armed forces that they were misused by politicians on that fateful date, which the military officer corps has deeply regretted ever since.

Even though a fair treatment of this case is beyond the scope of this chapter, it is important to draw a sharp distinction between that tragic evening and later events, most of them in the 1970s, during which the army faced internal subversion.[7] In most of the subsequent cases, particularly in the state of Guerrero, the choice to resort to violence was, for the most part, made by the small guerrilla groups themselves, though the methods used against them were a far cry from any politically acceptable response carried out today. The key argument, however, is that the logic of the authoritarian choreography of "democratic" practices and institutions in the 1970s and 1980s was incompatible with the overt existence of a violent opposition movement. Therefore, the civilian regime had strong political motives *not* to acknowledge the existence of guerrilla movements; therefore, public trials and a response in the form of appealing to an institutionalized rule of law were discouraged, as opposed to the blunt use of repression and extrajudicial killings in what became known as Mexico's version of the "dirty war." For this discussion, it is important to emphasize that the civilian political leadership clearly made this choice, and, for the most part, the armed forces carried out the decision in rural areas whereas the political police (the infamous Federal Security Directorate, DFS) did so in urban settings.

THE FOUNDATION OF CIVILIAN CONTROL OVER THE MEXICAN ARMED FORCES

The key characteristic of civil-military relations that emerged from this historical experience was the loyalty the armed forces bestowed upon the presidential institution, that is, upon the individual who bears that responsibility at the time. Until very recently, a strong presidential regime had simplified the practical mechanisms through which that loyalty was translated into a working chain of command. The centralization of the whole civil-military subordination equation in the presidential figure has historically simplified the management of the relationship by identifying one person with whom the military would deal, interact, and be accountable to. That arrangement has automatically placed a premium on the reliability of this individual as the manager of the civil-military interface and, naturally, on his acknowledgment and acceptance of that responsibility.

Mexico is one of the few countries that does not have a unified military command structure, with the army and air force housed under the Ministry of National Defense, separate from the navy, which has its own cabinet-level ministry. Neither of these two ministries has a single civilian official, either a political appointee or a career civil servant. The personal interaction between the president and the active-duty general and admiral who head these ministries has been based on military subordination to civilian control. Each new president has had a free hand to select the individual who will head each of the two ministries from the available pool of top generals and admirals. The practical expression of loyalty has come through the direct—and separate—interaction between these two military officials and the president. Any decision, including controversial ones, that has to be made is rendered within this framework, which consists of mostly verbal exchanges and is made regardless of its legal backing. That is why it has been so difficult, particularly for the army, to consider the operational consequences of having a civilian defense minister; in practice, presidents themselves are expected to be responsible for military policy. Naturally, the competing priorities of the president have typically limited his role in military policy to broad and rather passive or reactive oversight.

In addition to this decisionmaking process, civil-military relations also find daily reinforcement and expression of loyalty toward the presidential figure through the existence and activities of the Estado Mayor Presidencial. Even though the name of the unit is misleading, the EMP provides protection for the president, his family, and presidential facilities. The EMP, which is made up of a sizable all-military staff, is responsible for the planning and coordination of all presidential activities, presidential flights, and several battalions of presidential guards. Analysts of Mexico's presidential institution have seldom acknowledged the debt that this civilian center of power owes to the strength and stability provided by the EMP. As an institution in its own right, the EMP also serves as a permanent reminder to the politicians who live and work at any one time in the presidential compound at Los Pinos that they are only temporary occupants of the presidential institution, which imposes its own respect and logic.

Historically, the legislative consequences of military policy had been handled by a simple system based on the fact that the executive branch held a strong grip on the legislative agenda. Furthermore, the general who served as the minister of national defense would submit a list of several military officers whom he would like to become deputies or senators, thereby assuring that these officers would be included in the lists of candidates compiled by the Institutional Revolutionary Party (PRI). This was not a sizable group, but because a few generals and admirals would logically be assigned to defense committees in Congress, these officers would be able to provide the legislature with a voice that came from the armed forces. Eventually, some opposition parties began to include retired military officers in their own lists of recommended congressional candidates. These legislators' political role also allowed them to contribute remarks in the news media, where, given the absence of a visible National Defense and Navy Ministry communication policy, they could present almost the only opinion from the armed forces in matters like the situation in the state of Chiapas. The functionality of this arrangement depended, of course, on the predictability of electoral outcomes favoring the PRI.

Since the July 2000 election, political outcomes have become subject to a new environment of competitiveness that openly clashes with the assumptions under which the handful of military legislators had participated in Congress. Even so, the current 59th Legislature still includes a single army general from the Institutional Revolutionary Party who "represents" the military in the 500-strong Chamber of Deputies, as well as a PRI senator who is a retired army general. It is inconceivable that either of these two men could have decided to run without the approval, if not encouragement, of the defense minister. Aside from the implications of the specific party that was chosen, it is less likely that additional military candidacies will be presented in the future, because the whole idea of "military" representatives runs counter to any notion of democratic political practices that try to prevent the military from participating in politics. Furthermore, there is no meaningful evidence that "military" legislators ensure a level of communication and coordination between Congress and the military that warrants their presence in the legislature. On the contrary, in light of the political changes that are taking place in Mexico, it is far more consequential for civilian legislators from all political forces to become active stakeholders in defense and national security policies. Still, the quality of policy outcomes in this relationship will continue to be affected by the fact that the professional military communicates with Congress without the intervention of civilian officials who are knowledgeable and capable of articulating the relationship in political terms.

The significant changes that are taking place in Mexico's political system, as well as the evolving security requirements, are affecting the functionality of the entire framework of civil-military interaction, which, in the past, has been so crucial to governance in Mexico. But before exploring what viable options exist to update the arrangement, it is important to review how the first half of the Fox presidency has influenced the outcomes, as well as the mission and structure of the armed forces.

THE MEXICAN ARMED FORCES UNDER PRESIDENT FOX

In comparison with all previous Mexican presidents, Vicente Fox assumed the presidency without any working knowledge of the Mexican military. His contacts as governor with the local army commander do not seem to have paid off as an educational experience. A major feature of Fox's first reaction as a presidential candidate and as president-elect was a deep suspicion of the loyalty of the army to the PRI.

It is rumored that several signs along the way might have signaled that the military leadership could decide to take sides, and some generals who met with Vicente Fox during the campaign were chastised for doing so. Whatever the weight of each source of concern, Vicente Fox was the first official to consider publicly the appointment of a civilian defense minister. Fox's comment to the press might have been an off-the-cuff remark without an intended message, or maybe a signal designed to make the military wary of their position if they did not comply with democratic expectations. Furthermore, after the election, Fox and his advisers apparently were uncomfortable with the idea that the general and the admiral heading the armed forces would feel that they owed their designation as cabinet members to their own personal merits of having risen through the ranks.

Vicente Fox himself—or, to be more precise, his aides—handled the issue of succession in the army by adhering almost absolutely to the unwritten rule of choosing among the most senior generals to fill the post of defense minister. After the election and before the inauguration, Fox's team played an intense mind game with the military leadership. Newspaper stories abounded about the four or six top generals and how they were interviewed. Published résumés of the generals gave the public for the first time in the country's history a glimpse of who the top military brass was. The message was clear: Vicente Fox *would* choose among this small group for the selection of his defense minister.

A few days before the inauguration, Vicente Fox's office informed the public that General Gerardo Clemente Vega García had been designated as Fox's minister of national defense. Vega had been promoted to the rank of three-star general just over a year earlier, and in terms of seniority, he was among the more junior of the 25 three-star generals on active duty in the Mexican army.

Two individuals have either claimed or been credited for influencing the decision to name General Vega to the post of defense minister. One was the controversial presidential aide Carlos Rojas, who had a role in interviewing each of the several most senior generals allegedly in the running. The other adviser was Adolfo Aguilar Zinser, who became Fox's national security adviser for the brief time that this post was in existence. While this decision was being made, there is some indication that the outgoing defense minister, General Enrique Cervantes, might have played a role as well. As minister of defense during the Zedillo administration, General Cervantes had spent a term in office that was rather controversial because he was a strict disciplinarian and created a great deal of ill will among his peers. Aside from his right-hand man, General Juan Heriberto Salinas, who was the chief of the General Staff, none of the other senior candidates for the position of minister of national defense in 2000 would have been particularly concerned with watching his back when he left office, in the best of cases.

Given this perspective, it is possible to speculate that General Cervantes groomed General Vega to become a viable and attractive candidate to head up the Ministry of National Defense in case Vicente Fox won the election.[8] Up until two years before the election, General Vega was a respected two-star general who held a prestigious position on the General Staff. He earned his third star in fall 1999 and soon thereafter was designated commander of the First Army Corps, a surprising assignment for someone who had just joined the top tier of the army's leadership. A well-respected general officer with an uncommon background in military intellectual circles, his experience in commanding a unit was comparatively brief. Interestingly, General Cervantes himself became minister of defense in 1994, after some 16 years of experience as a three-star general; during that time he was also near the top of the seniority list. The same holds true for all other defense ministers over the past half-century.

In substantive terms, the military's organization did not even flinch in the face of what could be considered an unorthodox selection process, even when, in contrast to what happens in many armies around the world, all of the three-star generals who had more seniority than General Vega prior to his receiving the his fourth star (which is awarded only to Mexico's defense minister) remain on active duty until they reach retirement at 65 years of age. As General Mario Renán Castillo, one of the top generals at the time, said to a reporter in the days before General Vega's designation: "Whoever is chosen, we will all fall into line." The administration made a half-hearted attempt to appease some of the losing candidates; for example, General Mario Palmerin, who, according to leaks to the press, had been the top contender, was given the number-two spot as undersecretary of defense. The televised changing of command at the defense ministry included a very martial salute from General Palmerin to General Vega, thus signaling the former's subordination to the latter. Nevertheless, less than a year after that, Palmerin left his post at the ministry to become Mexico's military attaché in London.

With all but three of the initial group of three-star generals reaching the mandatory retirement age by the time the next administration takes office in 2006, General Vega has the opportunity to preside over an unprecedented generational change in the army's leadership. He is now in a position to determine who will be promoted during his tenure.

On the navy side, President Fox and his advisers went a step further. The administration selected Admiral Marco Antonio Peyrot to serve as the new minister of the navy. Admiral Peyrot was a vice admiral who had been passed up for promotion because of a confrontation with the former navy minister over differences about how a disciplinary issue had been handled. After being relieved of his command as vice admiral, he did not receive a new assignment. Admiral Peyrot was promoted to full admiral before he took office as head of the Navy Ministry, and a sizable number of the existing admirals retired.

For the purpose of this analysis, it should be noted that the new government started off with two military ministers who certainly owed their appointments to Vicente Fox. The relevant question is: Did President Fox need to name these two military men to cabinet posts in order to gain the loyalty of the armed forces? What may not be so obvious is that Mexico's military had been performing this ritual of "loyalty transfer" every time a new president took office. The loyalty of members of the armed forces has historically been directed to the presidential figure, not to a specific political party. For this reason, the military's full acceptance of the result of the 2000 presidential election should have come as no surprise. Furthermore, there is no evidence that either General Vega or Admiral Peyrot has gone out of their way to implement a policy agenda that another general or admiral would not otherwise have carried out. And neither of the two has experienced any insubordination or severe friction coming from the rest of the military leadership.

On the other hand, aside from some nuances about human rights and specific decisions related to the situation in Chiapas, President Fox has not had a military policy that he can claim as his own. Thus, even if Fox and his advisers wanted to have military leaders in the cabinet who would represent the president before the armed forces more than they would represent the armed forces before the civilian government, these ministers have not been faced with any real policy reform that they are expected to implement.

On the contrary, with so many other things not going the way he expected, President Fox seems to be increasingly comfortable with the reliability of the military, and he is content to leave the armed forces to their own devices. As far as the military leadership is concerned, any possibilities that existed to introduce substantial innovations have been put on hold as a result of the absence of a strong civilian leadership that can support any kind of reform. Inside the Fox cabinet, the relaxed discipline gives rise to the practice of "policy hijacking" by individual officials, who are not penalized for independent action. It takes no particular insight to realize the uneasiness that this power vacuum within the Mexican government generates for the top officers in the armed forces, and to understand why the military leadership has instead focused on ways to navigate the armed services through this period of uncertainty.

In early 2004, General Vega publicly stated his concern about the consequences of a climate of political confrontation. His rather cryptic message led to speculation about the appropriateness of the nation's top general speaking publicly about civilian political affairs, even if in the most abstract and nonpartisan terms. Controversy also abounded about the implicit subtext detected by many that linked his call for political reconciliation to the civilian investigations of the so-called "dirty war" of the 1970s and the possible indictment of army generals who had served at that time. The relevant issue from a policy standpoint, though, is that the military apparently lacks adequate channels of communication on policy matters, presumably because the existing channels (through President Fox) are no longer sufficient.

NATIONAL SECURITY POLICY AND THE ARMED SERVICES

Even though the concept of national security has hovered over military and security discussions and policies in Mexico for at least two decades, the fact is that no Mexican government has yet made the decisive move to turn national security into the organizing principle that can impose coherence upon the whole array of security, defense, and foreign policies. Instead, these policies remain fragmented and significantly lacking coordination. Whatever coherence is achieved comes from the individual federal agencies' institutional ownership of certain parts of the national security agenda, particularly the responsibilities assigned to the military. Even in this case, there is the fundamental divide resulting from the separation of the Ministry of National Defense and the Ministry of the Navy, each of which interprets its own policy responsibilities, with both ministries ending up with overlapping jurisdictions and policy differences.[9]

As there was no formal constitutional or legal definition or coherent body of doctrine until recently, the concept of national security has become part of a process of unstructured political discourse that signals the importance that the government would like the public to believe is being given to different issues. But this heightened visibility at the rhetorical level is seldom put through the more demanding paces of policy formulation and implementation. This discrepancy has become a source of confusion—as well as meager guidance—for those institutions that are more closely involved in providing national security, namely, the armed forces. An explicit and fully functional national security doctrine and policy can thus be seen not only as the missing link in the working relationship between military and civilian authorities but also as the stepping stone toward harmonizing the civil-military interface with the new, less predictable political environment.

For the past decade and a half, a National Security Cabinet has met regularly,[10] but it never evolved beyond its formal structure—consisting of the heads of the Government, Foreign Affairs, National Defense, and Navy Ministries, the Office of Attorney General, and, since its creation, the Ministry of Public Security—and sat down to discuss specific issues with the president. It has not had the support structure needed to proceed with its agenda, follow up on its implementation, and clarify the president's options. The executive assistant for this office's meetings has been the head of the civilian intelligence service, CISEN, an organization whose functional and administrative location inside the Government Ministry precludes its ability to be an honest broker for national security policy. All cabinet ministers continue to submit their own agendas directly to the president for discussion and authorization.

Beneath the surface, the government has almost never had an interagency process for coordinating policy. The Fox administration briefly considered the idea of elevating national security to a much more important level, but the combination of a failed implementation project and the president's lack of interest quickly made the effort evaporate.

The absence of civilian officials in the defense establishment has also removed national defense and the core national security issues from mainstream discussions of public policy. This state of affairs has capped the level of significance, visibility, and budgets that the military sector receives. With civilians remaining disengaged, defense issues continue to wither away in the backwaters of the military's autonomy. This situation has reinforced the visibility and legitimacy of the nonmilitary roles performed by the armed forces, constantly moving them away from their traditionally stated purpose and further into a gray area of responsibilities that are shared or overlap with those of civilian agencies that are much weaker.

The military's budgetary limitations, civilian agencies' institutional shortcomings, and the armed forces' discipline and organizational capabilities have all made it much easier for civilian authorities to continue to use the military as a "wide-spectrum" antibiotic for all sorts of institutional illnesses and policy demands. This situation has also allowed civilian authorities to protect some of their policy choices and decisions or hide them behind the institutional weight and prestige of the armed forces. Nevertheless, this practice of recurrent use of the military as a general-purpose public policy tool runs counter to the growing democratic demand to raise the level of accountability through the use of specialized public policy instruments that have an explicit regulatory and legal framework that supports and controls their activities.

As has been mentioned, there are two main structural differences between Mexico's armed forces and what has become the standard in almost every other democracy. These are the lack of a unified military command structure for the three services and the complete absence of civilians in the Ministry of National Defense and the Ministry of the Navy.

When the revolutionary forces unleashed in 1910 were finally able to re-create themselves into a professional military, the three armed services came under a War and Navy Ministry. Years later, President Lázaro Cárdenas, himself an army general, changed this arrangement when he separated the navy from the other armed services and established a cabinet-level department for it. Meanwhile, the air force has remained housed under the Ministry of National Defense, where it is under the overbearing control of the army.

Even though it is difficult to assess the specific costs and drawbacks that stem from this separation of the armed services, a comparison of the institutional development of the navy and the air force shows a profound difference between the two services. In spite of low budgets, the navy has been able to establish, for example, a shipbuilding industry that provides for the replacement of its main vessels, whereas the air force works at the management level like an army aviation component, with almost no ability to plan and implement its own acquisition, maintenance, and overall development policies—all of which are controlled by the army. Given current conditions, the relationship between the army and the air force leads the navy to view the possibility of being integrated with the other armed forces as a catastrophic event. The policy options regarding these two issues will be reviewed later in this chapter.

THE EVOLUTION OF THE MILITARY'S
COUNTERNARCOTICS MISSION AND POLICY

In the early 1970s, the extensive territorial deployment of the Mexican army gave rise to its original involvement in counternarcotics operations with its campaigns to eradicate marijuana and poppy fields, a mission that continues to this day. At any one time, between 15,000 and 25,000 troops carry out eradication and land interdiction operations throughout Mexico. Even though the military's methods of eradication are labor-intensive, no other organization is able to match its nationwide deployment.

In the mid-1980s, the introduction of large-scale cocaine trafficking through Mexican territory toward the U.S. market changed the volume of resources that traffickers devoted to corrupting members of Mexican law enforcement agencies and brought about a crisis from which these civilian organizations have yet to recover. Initially, the army was drawn into supporting the Office of the Attorney General (PGR) on several law enforcement activities like the interdiction of drug shipments, an activity that also involved the creation of a basic detection and monitoring infrastructure with military radars in the southern part of the country. While the military's human resources and infrastructure made them a natural participant in eradication and interdiction activities, an explicit decision was made initially to keep the police investigation and prosecution of drug traffickers within the Office of the Attorney General.

The repeated failures and internal turmoil of the Attorney General's Office eventually prompted President Ernesto Zedillo to authorize the creation of a significant counternarcotics intelligence and Special Forces capability within the Mexican army in 1995. To this date, this effort has been able to seriously damage every cartel and has led to the arrest of the most visible drug kingpins, like Benjamín Arellano, Osiel Cárdenas, and Armando Valencia. Recently, the ability to conduct simultaneous operations against different cartels has shown how this capability is maturing. The successes are also a signal that this operational intelligence asset could, if necessary, make a significant contribution in operations against terrorist organizations.

A feature that has changed since the end of the Zedillo administration is the way in which the army is now publicly acknowledging its role and responsibility in apprehending the drug kingpins; the army no longer needs to use the Office of the Attorney General for public relations efforts. With the army currently taking credit for its own success on the counternarcotics front, the reorganization of the Attorney General's Office—through the addition of an FBI-style force called the Federal Investigation Agency (AFI)—might provide the basis for the reemergence of a civilian law enforcement agency. However, it is too early to tell if this initiative will succeed as a permanent, structural reform, or if it will become part of the long list of failed efforts to revamp civilian law enforcement.

Part of the reason that the Office of the Attorney General has been unable to emerge from its internal crisis is because all of Mexico's attorney generals have retained the same broad set of institutional responsibilities and have therefore been unable to direct their meager resources and small core of capable and trustworthy personnel to priority areas. The Attorney General's Office has continued to be deeply involved in drug eradication throughout the country—a task that requires a sizable helicopter fleet—and to participate in staffing drug interdiction checkpoints along the national road network. The PGR has also kept a fleet of aircraft—which includes the only two units in Mexico that are equipped with relatively modern air combat radar—to be used for the interdiction of aircraft suspected of transporting illicit drugs. In the meantime, the army's counternarcotics intelligence and Special Forces units have carried out all major drug arrests, leaving the Office of the Attorney General the responsibility to conduct the legal prosecution of the drug kingpins who have been apprehended, but denying it a major role in the actual investigations.

It would appear that relinquishing the responsibility for both eradication of illicit crops and interdiction of drug shipments to the military could allow the Office of the Attorney General to focus on regaining the investigative and prosecutorial capabilities and expertise that are much closer to the office's legal mandate. However, even General Rafael Macedo de la Concha, Mexico's current attorney general and a former chief military prosecutor—a man who has gained experience in this field from working for both institutions—has not managed or desired to do so.

The different counternarcotics operations that these civilian and military institutions carry out—with varying degrees of success—

conform to a basic strategy that originated in the United States. When the Mexican government began to place greater importance on the drug issue, officials paid more attention to it as a result of the friction that the issue created with the United States. Mexico's civilian authorities saw drug trafficking as an obstacle to their political relationship with the United States and also an impediment to the potential development of trade that eventually led to NAFTA. Mexico responded by crafting a policy that was particularly receptive to what U.S. agencies involved in counternarcotics operations recommended as necessary.

In the first place, all of Mexico's territory was turned into a vast battlefield where drug interdiction activities were carried out. This allowed drug traffickers to choose where to establish the best-protected routes by corrupting the law enforcement authorities stationed along the way. The counternarcotics policy that Mexico adopted was based on a second fundamental assumption. The extent of the drug trade and the pervasive nature of the consumption market in the United States—as well as the visible limits on how far U.S. authorities were willing to carry out interdiction operations within U.S. territory—resulted in Mexico's acceptance of the fact that the illegal drug trade was a permanent issue that could at best be contained and mitigated but could not be resolved, as the term "war on drugs" seemed to suggest. Furthermore, the view from the Mexican side that the United States was unable to shut down the flow of cocaine into its territory, in spite of the sizable drug interdiction capability that U.S. military and law enforcement possesses, led to the simple conclusion that a far weaker nation like Mexico could not even pretend to do so. This interpretation, which is discussed below, implied that there was significant confusion about the strategic circumstances that motivate drug trafficking into the United States as compared with Mexico.

If Mexico's counternarcotics policy had no goal beyond containment, then it was clearly geared toward appeasing the U.S. government in what can best be described as a strategy of "visible effort," which held that the more visible an expense or action, the more effective the operation. This strategy made no assumption that counternarcotics operations could affect the structural dynamics of the drug trade. In other words, if reality could not be changed, then at least an attempt should be made to influence the perception of reality. It is notable that the whole array of U.S. agencies involved in counternarcotics activities operates—either consciously or not—under the same basic premise: need for containment and visible effort with no expectations of a successful or complete outcome.

Eventually, the relevant agencies in the United States themselves lost faith in interdiction and shifted their emphasis to the more visible task that might be labeled the "kingpin" strategy. This approach focused on bringing down the drug kingpins, who were brazenly challenging the authority of the state by flaunting their ability to corrupt authorities and by creating networks that started to infiltrate areas of political and economic power in the region. Therefore, if the government could not stop drug trafficking, at least authorities could prevent the principal beneficiaries of the drug trade from enjoying their money and extending their influence. U.S. agencies' motivation for developing this strategy was strongly influenced by the case of Pablo Escobar in Colombia, and Mexico adopted the approach for dealing with the likes of Amado Carrillo Fuentes. The kingpin strategy has also provided a much clearer scoreboard, which signals success by listing the arrests of individuals whose faces have become familiar to the public.

There is an inherent weakness, however, in an overall counternarcotics strategy that focuses on investigation and prosecution of drug kingpins. This strategy does not change the structural reasons for traffickers to seek to use Mexican territory on their way to the drug market in the United States. Every drug lord who is arrested or gunned down is swiftly replaced by one of his lieutenants, and when a complete cartel is taken down, others move in to take over their routes and distribution networks. Colombia's experience with its own cartel-busting operations shows that drug traffickers will continue to operate through smaller cells and discrete operators, because the level of risk for individual criminals will never be high enough to discourage participation. Thus the command-and-control structures of these groups will never run out of willing and eager substitutes to replenish their leadership.

If this assessment is correct, the volume of drug money used to corrupt authorities will remain relatively constant, and Mexico's law enforcement and judicial organizations will continue to be deeply corroded at all levels. The real threat that drug traffickers pose to the Mexican state is in direct proportion to the financial resources they can muster. As an example, the problem for Mexico is not that such characters as "El Chapo" Guzman exist, but that they have $2 million under the mattress with which to buy themselves out of a federal "maximum" security prison whenever they see fit. The main threat to Mexico is the level of corruption that drug traffickers can use to disrupt and neutralize law enforcement authorities and that makes it next to impossible for the Mexican government to regain full control of its police apparatus. This phenomenon has also severely restricted the government's capability to take effective action against other forms of criminal activity, such as kidnapping or bank robberies. The impact on the overall quality of governance in Mexico due to the resulting weakness of law enforcement is overwhelming. That is why the king-pin policy can be considered a necessary—but insufficient—part of Mexico's counternarcotics efforts: it prevents traffickers from consolidating their control over economic and political spheres but does not alter the reasons for the drug trade's continued existence throughout Mexico's territory and the traffickers' motivation to corrupt Mexican authorities.

In the late 1990s, authorities began to question the prevailing view that the flow of cocaine was a permanent and unavoidable feature in Mexico. An alternative counternarcotics strategy began to take shape, based on the idea that a significant increase in the effectiveness of air and maritime operations and drug interdiction capabilities on the border between Mexico and Central America—all activities focused on access points into Mexico—would be able to induce a shift of the cocaine flow away from Mexican territory by making it comparatively "riskier" for drug traffickers to pass through Mexico, in comparison to other available routes into the U.S. market. Given that the destination and source of profit is *inside* the United States and that Mexico is only *one* of several available routes, Mexico's policy would require a much lower level of interdiction effectiveness than the one that U.S. authorities have tried in vain to achieve in their attempt to shut down the flow of cocaine into their territory. In other words, Mexico would not need to make it physically impossible for traffickers to operate through its territory; it would only have to make it comparatively riskier and costlier for traffickers to attempt to do so.

The basis for this initiative lies in the experience that the U.S. government itself had in the 1980s, when it established an intense and successful drug interdiction operation that blocked the use of Florida as the gateway for cocaine to enter the United States. That effort was actually the principal reason for moving the cocaine route into Mexico in the first place. Surprisingly, in view of the contentiousness of anti-drug cooperation in the U.S.–Mexico bilateral relationship, one issue that has never been fully and publicly assessed or discussed is how such a locally successful strategy adopted by U.S. law enforcement could have such a devastating impact on Mexico with no perceptible reduction in the amount of cocaine available for consumption inside the United States.

Nevertheless, Mexico's new policy objective was inconsistent with its existing drug interdiction strategy, which, through its manpower-intensive and low-tech approach, had turned all of the Mexican territory into a battleground and exposed the vast majority of the police and military forces to the possibility of corruption. Moreover, the flow of interdiction information—gathered by U.S. agencies and provided to Mexico—has been seriously disrupted because of the change in the U.S. government's priorities, such as the need for heightened protection of U.S. air space since September 11, 2001, and events like the wars in Afghanistan and Iraq. These new demands caused the United States to redirect many of the resources that its original interdiction arrangement with Mexico had depended on, including information provided by the U.S. law enforcement infrastructure and U.S. military assets.

Furthermore, the United States' contribution to drug interdiction has been largely oversold. Because the United States currently has the more extensive infrastructure in the region, few realize that the U.S. government provides information on only a small fraction of the illicit movement of drugs that presumably occurs to move the 300-plus tons of cocaine a year that enter the United States through Mexico.

Moreover, even if every operation driven by the U.S. interdiction system ended in a successful seizure of drugs, Mexico's law enforcement institutions would continue to be vulnerable to corruption and payments from drug traffickers seeking to protect the flow of the remaining cocaine once it is inside Mexico's borders. The fluctuations in the presence of U.S. military assets and the limited efficiency of the current arrangement were therefore insufficient for implementing a new Mexican policy that aimed to shift the cocaine routes away from Mexico. The new initiative thus required Mexican institutions to develop their own modern interdiction infrastructure.

The Mexican armed forces have not yet wholeheartedly embraced the new initiative, and they have yet to develop, at the organizational level, a seamless interdiction system that integrates air, sea, and border capabilities. Nevertheless, the new strategy has triggered an institutional desire inside both the Defense Ministry and the Navy Ministry to invest in and acquire the means to carry out more effective and aggressive drug interdiction operations that transcend the limitations of the "end game" role that those ministries were assigned when Mexico depended on information provided by the United States. Mexico's relevant institutions will achieve this capability by acquiring their own intelligence-gathering assets, such as the Airborne Early-Warning system and maritime patrol aircraft, as well as dozens of fast interdiction "combat boats" deployed by the navy that can successfully seize drugs before they reach the Mexican road network, where they easily disappear. As in many historical experiences with doctrinal reform, the military and naval operators of this new interdiction infrastructure will become the real driving force for the consolidation of this shift in policy, and any successes they achieve will gradually help validate the concept.

The ultimate challenge for Mexico is that the viability of this new policy is limited because a window of opportunity is slowly closing. If the steady and determined development of a Mexican cocaine consumption market takes hold, the dynamics of the drug trade and the motivation for cocaine to reach Mexico's shores will change completely. It would be a cruel irony of fate that if the government hesitated to fully embrace the new interdiction initiative as the ruling paradigm for its counternarcotics strategy, Mexico could miss the chance to rid itself of the most damaging threat to its national security and to its prospects for development.

Perhaps now that the United States needs Mexico as a solid, capable, and enthusiastic partner in the war against terrorism—effectively denying the use of Mexican territory to terrorists who want to hurt the United States—both governments might find that the best way to cooperate is to fully recognize the security needs of both partners and to create a security perimeter that keeps out not only terrorists but also drugs. Mexico will be unable to become such an effective ally, however, if it cannot remove the devastating effect that illicit monies have on the integrity of its police forces.

Mexican governments have had little option but to recruit the military into the so-called war on drugs. Nevertheless, there is the very real fear that if a state assigns these missions to the military, it is exposing its ultimate defense resource to the corrosive threat of corruption. The Mexican armed forces have seen their share of problems, including the arrest of General Jesús Gutierrez Rebollo and the disbanding of the 65th Infantry Battalion following the discovery of widespread corruption. For the most part, however, these cases demonstrate that the armed forces themselves have the institutional strength to uncover problems and to solve them; that the military should use only specialized vetted units against drug trafficking, not regular army units, which are logically more vulnerable; and that top-level officials who are responsible for counternarcotics operations should also be vetted, regardless of their rank.

For Mexico's armed forces, eradication of drugs, counternarcotics intelligence gathering, and interdiction of drug shipments have become the defining operational environment that currently guides the military's institutional development, because the military's major role in the drug war cannot even be compared with the armed forces' minimal focus on its military defense capabilities. Even if civilian police organizations eventually gain the ability to stand on their own, it will be progressively more challenging to extract the Mexican military from the drug war and from other more general law enforcement duties, and with time this involvement will continue to alter the relative values of the civil-military equation.

NONMILITARY MISSIONS OF THE MEXICAN ARMED FORCES

Mexico's armed forces have been involved in law enforcement duties for a very long time. Lately, however, the way that the military is involved has been changing. Given the weakness of state and local governments in providing for law and order in nonurban regions, the army continues to play a quasi-police role by providing an armed federal presence in rural areas throughout Mexico. That mission has defined the Mexican army as a nationwide guarantor of stability and control and has imposed an internal organization that is heavily tilted toward territorial deployment, as opposed to a structure that is more suited to perform external military defense duties. The standard size of military units has been the battalion, which consists of 600 personnel. These units are individually deployed throughout Mexico's territory to provide a level of coverage and presence unmatched by any other federal force. This deployment structure both responds to the broad array of nonmilitary missions assigned to the armed forces and, conversely, makes these forces the most available instrument to fulfill those missions.

At the same time, the armed forces have historically been the general source of commanders for law enforcement organizations—mostly when officers leave active duty—because their management skills over subordinates are highly appreciated. Nevertheless, corruption at different levels in Mexico's police forces has reached several of these former military officers, and their links to the active-duty officers represent a vulnerability that the military leadership has to keep in mind.

In addition, the armed forces have also become suppliers of leadership and commanders for law enforcement agencies from an institutional perspective, by placing entire police forces under army management. This was the case, for example, with Mexico City's police force at the beginning of the Zedillo administration, when the defense minister had final responsibility for the performance of these police agencies. This specific activity does not follow a stable pattern and has varied over the years. The current case of the attorney general, General Rafael Macedo de la Concha, does not apply to this model, because President Fox selected him for this post for his own reasons, not at the suggestion of the minister of defense, as was done in the past for the position. The presence of another army general officer as a member of President Fox's cabinet has created a rather awkward situation for General Vega, the minister of national defense.

During President Zedillo's administration, the civilian intelligence service (Centro de Investigación y Seguridad Nacional or CISEN) developed a criminal intelligence capability, provided by mostly navy officers, which served as the core of the Federal Police Force when it was formalized around 1998. Together with this core, the PFP absorbed the Highway Police Force, which had been under the jurisdiction of the Transportation and Communications Ministry. But the main body of the PFP is the Federal Support Forces—military police battalions that, while using a new grey uniform, have kept their entire army command

and control structure, officer corps, equipment, and facilities. There is little evidence to suggest that their status will change in the near future.

These shortcomings inside the civilian law enforcement apparatus have led the army and navy to become involved in police activities. Part of the reason for this involvement is that Mexico has historically been unwilling to invest in creating a solid and professional police force and has considered the use of the armed forces an inexpensive way to address the shortcomings, because, according to this view, the government is already assuming the expenditures for the armed forces. The most important structural reason for drawing the military into nonmilitary missions and responsibilities lies in the weakness of civilian institutions, which have been unable to establish a career civil service system for their personnel. Because noninstitutional loyalties and incentives are able to compete strongly with organizational demands inside most police forces, reform efforts are usually superficial and short-lived. That is the defining difference between civilian police forces and professional armed forces.

However, the political discourse continues to emphasize the "temporary" nature of the military's involvement in law enforcement duties, even though no exit strategy can be identified.

Another sizable nonmilitary mission is disaster relief and civil protection duties performed by the armed forces. This mission comes from the federal government's responsibility to provide these services, given the weakness of local first-responders, and relies on the territorial deployment of the armed forces and their organizational skills as a disciplined and effective force. Whenever Mexico experiences a flood, an earthquake, an explosion, or any other major disaster, the army is the first responder to be deployed. The only case of the political leadership's hesitation in handing over control of the disaster relief operation to the military occurred after the earthquake in 1985, when President Miguel de la Madrid limited the military's activities in the Mexico City area, allegedly for fear of losing control. The resulting dismal failure of Mexico City's governor, a federal appointment at that time, only served to reinforce the practice of relying from then on on the military's infrastructure and command-and-control capabilities. In contrast, in the mid-1990s, the devastation caused by Hurricane Mitch in Central America led to the largest-ever foreign deployment of

Mexican troops, helicopters, and navy hospital ships to carry out rescue and relief operations in the affected region.

Participation in disaster relief has also allowed Mexico to garner support and legitimacy for the territorial deployment of the armed forces, which, along with providing social welfare in rural communities, is part of a policy that helps balance negative views of the military. Nevertheless, society's support for the armed forces is overwhelmingly attributable to the low- and middle-class origin of the members of the military—both its troops and its officer corps.

THE MEXICAN ARMED FORCES AS A MILITARY FORCE

Since the consolidation brought about by the Mexican Revolution, the external military challenges facing the country's armed forces have been mostly irrelevant, although counternarcotics operations have demanded a substantial investment in personnel, equipment, and technology. As a result of Mexico's geostrategic location, the government has been able to make a fairly minor investment in the military budget, and, as discussed above, this has led to weak public awareness and support for the strictly military capabilities of the armed forces, and particularly for the budgetary consequences of maintaining those capabilities. Nevertheless, the military's responsibility for defending the integrity of Mexico's territory continues to be a strong political value. It is the absence of specifically identified threats, or their conceptualization, that inhibits the formulation of a clear and solid defense policy.

Consequently, Mexico does not possess the military equipment that is usually associated at the international level with a country of its size and importance. If the regional situation were to deteriorate to such an extreme that a military buildup was necessary, the successful incorporation of new hardware would not be beyond the reach of the military's professional officer corps. Indeed, some new technologies are being introduced, such as those developed for the military's counternarcotics mission.

It is well known that most Latin American military forces believe that there is a U. S.–led conspiracy to turn them into police forces and steer them away from any true military capability. Repeated statements along these lines by individuals inside the U.S. military establishment fuel this concern. The purported goal of the effort to dilute Latin America's military capabilities is to minimize the potential for armed conflict between neighbors, as would be the case of Ecuador and Peru, and to divert budgetary resources to development issues.

Mexico's military leadership is deeply concerned and suspicious about this perceived policy, but its concern does not seem to influence the way military leaders and the civilian government articulate defense policy. In other words, in a case of a "self-fulfilling prophecy," not only does the army embrace its nonmilitary mission portfolio, but it is also almost the only argument that the army uses when presenting itself to society. Almost every publication or statement coming from the Defense Ministry plays up the armed forces' nonmilitary role and mentions their national defense responsibilities only as an afterthought. The relevance of this nonmilitary role is not just an issue of communication; it reflects the government's funding priorities. Paradoxically, at the operational and conceptual level, the decision of the Mexican armed forces to publicly downplay their military role and instead highlight their nonmilitary missions is entirely consistent with the perceived U.S. policy that they view as so threatening.

The area of activity carried out by the armed forces that is most closely related to the defense of territorial integrity is protection of Mexico's borders, a mission that is performed by the string of motorized cavalry regiments and infantry battalions located along both the southern and the northern borders. On the U.S.–Mexican border, these units become involved in counternarcotics operations and also face a challenge seldom assessed in the bilateral relationship: trafficking in small arms, which supports criminal activities in Mexico and flows from the north because of the ample supply of firearms inside the United States and easy access to them. Another serious challenge is the establishment of a working arrangement for communication and coordination of duties with U.S. authorities—particularly the U.S. Border Patrol, which is now part of the U.S. Department of Homeland Security—to prevent possible confusion and even incidents of friendly fire when concurrent operations are undertaken.

Another major area of military responsibility is maintaining effective control of Mexican air space. Because of Mexico's geographic proximity to the United States, the military not only must deal with the existing threat of flights transporting drugs but is also forced to

prepare for the possibility of Mexican airspace being used for a terrorist attack. The infrastructure and policy that were developed in the
first case do not provide a coherent response to the more recent threat.
Mexico has three land-based military radars in the south, and everything other than drugs and terrorists that enters Mexican air space falls
under the air safety and navigational requirements of civil aviation authorities. Hence, flights that contain either drugs or terrorists can pass
through without detection if they do not willingly identify themselves.
In fact, U.S. authorities have long insisted that drug traffickers carry
out hundreds of illicit flights a year in order to move drugs from different parts of Mexico to just a few miles from the U.S. border, from
which the drugs are smuggled into the United States via land routes.
To date, Mexico's army and air force do not have the capability to assess the intensity and pattern of these flights. Even the introduction of
a few airborne assets equipped with radar would simply stretch this
capability too thin, given the extent of Mexican air space and the areas
through which drugs are introduced into the country.

Furthermore, because of its very limited fleet of combat aircraft
with obsolete avionics and electronics, the air force would be unable to
intercept either type of illicit flight successfully.[11] Neither the armed
forces nor the civilian authorities have articulated a policy that could
eventually lead Congress and the public at large to support the modernization of even a modest combat aircraft capability; as a result, the
government will probably not address this strategic vulnerability in
the near future. It is worth noting that, in the past few years, many
countries like Poland, South Africa, Brazil, Chile, the Czech Republic,
Hungary, and Austria have been undergoing substantial modernization programs to enable them to guarantee control over their air space,
under stringent conditions of democratic debate and oversight.

The protection of the country's critical infrastructure is another
strategic role assigned to the Mexican armed forces. Most of the time,
this task involves simply stationing a detachment of troops next to the
facility to be protected. The terrorist attacks on the United States and
the war in Iraq have recently created the perception that Mexico's oil
facilities— particularly offshore oil rigs in the Gulf of Mexico—face a
substantial threat. This perception has prompted the Mexican navy to
concentrate a good portion of its ships in the area and to acquire small
numbers of antiaircraft missiles (Russian SA-18 Igla shoulder-

launched missiles and launchers), the first time Mexico has possessed such weaponry. This mission to protect Mexico's infrastructure apparently also triggered the decision to buy three first-generation Northrop Grumman E-2C Hawkeye airborne early-warning aircraft from Israel, but the high operating cost of this type of equipment will make it difficult to provide permanent coverage of the area. It is still too soon to determine if this specific mission will become the Mexican navy's permanent core responsibility or if the mission only emerged as a temporary response to the terrorist attacks of 2001.

Another part of the armed forces' military mission involves confronting the small subversive movements around the country. For the past three decades, there has been a small but durable guerrilla presence in the state of Guerrero, where the Popular Revolutionary Army (EPR) and splinter groups continue to carry out violent confrontations with army units. The link between poverty and social unrest in this region has kept these movements alive, but they have not grown into a challenge whose magnitude would seriously jeopardize governance, even inside the state of Guerrero.

The army has had a different experience in Chiapas, where the 1994 uprising quickly developed into a political stalemate that has yet to be resolved. This situation and the proximity of the Chiapas border with Guatemala have forced the Mexican army to maintain an extensive deployment in the area, providing a presence that contains the Zapatista-held territory. The presence of the army has also served to keep rival communities apart and to inhibit overt violence among them but did not preclude the killing spree that took place in Acteal in December 1997. Whether a smaller presence of the Mexican army would lead to many more of these clashes is an open question.

Because the Zapatista movement has become a local issue, it has steadily left the mainstream agenda and has been reduced to a footnote of history, squandering the potential that Zapatista supporters in Mexico City and abroad had hoped would turn into an alternative for political activism at the national level. Few on the left can say that the Zapatistas—and "Subcomandante" Marcos in particular—have fulfilled the expectations that they had generated. The army, in the meantime, is stuck with a deployment structure that, for all practical purposes, has become permanent.

SECURITY RELATIONS BETWEEN THE UNITED STATES AND MEXICO AND THE WAR AGAINST TERRORISM

During most of the twentieth century, Mexico and the United States did not need to address the implications of their geographic proximity in terms of the security of both nations. Even during World War II only token steps were taken to prepare for a potential territorial defense before the tide turned against Japan. Thereafter, aside from some cooperation on specific intelligence gathered during the Cold War, the United States had no defense concerns related to Mexico. Thus neither country saw a need to coordinate defense policies.

Even though both parties may have not fully recognized it, the era ushered in by the terrorist attacks of September 11 has created a new and powerful bond between Mexico and the United States. The cooperation on counternarcotics operations since the mid-1990s has provided some useful lessons. On the one hand, Mexican authorities, including the military leadership, have proved to be far more pragmatic when it comes to actual cooperation than anyone could have expected from the political discourse that has taken place. National security and Homeland Security officials in the Bush administration go out of their way to praise the level of cooperation that Mexican authorities are providing. On the other hand, as in the case of counternarcotics programs in the past, if Mexican officials' pragmatism does not find some level of explicit political support within Mexico that helps to explain the reasons for this cooperation, democratic accountability will be damaged. Moreover, the lack of political support will provide a fragile basis for cooperation, because bilateral cooperation will constantly run the risk of being exposed and becoming politically controversial. Mexico's civilian authorities have created this vulnerability, because they have done little to build political support for bilateral cooperation on security issues.

Cooperation between Mexico and the United States on matters of national security is likely to evolve through the implementation of specific programs and initiatives. Mexico's political leaders do not appear to be considering a framework agreement that would otherwise guide and regulate a more coherent process. Nevertheless, it is important to bear in mind that the level of commitment that Mexico can develop with regard to counterterrorism policy and capabilities is directly tied to the perceived benefits that the country could reap from addressing threats to its own security.

Nevertheless, there are significant obstacles to establishing a meaningful dialogue on security. The extreme centralization of the command structure in the Mexican Department of National Defense prevents anyone except the defense minister, General Vega, from discussing possible ways to cooperate with the United States on issues related to national security. At the same time, the U.S. secretary of defense, Donald Rumsfeld, has been so focused on his agenda's grand-strategy items halfway around the world that he pays little or no attention to the U.S. relationship with Mexico, delegating the task to the commander of the new U.S. Northern Command, who is also responsible for coordinating U.S. defense policy with Canada. The mismatch between expectations and military protocol has apparently prevented the militaries of both countries from engaging in a substantive dialogue.

Aside from strategic considerations, it is still surprising how much influence the personality and individual policy priorities of the defense leadership have in shaping cooperation policy. In 1995, William Perry was the first U.S. secretary of defense to visit Mexico as part of his overall policy of expanding defense relations throughout Latin America. This meeting prompted General Enrique Cervantes, Mexico's minister of national defense at the time, to visit the United States soon thereafter. The rapport established between the two officials gave rise to the most important bilateral cooperative relationship on military matters since World War II. Counternarcotics operations became the prime area of cooperation, because this effort included specialized training for Mexico's newly created Special Forces units as well as the transfer of 73 U.S. Army helicopters to Mexico. (Unfortunately, the unforeseen expense and intensity of operating these vintage machines, as well as fleetwide mechanical needs for this type of helicopter, prompted the Mexican military to return all of them after a few years.) As an indication of the political sensitivities, Mexico's military leadership did not want U.S. instructors inside Mexico, and training for both Special Forces personnel and helicopter pilots was provided at military facilities in the United States.

Another case of significant cooperation was the streamlining of information flows regarding the detection and monitoring by U.S. assets of aircraft and ships suspected of transporting drugs from South America as they approached Mexican territory. During these years, the Mexican military received widely different levels of support from civilian authorities—both for the military's political articulation of defense policies in general and for its cooperation with the United States in particular. Lack of political coverage partially explains the downscaling of cooperative efforts during the latter part of the Zedillo administration.

As it stands today, U.S.–Mexican cooperation on security matters has had to deal with a major structural reform in the United States: the creation of the U.S. Department of Homeland Security. This overhaul of the U.S. security apparatus has prompted Mexico's minister of government, Santiago Creel, to take the lead in becoming the government's main interlocutor with the United States and in using the intelligence service (CISEN) to coordinate the tasks involved in providing for the country's national security.

The current nature and extent of bilateral cooperation on national security appears to be largely driven by the U.S. government's assessment of it own needs for the war against terrorism. Mexico has been reluctant or unable to broaden the scope of the dialogue to include its own security concerns related to drug interdiction operations. This situation is also partly attributable to the low level of internal coordination inside Fox's cabinet and the lack of specific guidance and follow-up provided by the president himself, which induces individual agencies to take full control of their own international cooperation programs.

Aside from the political willingness to cooperate, Mexico faces a huge challenge because of the country's limited capabilities. A case in point is related to the specific delivery method used by the September 11 terrorists, which triggered substantial changes inside the United States with regard to controlling air space. Even if Mexico were to consider the move to be in its own best interest, the government could not hope to be a partner in a NORAD-type trilateral effort to control air space, alongside the United States and Canada, if Mexico continues to have a token air force that has no real interception capabilities. Achieving this capability would require investing in maintainable, long-range combat aircraft and air-refueling capabilities in order to ensure adequate and timely coverage of all of Mexico's air space. Obviously, this infrastructure would also be instrumental in denying the use of Mexican air space to drug traffickers for the introduction of cocaine into Mexican territory as well as for the internal movement of drug shipments. These interceptors would be the logical complement to the Airborne Early-Warning systems that Mexico has purchased, which became operational in mid-2004.

THE FUTURE OF THE CIVIL-MILITARY EQUATION AND SECURITY POLICY IN MEXICO

As opposed to the experiences of other Latin American countries, civil-military reform in Mexico would appear not to be focused solely on subjecting an autonomous military to democratic civilian control, but rather on the twin goals of protecting a professional military from a process of politicization and assuring that the military can contribute to enhancing the effectiveness of security policy under the premises of democratic accountability.

During the next presidential campaign—in 2006—the functionality of the civil-military framework will be put to the test. Through the legacy of the Fox administration, the political system has sent out a message that whoever wants to head the armed forces might have to "earn" the post through his allegiance to the winning presidential candidate rather than through his seniority or professional track record. Since the new democratic environment makes it difficult to predict which political party will win, the stage is set for the military leadership to become politically active. Clearly, expectations of self-restraint do not constitute a policy as no alternative set of rules is being even discussed.

On the other hand, the security challenges that the Mexican state has to address will also demand institutional reforms and increased budgets. The need to move defense and national security policy into the mainstream discourse will require a completely new level of political articulation. For this to happen, civilians will have to feel co-ownership of these policies and not consider them the exclusive purview of an isolated interest group that only seeks to protect and promote its parochial interests.

The almost exclusive subordination of the military to civilians through the armed forces' loyalty to the president is not longer able to provide this level of political articulation. A very strong presidential regime is gradually coexisting and interacting with a wider set of sources of political and institutional power. It would appear that the key to reestablishing the functionality of the civil-military equation in this new era is for the military to transfer its loyalty from the individual who is president to the institutions that make up the state, thereby broadening the base of stakeholders to better anchor defense and national security policy and safeguard the institutional role of the professional military. This transition would require defining a clear and specific set of rules that will provide guidance and make the relationship predictable, because the rules will determine the nature of civilian co-responsibility for defense and national security policy. Because the transition is a political process, it is wrong to expect the armed forces to initiate such a reform. If they did, the armed services would be behaving as politicians do, not as a professional military should.

Notes

[1] Surprisingly, this lack of appreciation for the relevance of the Mexican military is also evident in the large and well-established school of civil-military studies in Latin America. Over the years, the region's historical development has provided significant material for analysis—from coup theories to the transition back to civilian rule. But it is almost impossible to find the Mexican case even in the most recent collections of studies on this topic. A case in point is a book published in 2001, *Civil-military Relations in Latin America: New Analytical Perspectives* (David Pion-Berlin, ed. [Chapel Hill: The University of North Carolina Press, 2001]), whose editor did not even think it necessary to explain in the introduction why the second-largest country in the region and the second-largest trading partner of the United States is excluded.

[2] It is interesting to note that in few fields other than Latin American civil-military studies can political scientists express so uninhibitedly their own cognitive preferences without contestation, as the military leadership almost never engages in a dialogue by answering back with a critique in the political scientists' own academic "language." Likewise, political scientists quite often do not incorporate the military's threat assessment and strategic views in explaining their policy preferences.

[3] There is, of course, no "objective" assessment of security threats, because they almost always deal with potential events that have not taken place or may

or may not take place again. Nevertheless, the occurrence of such events is influenced by preparedness, because tangible measures, capabilities, and policies can deter potential aggressors. This comment refers to the increasing asymmetry of antiterrorist preparedness that is currently developing in the North American region.

[4]Adolfo Aguilar Zinser's definition of his role reflected more of a personal power play, which had no substantial backing from President Fox, a fact that soon led the different ministries to ignore and isolate Zinser. One key battle that he lost was the attempt to transfer the intelligence service out of the Government Ministry and place the service under his control. The idea of a national security adviser inside the president's office was severely damaged by this brief experience and Zinser's personality traits, and also by the fact that President Fox did not consider national security an organizing concept for the whole set of security and defense policies and organizations. Thus, Fox preferred to eliminate the position after Zinser left for New York to serve as Mexico's envoy to the United Nations.

[5]Here again, Castañeda appears to have overtly disregarded any internal consensus-building process by publicly presenting Mexico's commitment to multilateral peacekeeping operations without obtaining the armed forces' endorsement first. An indication that President Fox accepted the idea was probably not followed through by a direct and precise presidential instruction to the armed forces. One possible explanation is that General Ricardo Clemente Vega probably felt that, if Castañeda had not even coordinated this significant policy announcement with the National Defense Ministry, then any sign of acceptance would lead him to volunteer Mexican troops to the UN mission without internal consultation, putting them at risk both physically and institutionally.

[6]A showcase for these alternative expressions of power and their leadership took place when the Fox administration announced its decision to build the new Mexico City airport in the area of nearby Texcoco and the community of San Salvador Atenco strongly opposed the decision. The early stages of the local opposition quickly drew in a myriad of confrontational activists—from radical student groups (the General Strike Council [CGH] from the National Autonomous University of Mexico) to others involved in urban property disputes. In a short time, an otherwise unknown rural community on the outskirts of Mexico City turned into a hotbed of activism that, through strong-armed confrontational politics and violence, essentially forced the Fox administration to backtrack on its decision and cancel the project for a new airport. The fact that the Fox administration does not have the political expertise to deactivate situations like these also hurts the notion of the rule of law and the investment environment for the country.

[7]International press accounts put the number of persons listed as having disappeared in the 1970s at 543, 300 of them in the state of Guerrero. As a stark comparison, the Argentinean "dirty war" involved the death of 30,000 persons.

[8]General Enrique Cervantes retired as soon as he left office, and he has remained an adviser to the minister of national defense, a common practice among former ministers. This amicable relationship stands in sharp contrast to the confrontation between the former and current navy ministers.

[9]The most visible jurisdictional overlap was the creation in about 1997 of the army's amphibious Special Forces units (GANFES) that used small boats to establish a presence all along the Mexican coastline, much to the annoyance of the Mexican navy. On the other hand, prior to 1997, the lack of navy interest in establishing its own presence in these coastal areas is cited by the army as the reason it became necessary to create the GANFES. Less than a year afterward, the navy created its own fast interdiction capability using more capable equipment and expertise. Even though this case took place during the past administration, both services continue to coexist in the same operational environment under the Fox government. On policy, the navy appears to welcome multinational cooperation with other navies, whereas the army remains visibly opposed to participation by the Mexican military in multinational peacekeeping operations.

[10]The National Security Cabinet ceased to operate during the brief existence of the position of national security adviser in the person of Adolfo Aguilar Zinser.

[11]The Mexican air force currently has only 10 jet combat aircraft (Northrop Grumman F-5E/F Tiger II, a small, short-range aircraft unsuited for long-endurance patrol and interception missions), which are also concentrated close to Mexico City.

SIX

———

THE EVOLVING RELATIONSHIP BETWEEN CHURCH AND STATE

Raúl González Schmal

The problem of church-state relations, which came to be known as the religion issue, has been at the center of Mexico's history. While Mexico was under the rule of Spain and for a significant part of the period after gaining its independence, the religion factor—originally manifested by the monolithic Roman Catholic religion—was the single strongest element contributing to national cohesiveness. Religion is the social glue that holds Mexican society together and endows it with a specific identity.

With the forbearance of the Catholic Church, a process of miscegenation began to take place between the ranks of the Spanish conquistadores and the peoples they had subjugated. Thus, a mestizo (racially blended) culture was created in which European elements dominated. The outcome can simply be called "Mexican culture."

HISTORICAL POINTS OF REFERENCE

In contrast to the United States, Mexico took shape under the banner of religious unity that, in accordance with the concepts of Roman Catholicism that were produced by the Counter-Reformation in the sixteenth century, would not abide the presence of any other religion.[1] The United States, on the other hand, developed under the banner of religious pluralism, with no mixing of races. Anglo-Saxon culture was transplanted to the newly colonized lands. The Pilgrims who arrived on the *Mayflower* in the mid-seventeenth century had fled the religious intolerance they faced in England and set about to make their fortunes in the New World.

Translated by Charles J. Becker

Religious pluralism typified the colonization of the New World: in 1605, Anglicans settled in Jamestown; by 1611, Presbyterians settled in New England (after first fleeing Scotland and later Ireland); by 1620, Congregationalists settled in New Plymouth (after leaving Holland, they had fled from William Laud, an avowed enemy of Puritanism and the archbishop of Canterbury); in 1634, Catholics had established themselves in Maryland; in 1639, Baptists settled in Providence; in 1656, the Society of Friends (Quakers) settled in New England; and in 1683, Mennonites settled in Pennsylvania. The German Lutheran church, which was alien to the English Protestant tradition, was established in New Amsterdam in 1649; the French Reformist church reached New Holland in 1626 and New York (formerly New Amsterdam) in 1683; and a Jewish congregation moved from Brazil to New Amsterdam in 1664.[2] Tolerance was to become essential to the cross-cutting pluralism required for coexistence among so many different religious groups. Nevertheless, the road to religious tolerance in the United States was long and arduous.

Those who had fled religious intolerance in England embraced the paradox that cloaks all fanaticism and immediately began to establish an even greater level of intolerance. Whoever was not of the faith was not of the congregation, and whoever was not of the congregation was not of this world.[3] A clear example of such intolerance occurred between 1659 and 1663, when the Virginia Assembly prohibited the Society of Friends from so much as setting foot in the colony and subjecting three-time offenders to the death penalty. As for Catholics, at the outset of Colonial history, they were generally banned from the colonies, with the exception of Maryland and Pennsylvania, where the Catholic Church was allowed to function.

During the American Revolution (1775–1783), religious groups had to ignore their differences in the interest of making common cause. Independence had a dual purpose: the colonists were opposed to the British Crown and the various other religions opposed the Anglican Church.[4] Thus, this period was the first time that the ideals of civil liberties and religious freedom arose together.[5]

In Mexico, history unfolded quite differently. Throughout the three centuries of the viceroyalty in what was then called New Spain, the Catholic Church was governed by the Royal Trust (Patronato) of the Indies, established under the papal bull *Universalis Ecclesiae,* issued by

Julius II on June 28, 1508. In this edict, the papacy extended a series of privileges and obligations to the Spanish Crown with respect to the evangelization of the native peoples. These rights and responsibilities included the appointment of bishops, establishment of dioceses and parishes, and administration of tithes that the church collected each year.

During this extended period, the Royal Trust unilaterally increased its own powers and authority, for example—

- convening provincial councils that the viceroy presided over and also censured;

- exercising the right to award or retain papal bulls and other papal documents that the Crown issued to deal with matters in the Americas; and

- prohibiting prelates in the Americas from communicating with the Holy See.

Thus, the king of Spain virtually assumed the role of the pope's representative, or vicar, which is why some authors refer to this period of the council, which corresponds to the reign of the Bourbons, as the Royal Vicariate. The church was entirely subject to, and under the total domination of, the Spanish monarchs. This phenomenon—referred to as *royalism*—reached its zenith under King Carlos III, who expelled the Jesuits from his domains in New Spain in 1763. A number of historians consider this action one of the root causes of the movement toward national independence.

It is important to note that, in effect, Miguel Hidalgo (just as José María Morelos)[6] was a follower of the Jesuits,[7] as was Francisco Javier Clavijero. Moreover, because most of the disciples of the Jesuits were Mexican-born Creoles, it is safe to say that this group of revolutionaries was the first to forge a Mexican national consciousness. Religion, without a doubt, was a factor in Mexico's war of independence not only because the principal advocates of Mexican independence came from the ranks of the clergy but also because the religion factor was clearly instilled from the beginning to the end of the struggle for independence. The insurrection in Mexico began in the early morning hours of September 16, 1810, with shouts of "Long Live Our Lady, the Virgin of Guadalupe! Long Live Our King Fernando VII!" and "Death to Bad Government!"[8] Jean Meyer relates that when Hidalgo passed the famous sanctuary of Atotonilco,

Hidalgo took an image of the Virgin of Guadalupe from the sacristy, had it held aloft on the tip of a lance, and displayed it to his army, which was roused to cheer: Long live the Virgin of Guadalupe! . . . What is certain is that at that time worship of the Virgin of Guadalupe was so widespread that one could say, "Mexico is Guadalupan." Even the foes of independence, even the royalist Creoles and indigenous peoples, raised the banner of the Virgin of Guadalupe![9]

In fact, the banner of the army of the "three guarantees," at whose command Agustín Itúrbide, later the emperor of Mexico, achieved independence, proclaimed the three guarantees: "Religion, Unity, Independence."

Even agnostic liberals subsequently announced that they were Guadalupan; Ignacio Manuel Altamirano wrote: "The day that the Virgin of Tepeyac is no longer worshipped in this land, not only will Mexican nationality certainly have disappeared, but so too the memory among those who currently dwell in Mexico."[10] On the occasion of Pope John Paul II's fifth visit to Mexico for the canonization of Juan Diego and the beatification of two other indigenous Mexicans, which took place in July 2002, Joel Ortega—a leftist leader of the Democratic Revolutionary Party (PRD) and head of the delegation from Gustavo A. Madero's district (which houses the Shrine of Guadalupe)—declared himself to be "Guadalupan and a Juarista."[11] For his part, the vice mayor of Mexico City, Alejandro Encinas (deputy secretary of the government of the Federal District), who is a leftist, stated that "not being Catholic does not mean that you cannot see that, as Herbert Castillo once said, even the Marxists are Guadalupans.... The Virgin of Guadalupe is in the marrow of our bones."[12]

After a time, a process of reform—referred to as secularization—began in Mexico with the confrontation between two mutually irreconcilable visions for the nation: the liberals' view and the conservatives' view. This conflict, arising from an absence of dialogue and an excess of mutual incomprehension, would soon sweep the country in an internecine struggle that would ultimately see the liberal camp prevail and punish the Catholic Church for all the "historical sins" it had committed. During this period of domestic discord, Mexico would lose a bit more than half of its national territory—2 million square kilometers—to the United States as a result of the War of 1846–1848 (the Mexican–American War).

RELIGION IN MEXICO'S CONSTITUTIONAL HISTORY

From the time Mexico gained its independence from Spain in 1821 to the passage of the current Constitution in 1917, the constitutional status of the church in Mexico passed through three stages:

- recognition of Catholicism as the only religion in the country and the prohibition of all other faiths, as established in the 1824 federal Constitution and the centralist Constitutions of 1836 and 1843;

- separation of church and state and theoretical recognition of freedom to worship in the religion of one's choice, but with serious constraints on many areas of religious freedom, as established by the Reform Laws and in the 1857 Constitution;[13] and

- withdrawal of the legal status of the Catholic Church and other religious organizations, with ensuing violations of religious freedom in various areas, such as bans on public worship, religious association, religious instruction in private schools, and granting of authority to the state to determine the number of religious officials in each jurisdiction, as established in the 1917 Constitution.[14]

The decisive point in the conflict between the public sector and the Catholic Church occurred in 1926, with the passage of several regulatory laws that were even more restrictive than the constitutional provisions were. The Catholic Church's response was to suspend public worship services, and many Catholic groups, particularly in the countryside, rose up in arms against the government in what became known as the Cristera Rebellion, or, simply, *La Cristiada*.[15]

The armed conflict concluded in 1929 with the so-called Arrangements agreed to by church representatives and the administration of President Portes Gil. A modus vivendi was established between the church and the state: the antireligious legislation was not repealed, but it was no longer vigorously enforced. The state demonstrated an extralegal tolerance for certain public religious displays that were prohibited by law. This modus vivendi endured tense moments and even conflict, alleviated from time to time by a period of détente, from 1929 to 1992, during which time several amendments dealing with religion were added to the 1917 Constitution (Articles 3, 5, 24, 27.II and 27.III, and 130) and the Law on Religious Organizations and Public Worship was issued.

THE NEW LEGAL FRAMEWORK

President Carlos Salinas inaugurated the new phase of modernization in relations between, first, the church and the state, and later, the churches and the state. Upon his election, Salinas's legitimacy was open to serious questions, given the widespread perception that his opponent, Cuauhtémoc Cárdenas, had won the contest. Salinas invited key members of the Catholic Church's hierarchy to his inauguration on November 1, 1988. The guests included Apostolic Delegate Girolano Prigione, who was to play a major role in the new approach to the situation. In an effort to establish future relations with the Holy See, which was one of the components of a policy leading to globalization, Salinas appointed a personal representative to the papacy. It was later learned that, in return for reestablishing relations with the Mexican government, the pope insisted that Mexico's Constitution first be reformed to allow a wider berth for religious freedom. In December 1991, Salinas presented his package of constitutional reforms, which the Permanent Constitutional Congress passed on January 28, 1992; six months later—on July 15, 1992—the Mexican Congress passed the corresponding enabling regulations. As a result, on September 20, 1992, diplomatic relations between Mexico and the Holy See were reestablished after a 127-year interruption.[16]

The constitutional reforms contained in Articles 3, 5, 24, 27.II and 27.III, and 130 can be summed up as follows:

- The right to profess religious belief and to attend public worship services has been preserved in its original form, including the possibility—which is not mentioned in the amended text, however—to hold worship services of an "exceptional nature" outside of the churches.

- The ban on religious instruction has been lifted for private schools but has remained in effect for public schools.

- The ban on taking religious vows and on establishing religious orders has been repealed.

- The ban on participation by religious officials in charitable, scientific, or educational institutions has been lifted.

- The right of legally constituted religious organizations to acquire property that is essential to their mission has been recognized.

- The legal status of religious organizations is to be recognized, provided the organization is registered. In addition, government authorities are prohibited from interfering in the internal activities of religious organizations.

- The right of foreign nationals to practice their ministry in any religious group has been recognized.

- Religious officials are entitled to vote in elections but not to stand as candidates for elections, unless they have resigned from their ministry at least five years prior to the date of the election.

- Religious officials are prohibited from opposing the laws of the country or its institutions and may not disrespect patriotic symbols in any way.

- The restriction on religious officials' rights of inheritance has been reaffirmed and has been extended to cover religious associations in the amended regulations.[17]

The new legal framework ushered in a new, unprecedented stage in relations between the political and religious spheres. Although the state's relations are no longer exclusively with the Catholic Church, this relationship remains the dominant one. The state also maintains relations with several different religious faiths that are woven into the fabric of religious pluralism in Mexican society. According to the 2000 census, 87.99 percent of the Mexican people still identify themselves as Catholics, but other denominations have been making gradual headway: 5.2 percent are listed as Protestants (including members of the traditional religions, Pentecostals, and Neo-Pentecostals, as well as members of the Church of the Living God [Iglesia del Dios vivo], the Pillar and Support of Truth [Columna y Apoyo de la Verdad], the Light of the World [la Luz del Mundo], and other proselytizing groups); 2.07 percent are listed as followers of non-Evangelical biblical religions (such as Seventh-day Adventists, members of the Church of Jesus Christ of Latter-day Saints [Mormons], and Jehovah's Witnesses); 0.05 percent were listed as Jewish; 0.31 percent did not specify a religious affiliation; and 3.52 percent claimed to have no religion.[18]

It is important to note that, despite the significant progress in guaranteeing religious freedom that the new legislation made possible, a number of roadblocks, constraints, and ambiguities must still be overcome. The state held on to perhaps too much authority, which could actually restrict freedom of religion in the future.[19] The fact that the law places responsibility for religious matters under the purview of the secretary of the interior suggests that the balance was tilted toward controlling the freedom that the law granted.[20] Traditionally, the Ministry of Government has served as an organ of government intelligence; it has been the center of control, surveillance, and espionage on citizens and political or religious groups that were considered to be in any real or potential way opponents of the ruling group. The ministry's activities have historically even extended to include ordering the physical disappearance of political adversaries, first through the sinister and now defunct Federal Security Directorate (DFS) and later through the Center for Investigation and National Security (CISEN), which has now been transformed into an agency that operates under a democratic regime.[21] Therefore, this ministry does not seem to be the most appropriate one to guard religious freedom, when historically, under the principle of "reason of the state," it has had the responsibility for repressing religious freedoms as well as other human rights.

Moreover, Mexico has signed and ratified international instruments designed to protect human rights that cover the area of religious freedom much more broadly than Mexico's own domestic legislation does. These global commitments impose two types of obligations on the Mexican state: (1) the instruments, which include agreements, conventions, and treaties, must be considered part and parcel of the domestic constitutional and legal framework; and (2) constitutional and legal reforms are needed in order to ensure that the domestic legal system will be consistent with the text of these international documents.

VICENTE FOX'S CAMPAIGN PROMISES

Vicente Fox's campaign for the presidency emerged against the backdrop of this new stage in relations between the church and the state. Fox—the candidate of the National Action Party (PAN)—not only boasted of his religious convictions but also used religious symbols as testimony of his faith on more than one occasion,[22] thereby arousing the concerns of not just non-Catholics but also several Catholic sectors that feared that the candidate was assuming a preconciliar position.

It is revealing that, from 1917, when the current Constitution was enacted, until the year 2000, when Fox was inaugurated, of the 18 presidents who served over a period of 83 years, virtually all considered themselves to be atheists, agnostics, or freethinkers. Only one, Manuel Ávila Camacho, publicly announced that he was a "believer"—whatever that means. In response to a newspaper editor's question at the conclusion of his term, "Are you religious?" another Mexican president, Miguel de la Madrid, simply replied, "Vaguely." It is both curious and unsettling to witness the incongruity of so many non-Catholic and even anti-Catholic leaders presiding over a nation of people that is predominantly Catholic, as indicated by four censuses conducted over the past 40 years: 96.2 percent in 1970; 92.62 percent in 1980; 89.69 percent in 1990; and, as cited above, 87.99 percent in 2000.[23]

Under the democratic rule of law, the religious convictions of a nation's president should be irrelevant. A political leader should not necessarily reflect the religious beliefs of the majority of the nation's citizens. It is enough for a country to have democratic values guiding the business of government and for citizens' rights—starting with the keystone of all rights, religious freedom—to be respected. The problem is that, in the past, Mexico did not have a democratic system of government but, rather, an authoritarian regime that had begun to make the transition to democracy only in the past decade. Nor did Mexico operate within a framework of respect for citizens' religious rights or provide legal and constitutional safeguards to protect those rights. All these features indicate that there had been a protracted rift between the government and the nation itself.

Nevertheless, despite certain imprudent actions that have since been corrected, Fox has not given in to the temptation to create a "Catholic" government in Mexico. His campaign message made it quite clear that he offered to guarantee the right to religious freedom in the broadest terms possible as a condition of "an authentic acceptance in the context of an open, respectful, and tolerant society." On several occasions during the campaign, Fox met with representatives of different religious denominations who viewed his candidacy favorably, and he voiced his opinion that the right to religious freedom was only partially protected under Mexico's legal framework, because the population's exercise of this right "has been left in the hands of a bureaucracy with burdensome procedures and broad discretional power to create files in the interests of control by the use of information."

Fox also offered "to promote relations between the state and religious organizations, respecting their separation and independence, and encouraging them to engage in broad cooperation." With keen conceptual aim, he averred: "the secular and the religious spheres must set aside a conflict that makes no sense in a pluralistic, free, and democratic society...." However, he believes that "current legal doctrine places constraints on religious freedom..." and therefore committed himself "to promoting human rights, including the right to religious freedom, so that Mexico can truly achieve the rule of law."

During his campaign for the presidency, Fox distilled his public policy into 10 points, which some in the media somewhat sarcastically dubbed "Fox's Ten Commandments." These are listed below, along with commentaries that provide a frame of reference with which to compare what Fox proposed as a candidate and what he has actually accomplished so far as president.

Before discussing Fox's so-called Ten Commandments, however, it would be worthwhile to review briefly the seven points that Francisco Labastida, the presidential candidate of the Institutional Revolutionary Party (PRI), proposed, which might be termed "Labastida's Seven Commandments." These points, listed below, were not made public at first; rather, as far as can be ascertained, they were conveyed only to the leadership of the Catholic Church:

1. official recognition of ecclesiastical and religious studies provided in church seminaries and educational institutions;

2. submission for comment and consensus of the regulatory legislation on religious associations;

3. recognition of tax deductions for religious organizations;

4. substantial advancements in the right to religious freedom;

5. overhaul of protracted bureaucratic processes in order to facilitate placing priests from overseas in Mexico;

6. permanent space in the mass media for different religious and apostolic groups to promote values, ethics, and religion; and

7. removal of restrictions on schools so that parents may conduct classes in religion.[24]

Apart from the vagueness of some of these proposals, the seventh point—the reference to the freedom of parents to conduct religious instruction in schools—is intriguing because, even though it does not explicitly state it, the proposal can refer only to public schools, given that the right is already recognized in private schools. The PRI's government program forbids secular education from including any kind of religious instruction in public schools. Hence, Labastida's proposal contradicted the position of his own party.

As for the 10 proposals that Fox included in his electoral platform—several listed under the title of "Religious Freedom and Church-State Relations"[25]—some of them suffer from a certain opaqueness and ambiguity, and even a lack of connection to the issue at hand, which may be attributable to haste in the heat of the campaign. Nevertheless, a number of his proposals specify emphatically Fox's political will to broaden the scope of religious freedom for a pluralistic society and to create and maintain an openly secular and democratic system of government. Given that the points represent Fox's view of the issue that is the subject of this chapter, it is helpful to examine the text of the proposals themselves.

1. *I will promote respect for the right to life from the moment of conception until the moment of natural death.*[26]
   This point relates to an extremely important right—one that is the basis of all human rights—which Mexico's own Constitution does not directly and unconditionally uphold; instead, the right to life is mentioned in an indirect and conditional manner.[27] In any event, the point does not specifically refer to religious freedom. It is very likely that the issue of abortion underlies the proposal and is disguised to avoid exposing a vulnerable side to anti-abortion groups.

2. *I will support the strengthening of the family unit.*
   This is an abstraction that has no relevance to the issue under consideration.

3. *I will respect the rights of parents to make decisions on the education of their children.*
   Clearly this point refers, albeit obliquely, to the possibility of permitting religious instruction in public schools, which has been the most consistent and vigorously expressed demand of the Catholic hierarchy and would require an amendment to the Constitution, which, as it now stands, prohibits teaching religion in public schools.[28]

4. *I will promote free access to spiritual and religious counsel in health centers, correctional institutions, and institutions of assistance, such as orphanages and nursing homes.*

Mexico has no laws that expressly recognize this area under the rubric of freedom of religion; nor are such activities legally restricted. Thus, legislation would have to be enacted to implement this reform and to establish the corresponding regulatory procedures.[29]

5. *I will respond to the interest expressed by the churches to promote a broad margin of religious freedom, on the basis of Article 24 of the Constitution.*

This point tacitly acknowledges that religious freedom is not currently sufficient; thus, during the campaign, Fox proposed expanding this right in accordance with demands made by the churches. Because there is no indication as to what the churches' demands might be, a review of the claims that religious organizations, especially the Catholic Church, have announced will have to suffice for this discussion. The demands, which may not necessarily enjoy universal support among the other religious groups, are listed below:

- the right, as indicated above, to provide religious education in government schools (the Catholic Church has insisted that this right must apply to all religious professions, but the Evangelical Church generally opposes it out of fear that Catholicism would exercise a monopoly);

- the right, also indicated above, to spiritual counseling in correctional institutions as well as those that deal with social welfare;

- the right to obtain the government concession in order to own and operate a mass media company;

- the right to public worship (that is, hold services outside a congregational setting), which would repeal the "exceptional nature" condition set forth under Article 24 of the Constitution and the corresponding regulatory legislation;

- the right to conscientious objection that churches have generally demanded without particular emphasis, but one that has been the object of incisive and vigorous demand by the Jehovah's Witnesses and is manifested in their opposition to showing reverence for patriotic symbols and to allowing blood transfusions, even when they are required to save a human life;

- the right to extensive freedom of protest, which is restricted under Article 130 of the Constitution; and

- full political rights of citizenship for religious officials, which under Article 130 are limited to the right of these officials to vote. (Not all the churches embrace this demand. In fact, this measure is not even universally supported by the Catholic Church, with several prominent experts in canon law opposed to this demand.[30] When the reform was debated in the Chamber of Deputies, the supporters of the measure to grant full political rights of citizenship to religious officials were left-wing deputies. For example, Deputy Gilberto Rincón Gallardo proposed that religious officials receive equal treatment under "the legal framework that governs the armed forces; that is, to submit a request for personal leave six months prior to elections [current law requires five years] and to refrain from exercising their ministry during their term in civil office." According to Deputy Cecilia Soto, "There are other countries where there's a perfect separation between the state and the churches; nevertheless, the religious officials enjoy full civil rights, both to vote and to be voted for."[31] On November 1, 1999, Cuauhtémoc Cárdenas, the founder and a leading figure of the Democratic Revolutionary Party, came out in favor of reforming the Constitution to allow religious officials to take part in politics. The papal nuncio, Justo Mullor, characterized the proposal as "inadvisable," given the canon law's ban on church officials' participation in politics.[32])

Don Benito Juárez himself—in the electoral law of August 14, 1867—expressly recognized the right of "the citizens who hold ecclesiastical status" to serve in the legislature; supplemental documents explaining the law contain his reasoning for acknowledging that right:

> With regard to the clergy, because they are citizens, it did not seem fair to deprive them of one of the most important rights of citizenship. Moreover, the presumption that they would exercise an illegitimate influence in order to get themselves appointed as deputies would seem insufficient reason to deprive them of this right, because the act of appointing a deputy must, of necessity, be entrusted to the discretion of

the voters, and because it has not commonly been deemed to be a danger, nor have members of the clergy often been assumed to have exercised an illegitimate influence in order to get themselves elected, but rather to get people elected who enjoy their trust.[33]

6. *Consistent with the human right to freedom of worship and the international agreements in this regard to which Mexico is signatory, I shall promote the elimination of the inconsistencies in Articles 24 and 130 of the Constitution by amending that part of Article 130 that restricts the religious freedom decreed under Article 24. Along these lines, I will seek to*

- *reform the registry system of incorporation in favor of a simplified voluntary registration that would recognize the nature of religious organizations as legally entitled institutions;*

- *ensure that churches exercise full freedom and independence in appointing their own officials and defining their responsibilities;*

- *eliminate all forms of discrimination based on religious affiliation; and*

- *review the financial standing of religious associations.*

Several observations spring to mind in response to this sixth proposal from the candidate and now President Fox. The proposal fails to explain what the inconsistencies in Articles 24 and 130 of the Constitution are, but the reference is most likely to the following: (1) restrictions that Article 130 places on church officials' civic rights and freedom of expression and dissent; (2) the curbs placed on the right of church officials and religious associations to receive an inheritance from estates; (3) the tacit denial of legal civil status to religious wedding ceremonies; and (4) the authority of the state to award—not simply acknowledge—the legal status of religious associations. The last item relates to Fox's confusing proposal to substitute voluntary registration for the existing registry system of incorporation of religious organizations.

It is also unclear what Fox meant by his proposal to permit churches to exercise full freedom and independence in appointing their own officials—a right that is already guaranteed—or by his proposal to review the financial standing of religious associations. With regard to the discrimination clause, the Constitution already provides for the elimination of all forms of religious discrimination, a provision that was achieved not through Fox's reform proposals but as a result of the conflict with the indigenous peoples in Chiapas.[34]

7. *I will provide the churches with open access to the mass media, so that they may publicize their principles and activities.... I will encourage their ability to enjoy access to the mass media.*
This point has already been mentioned, but it should be noted that church groups' access to the mass media would not depend exclusively on the president's willingness to put this proposal into effect. Rather, such access would require congressional approval of a modification to the applicable laws.[35]

8. *I will promote, within the framework of a comprehensive tax reform, a tax structure to be worked out for the churches, allowing tax credits when church activities contribute to human development.*
This proposal relates to a source of indirect financing for religious associations as a way to promote the right to religious freedom, as is already the case, for example, with political parties. In the case of churches, however, the funding awarded is not only indirect— that is, it is granted by means of tax credits—but also direct, because of the belief that it is the state's obligation to promote the political rights of its citizens.

9. *I will put an end to the state's power of discretion to authorize the placement and permanent residence of foreign religious officials in Mexico.*
Legally, the placement and permanent residence of church officials from other countries are subject to the laws governing the status of foreign citizens as established by the General Law on Population and enforced under the jurisdiction of the Ministry of Government. Here too, the proposal would probably require an amendment to this law, which the president could submit to Congress for its approval.

10. *I will promote the voluntary mainstreaming of religious studies in the civil sphere, respecting the curriculum and subject matter taught in the seminaries and institutions for religious education.*
This is a praiseworthy proposal that responds to a demand for religious freedom made by several religious denominations.

Candidate Fox concluded his proposals on church-state relations and freedom of worship by underscoring in a conversational tone the importance of religious freedom: "This is why it is so important for Mexicans, for our families, for you and for me, that there be full enjoyment of the right to religious freedom."

IMPLEMENTATION OF CHANGES

After his election, Fox put together a transition team, which he named the Consultative Group on Religious Affairs. This group's task was to incorporate the 10 campaign proposals, fine-tune them, and render them into a program for government reform whose implementation would begin as soon as the new president assumed office on December 1, 2000. A noteworthy and unprecedented aspect was the group's composition: its members belonged to the major religious groups established in the country, in addition to the Catholic Church. Even so, the group's work was marked by an exemplary spirit of dedication and harmony. The group's coordinator was Dr. Alberto Ortega Venzor and its technical secretary was Ernesto Espejel Alva, a political scientist, a graduate in theology, and a member of the Presbyterian faith.

Among the proposals developed by a consensus of the group was the creation of a National Council for Religious Freedom as a decentralized agency operating under the Ministry of Government. The task of the council was to study, formulate, plan, report, propose, implement, and control all matters concerning the effect of the Law on Religious Associations and its corresponding regulations. The idea was that, after an assessment of its track record, the council would become an independent constitutional agency. This innovative proposal was based on the assumption that the right to religious freedom of Mexican citizens and religious groups and the relations between these groups and public authorities should have as a framework the modern secular state—based on the separation of church and state—and the recognition that religious freedom is not only a fundamental human right but also a formative principle in society and a governing principle of an open secular state. The council was to be a viable and effective instrument for achieving full assurance of the right to religious freedom—one that was decisively aimed at preserving the values of religious equality, autonomy, identity, equity, nondiscrimination, and pluralism.

Fox's Consultative Group also had plans to conduct several studies on constitutional and legislative reforms pertaining to different aspects of religious freedom and relations between religious institutions and public authorities. Although the particulars are not really relevant to this discussion, a plan to legislate specific crimes of discrimination—proposed by members of the Jewish community—should be mentioned because of the seriousness with which the project was undertaken. Another plan proposed the creation of a body to be called the Mexican Institute for the Study and Promotion of Religious Freedom, which included proposed draft legislation that would govern the organization and the operational role of the institute.

At the same time that the Consultative Group on Religious Affairs was formed, the Commission for Reform of the State was also created, with Porfirio Muñoz Ledo, then a congressman, serving as its coordinator.[36] The original underlying objective was to develop either a draft for a new constitution or a thorough revision of the existing one—a task that was considered the sine qua non for a true democratic transition. This commission was organized into several working groups—officially called "transition panels"—each of which was assigned a specific constitutional area to study.[37] The theme of religious freedom and relations between church and state was included under the commission's Panel on Human Rights.[38] However, church-state relations were only covered in a brief study of secularism, some oral comments on freedom of conscience, and a plan entitled "Religious Freedom and Church Relations," drafted by Dr. Alberto Athié, in which, among other proposals, he embraced the plan developed by the Consultative Group, in which he was already participating. Dr. Athié also recommended the creation of a Commission on Religious Freedom.

PRESERVATION OF THE STATUS QUO

It is surprising that the Fox administration did not take up any of the proposals developed by the Consultative Group on Religious Affairs or the Commission for Reform of the State. Nor have any steps been taken to implement the 10 proposals on religious freedom and church-state relations that Fox had featured in his presidential campaign. Having failed to seize the opportunity to act on this issue when he first assumed office, President Fox is unlikely to do so in what remains of his term. In view of the fact that an opposition party has a majority in Congress, the complex and controversial nature of the issue is bound to provide fertile ground for demagoguery that would arise at the president's expense.

What happened? Why did Fox accept this apparent contradiction between what initially appeared to be his modern concept of the right to religious freedom and of the relationship between the church and the state and what seems like his lack of concern over this issue today? Religious freedom has not deteriorated, but at the same time, no action has been taken to advance any of Fox's proposals. Instead, the status quo has been accepted. Having said that, however, the officials who are responsible within the current legal framework should be recognized for the work they have carried out to date.[39]

Does the president's public status as a Catholic make him a hostage to certain groups of a liberal nineteenth-century persuasion who are beholden to a "private" or "intimate" concept of religion and who see former President Salinas's opening to the Vatican as a betrayal of Benito Juárez's principles? Or is Fox being held hostage to traditionalist or absolutist Catholics who expected a Catholic president to restore the erstwhile privileges that the Catholic Church once enjoyed? Do the liberals who are more Juárez-like than Juárez was and the Catholics who are more Catholic than the pope is continue to feed the flames of historical injustice?

Octavio Paz was on target when he said that in Mexico what is past is present. Mexico still has currents of thought—held by many—that continue to present the issue of relations between church and state as though it were still the middle of the nineteenth century; the Catholic Church, in particular, has had a leading role in this way of thinking. A number of writers, historians, sociologists of religion, and, of course, Catholic clergy, as well as officials of other religions, behave as if they were "latter-day Jacobins and Catholic followers of Peter the Hermit," incapable of transcending a historical path that no longer exists, and one that, given the nature of the situation, cannot be repeated.

The historical clash continues. On one side of the debate, the state is seen as the pristine and immaculate defender of the people's freedoms and the church is considered monolithic and insensitive, always waiting for the opportunity to assault public authority. On the other side of the debate, the state is viewed as a diabolical manifestation and the church as an ever-faithful follower of its mission of salvation. These Manichaean perspectives forget that the "people" at the heart of the debate are human beings whom both institutions are meant to serve and also members of both the church and the state—as both worshippers and citizens.

It seems ironic that those who would wear the mantle of liberalism are sometimes the most steadfast opponents of the spiritual freedoms to which people and religious communities have a right. Such opponents often come to idolize a state that they would like to see exercise maximum possible control over the churches, especially the Catholic Church. Those who hold this view do so all in the name of history, and they consider themselves, of course, the most sacred guardians and exclusive interpreters of that history. They would counter the human aspect of religion with a civic religion, and counter religious dogmas (which legitimately define religions) with historical dogmas (which are illegitimate from the standpoint of the science of history). These critics are the ones who would oppose expanding any aspect of religious freedom on behalf of an orthodoxy attributed to the legacy of Benito Juárez. They are the polar opposite of libertarians; these liberals would have the state exercise every possible constraint and control and allow only the freedoms that are absolutely essential. They have condemned, for example, the spiritual counsel provided by religious communities in public agencies—such as hospitals and prisons—as instances of government-sponsored "religious activities." And they have qualified the Fox administration as denominational because of the president's attendance at religious services, which has received media coverage, or because the president speaks of the common good and "subsidiarity" as theological virtues. Curiously enough, these same critics, who are so ready to condemn the Fox administration for being denominational, never protested the 60-plus years of constitutional regulations that violated religious freedom, perhaps because they considered that situation to be history's punishment of those who had been on the wrong side of this same history.

THE EFFECT OF THE REFORMS AFTER TEN YEARS

In any event, it has been more than a decade since the enactment of the constitutional reforms and the Law on Religious Associations and

Public Worship, which transformed the legal framework and the objective conditions for church-state relations—specifically, the state's relations with the Catholic Church, because this was and remains the faith to which the vast majority of the Mexican population belongs, and in particular, because it was with the Catholic Church that 150 years of conflict arose.[40]

Even though the reforms that were passed are insufficient from the modern standpoint of the human right to religious freedom, the changes have had an enormous impact. The reforms brought to an end an era marked by legal schizophrenia—that is, the state's dissociation with constitutional regulations that, while officially in force, were contravened by public authorities themselves in order to allow a measure of religious freedom. During this period, the right to religious freedom was granted, under the label of extralegal tolerance, to citizens and religious communities, which were considered "not legal," because the Constitution did not acknowledge their legal standing.[41] In the 10-plus years that have passed since the reforms were enacted, no changes have been made to this part of the Constitution, the corresponding legislation, or any of the regulations issued to put the law into effect.[42]

On July 2, 2000, after a protracted process, Mexico consummated its transition to democracy as a result of the creation of new electoral institutions—the Federal Electoral Institute (IFE) and the Federal Electoral Tribunal (TRIFE)—that guaranteed the possibility that nonincumbent political parties could win control of the executive branch of Mexico's government. The major outcome of this process was the election of an opposition candidate, Vicente Fox. The opposition's electoral victory gave rise to high levels of both expectation and fear—neither of which has been borne out: the expectations were not based on objective political circumstances, and the fears were simply unfounded.

THE POSITION OF THE CATHOLIC CHURCH

In the decade or more since the enactment of the constitutional reforms (a period that includes the first half of Fox's presidential term), what has been the vision and position of the Catholic Church as shown by its response? One answer may be found in the discussion and outcome of the 73rd Assembly of the Mexican Conference of

Catholic Bishops, the highest governing body in the Mexican Catholic church. This meeting, held April 8–12, 2002, was devoted to a comprehensive study and assessment of the church's relations with the state and the issue of religious freedom in the decade that had just ended. In fact, the assembly itself was entitled "Ten Years after the Constitutional Reforms." An eloquent indication of the church's willingness to consider change and the positive response to this phenomenon by both academia and the executive and legislative branches of the Mexican government was the participation in the assembly of various experts, the Secretary of Government, and representatives and senators from several political parties.

The Focus of the Mexican Conference of Catholic Bishops

In his keynote address to the assembly, the president of the Mexican Conference of Catholic Bishops, Archbishop Luis Morales Reyes, stated that the focus of the assembly was to look at the current status of religious freedom in the country and to review objectively what had happened in the 10 years since the enactment of the constitutional reforms. The assessment was to be conducted so that the bishops could suggest standards by which to advance the legal procedures that guarantee the right to religious freedom "not just of Catholics" but of all Mexicans. Archbishop Morales Reyes noted that the Mexican Conference of Catholic Bishops did not intend to take over legislators' responsibilities, but rather—with the help of experts and political figures and on the basis of the universal magisterial doctrine of the church and the United Nations Universal Declaration of Human Rights passed in 1948—to offer the country some illumination on the implications of the human right to religious freedom.

In his message, Archbishop Morales Reyes recalled "with gratitude and admiration so many martyrs who gave their lives to defend the sacred right to practice their religion in public life and not only in their conscience and in their homes or temples." He expressly acknowledged "the legislators who 10 years earlier were able to give Mexico the legal framework that was justly being claimed; . . . [and that] after a decade we undoubtedly enjoy greater religious freedom. All of us, not only Catholics, have a new legal system that recognizes some of our rights...." However, the archbishop observed that "there are some still pending...."[43]

One of those rights that was "pending"—and, in fact, Archbishop Morales Reyes devoted the main thrust and most relevant part of his message to this topic—was religious freedom in education: "Without wishing to anticipate what the Assembly may discuss on the matter, allow me to share with you some thoughts on one of the most sensitive issues in Mexico, which is precisely religious freedom in education." The demand that this right be recognized, not just for Catholics but for followers of all religious beliefs as well as for "parents who do not want any religion for their children in the schools," is founded on the United Nations Universal Declaration of Human Rights and international agreements on human rights, as well as the teachings of the Catholic Church.

Obviously, this issue is an insistent, but measured, demand made of the state and accorded absolute priority by the Catholic Church. With a realistic and clear-eyed view of the complexity of the question and the difficulty in responding to it, the president of the Mexican Conference of Catholic Bishops expressed the following in his message:

> I am aware that this issue is one of the most debated in the past and present history of the country. There will always be those who interpret this demand for justice and freedom as a desire to reclaim special legal exemptions and privileges or as a way by which to return to bygone days and to ambitions for dominion and power over peoples' consciousness. Others will imagine that the desire is to impose the Catholic religion in all public schools, regardless of the current religious plurality that shapes the country.[44]

In a tone similar to the one used by Archbishop Morales Reyes in his keynote address to the Assembly of the Mexican Conference of Catholic Bishops, the current papal nuncio, Monsignor Giuseppe Bertello, also insisted on the need to recognize the right to religious freedom within the sphere of education as an inherent requirement of its social dimension, even though "many, in the name of the intellectual pluralism characteristic of contemporary society, would like to restrict it to the sphere of individual conscience, depriving it of any social dimension." In his address, Monsignor Bertello presented a concise summary of his vision of religious freedom in Mexico as well as his view of relations between the church and the state:

Throughout the breadth of Mexican history, the exercise of religious freedom has undergone difficult stages, and, as a consequence, relations between the church and the state have not always been peaceful, in recent times passing through a number of phases running the gamut from actual tolerance and close coexistence—within an adverse legal framework—to the current situation that has transcended the prior dialectic of at least official confrontation between the two entities.[45]

Thus, there can be no doubt that the Catholic Church's central concern regarding religious freedom was that the law should recognize the human right of parents to determine the type of education that they should provide their children and that the law should allow for the possibility of conducting religious classes in public schools—"open to all beliefs," as the bishops insisted—as an extracurricular activity outside the regular class schedule. This concern was also made clear throughout the discussion among the bishops themselves and between their interlocutors and the experts and public officials and legislators who were in attendance at various times during the assembly. Nevertheless, it is surprising that the final official document issued at the conclusion of the assembly did not place any demands on President Fox to fulfill or, at least, attempt to fulfill the third of his 10 points that dealt with the issue of church-state relations, despite the assembly's repeated calls for such action—calls that were not addressed to anyone in particular. Because the final report of the Conference constitutes the official general position of the Catholic Church in this stage of Mexico's history, this chapter will discuss this document in greater depth.

Government Representatives' Positions on Religious Instruction

Before examining the assembly's final official report, it is helpful to review some of the positions on religious education that were taken by the most relevant interlocutors from the government and the political parties who attended the Mexican Conference of Catholic Bishops. Their positions may explain why the issue of religious education was omitted from the final report.

During the session that took place on April 10, 2002, representatives of the three major political parties—PAN, PRI, and PRD—explained that the issue of religious freedom, particularly as it applies to religious education, was not on the legislative agenda of any of the parliamentary groups. A number of officials indicated that they had no interest in having the Catholic Church's proposal to teach religion in public schools presented for debate. Specific responses to the bishops' position included the following viewpoints:

- Martí Batres, then the leader of the PRD in the Chamber of Deputies, stated his belief that education should be secular and that no constitutional reforms related to this issue should be enacted. He indicated that religious education should be conducted within the family setting and that the principle of maintaining a secular state and secular public education should be preserved.

- PAN senator Diego Fernández de Cevallos, then chairman of the Senate, argued that no issue should be forbidden or prohibited from legislative debate, even if religious freedom is not under consideration.

- Felipe Calderón, then coordinator of the PAN in the Chamber of Deputies, noted that, in light of Mexico's educational system in which religious instruction is reserved for those who can afford to pay for it, the state—functioning in subsidiarity—should guarantee every human being access to the religion that his or her convictions may dictate. He added that education could be secular without necessarily being atheistic, but that there should not be any official or state-sponsored religious education. He added that "there are things in the law that could be improved in order to extend full religious freedom, but it is a complicated issue, which must be treated prudently."

Other government officials who were unwilling to include the issue on Congress's agenda included Beatriz Paredes, then president of the Chamber's steering committee, and José Natividad González Parás, then a PRI senator.

Representing the executive branch was Santiago Creel, secretary of government, who—in addition to attending all the sessions of the Assembly—met separately with the bishops. Creel made a commitment to see that the issue would be discussed under the Political Accord for National Development. According to Creel, "It is fitting that it be subject to extensive reflection in order to see what we should change and how to improve relations with the church under the precept of freedom of religion for all Mexicans. No issue can, a priori, be placed off limits for discussion. This is a good time to see how to safeguard religious freedom." [46]

Major Points in the Final Report of the Mexican Conference of Catholic Bishops

The final official report of the Mexican Conference of Catholic Bishops, titled "Religious Freedom in Democratic Mexico: A Message from the Mexican Bishops Ten Years after the Constitutional Reforms," includes several points that should be emphasized:

- The conference acknowledged that, after so many years of legislation that reined in religious freedoms, with the enactment 10 years ago of legal reforms, "Mexico has left behind an anachronistic situation by recognizing the right of its citizens to religious freedom . . . [which] may be considered daring given that, with such a heavy historical burden, broaching these issues used to seem verboten. Just the same, the new laws could be improved." The bishops acknowledged that "a ten-year period is a relatively short time to achieve a change in mentality and a new culture in our Mexican society, accustomed to pretense and habituated to a certain contempt for laws."

- The conference insisted that the principle of the separation of church and state should be maintained but pointed out that "separation does not spell subordination or confrontation, but rather respect and collaboration, each from its own sphere. . . . The State should not be denominational, but should maintain its secular character, which in no way means that it is antireligious; rather, it is respectful of the different religious choices exercised by individuals and groups."

- The bishops particularly stressed that in promoting the right to greater religious freedom, they "do so for all Mexicans, Catholics and non-Catholics, believers and nonbelievers, because this concerns a natural right of the individual." The bishops emphasized that they in no way "seek to see the Catholic religion imposed on everyone, but we do claim the right to freely advocate it."

- The bishops recognized that they have to "learn to live in a more ecumenical spirit, to respect those who choose a different belief." Accordingly, they believe that their efforts must be made in common "with leaders of other religious denominations in order to achieve greater progress toward full recognition of this fundamental right to religious freedom."

- They acknowledged that "the new atmosphere in which we live with regard to the exercise of religious freedom is due, among other factors, to the dialogue and collaboration of the Catholic Church with different sectors of society," and they added that "dialogue, respect, and collaboration with other actors in society will allow us to know ourselves better and to uproot prejudices."

- On the key question of religious freedom in education, the bishops said: "We reiterate our recognition of the natural right parents have to educate their children comprehensively; also in the religious sphere. This right must be recognized, guaranteed, and supported by the state, the religious associations, and other institutions, as provided for under Article 26.3 of the Universal Declaration of Human Rights. . . ." Furthermore, they noted that "the reform is contributing to overcoming a secular mentality and respect for secular education. In other words, preserving the constitutional provision that education provided by the state must be free of charge, compulsory, and secular; we are certain that secularity in education, which had almost always been understood to mean antireligious and anti-Catholic or anticlerical, is, little by little, being overcome." Demonstrating profound understanding of the complexity of the problem, the bishops went on to state: "Nevertheless, still recognizing the sensitivity of the issue, owing to the historic burden of our past, we, the bishops of Mexico, have great hope that we may encourage different sectors that are interested to expand the dialogue about this right to religious freedom in educational affairs in our Constitution."

The bishops concluded their message with a series of exhortations, such as the following:

- "We call upon everyone to educate us and instruct us for the new stage of religious liberty in which we are living, because the change that we yearn for in our fatherland depends on more than a modification to the laws, on interior conversion, of a new mentality, to live more coherently with the Gospel."

- "We must continue to overcome the historic prejudices that did so much harm to the country."

- "We encourage the authorities and the legislators to continue the dialogue that we have initiated on this matter, which shall redound to the benefit of the country."

Finally, the bishops issued a call to all Mexicans in anticipation of the July 2002 visit of Pope John Paul II for the canonization of Juan Diego and two other indigenous Mexicans, that it "take place in an atmosphere of faith, of joy, of liberty, and fraternal harmony."[47]

In the opinion of this author, this message from the Mexican Conference of Catholic Bishops represents a historic document of the highest value. Unfortunately, analysts have failed to recognize its importance. Without ignoring the Catholic Church's demand that the right to religious freedom meet the requirements of international instruments in this area, the bishops also claimed this right on behalf of the other religious denominations and for those who do not profess any religious belief. Ever since the enactment of the 1992 reforms, opportunities have arisen for the exercise of this right. The Catholic Church, in particular, has called on others and on its own members to become educated about the new stage of religious freedom and to adopt a new mentality that will allow the historical prejudices that have so hurt the country to be overcome. The Catholic hierarchy accords priority to entering into a dialogue and also closing the gap between the church and those who think differently as a way to gain true knowledge and comprehension of one another and to strengthen the commitment to coexist in an ecumenical spirit.

At the assembly, the bishops did not angrily demand that the Fox administration make good on what it had offered to do during the presidential campaign. Such a demand would only have strained relations between the Catholic Church and the state. Rather, the bishops expressed an attitude of openness, an invitation toward reconciliation, and a measured demand to continue to move forward.

RELIGIOUS MINORITIES

It should be noted that the same attitude and vision are not evident among all the religious minorities. This chapter is not the place to undertake broad specific research and opinion surveys among the dozens of non-Catholic religious denominations. However, one individual who might be representative of many of them—particularly the evangelical churches—is Isaías Ramos, the bishop of the Methodist church, one of the denominations that has numerous members in Mexico.[48]

Bishop Ramos admits that as a non-Catholic church, the Methodist church did not agree with the 1992 constitutional reforms, but he recognizes that since his church has gained legal status and the ministers have obtained citizenship status, a number of rights they used to lack have now been recognized. Their opposition to the reform responded to their concern over the possibility that religion would have a role in matters that were strictly secular. Bishop Ramos considers the relationship between the current administration and the churches cordial but inequitable. As an example, he has cited the renovation project for the historic downtown area of Mexico City undertaken by the city's municipal government. A Catholic cardinal is a member of the committee created to advise on the project, but no one from the hierarchy of any of the evangelical churches has ever been invited to participate, notwithstanding the presence in the area of some of the most important and historic houses of worship. Bishop Ramos complains that non-Catholic officials were never asked to offer their opinions, much less participate in making decisions about the renovation project.

According to Bishop Ramos, non-Catholic denominations had the same kinds of relations—cordial but distant—with PRI governments in the past. The Methodist leader believes that the current government has shown a marked preference for the Catholic Church, when—despite the Constitution—the chief executive and some of his cabinet members publicly express their faith, thus suggesting that presidential policies and attitudes exclude other religions. In Bishop Ramos's opinion, the legal statutes need to be reformed in order to establish standards that are equitable for all Mexican citizens. Although he concedes that the legal framework provides the necessary conditions for guaranteeing and protecting religious freedom in Mexico, in practice the government is promoting a different policy when public servants publicly display their religious preferences.

Bishop Ramos asserts that relations with members of the Catholic Church are excellent; he sees an increasing level of openness to enter a dialogue in matters of faith. However, other religions' relations with the hierarchy of the Catholic Church are quite distant because of the regrettable absence of an ecumenical spirit among the hierarchy of all the churches.

In addition, the Methodist bishop also regrets that outbreaks of religious intolerance still occur among groups that are closed off to the new era and its pluralistic and democratic atmosphere. What is worse, he believes that politicians and religious leaders sometimes encourage these incidents. Finally, Bishop Ramos sees the need to pay special attention to the economic and political discrimination that is directed at the indigenous peoples—mainly in Chiapas and Oaxaca—under the guise of religion.

THE NEW SECULAR STATE

Twenty centuries have passed since Christianity first separated the temporal and the spiritual spheres, as proclaimed in the gospel: "Render therefore unto Caesar the things which are Caesar's and unto God the things that are God's." The primary guideline that people belonging to all camps have accepted and followed in theory is just that: the political sphere is one thing, the religious sphere is another. Thus, the state is one institution and the church is another—or, more accurately, the churches, after religious unity was split asunder in Europe in order to give way to religious pluralism.

Nevertheless, in the historical recounting of what conventionally is called Western civilization—in different places, times, and circumstances—political power has invaded the spiritual sphere or the spiritual sphere has occupied the political arena. The nature of politics and the nature of religion are prone to provoking activities that correspond to the other's sphere, thereby causing them to come into contact with each other, resulting in interference, conflict, and even serious collision, which in some extreme instances may even lead to violence. Nineteenth- and twentieth-century Mexico experienced painful confrontations between these spheres that divided the country throughout much of its history.

As ideological positions are staked out on this issue and historical phenomena designated, borders drawn, and the type of ideal state described, terms have been coined such as "liberalism," "laity," "secularity," "secularization," "reform," "denominationalism," and so forth—all of which tend to have multiple meanings. As these concepts are adopted, they are assigned different meanings by different authors, making it necessary to attempt to define them more precisely before even initiating a discussion. One term above all others, in one way or another, embraces all these terms and, in Mexico's case, is especially relevant, is particularly loaded, and must be fine-tuned and clarified before a desirable framework for relations between political powers and religious communities can be established. That term is "secular state," and it has recently been the subject of study under the new area of law known as the ecclesiastical law of the state.[49]

What, then, is the secular state? What is the modern conception of the secular state? As it turns out, this point is most likely the source of the problem for many sectors when it comes to accepting new guidelines and new practices in the relationship between politics and religion. No thought is given to continued adherence to the notion, now in decline, that the state is alien to all religion or that a secularized society is one in which religion constitutes a sentiment—or, in the best case, a right—but that, in any event, the practice of religion must be confined to an individual's privacy.

The term "secular state" has been used to refer to different ideological positions and different concrete historical realities:

- the secular state manifest in the two stages (anticlerical and antireligious) of the French Revolution;

- a nonrevolutionary, liberal secular state that is indifferent to religion and religious activities;

- the atheistic secular state of Marxist-Leninist regimes;

- the secular state that takes a neutral position on any religious denomination but a negative one on promoting the right to religious freedom as a public right; and

- the secular state that is neutral but, in principle, takes a positive approach toward religious activities.

The typology of the secular state includes several other forms and nuances that do not need to be discussed here. What is important is to identify, by way of comparison, the nature of the new concept of the secular state that some authors propose as a way to avoid confusing the idea of the secular states with the obsolete historical examples. Accordingly, the concept can be referred to as the "state of religious freedom," and its strongest element can be underscored by calling it the "open secular state." This concept is naturally included in the framework of constitutional democracy.

This last type of secular state is predicated on religious freedom, which in this context is considered a fundamental human right and a principle of social organization and political configuration, containing as it does the idea or definition of the state. Because of the democratic legitimacy of the Fox administration, the PAN's minority status in Congress, and the fact that the government recognizes and is recognized by a society that enjoys religious pluralism, President Fox could do a great deal to advance the shape of this type of secular state.[50]

The principle of the secular status of the state is realized when the government peacefully recognizes the decisive and particular social contribution that is inherent in the set of spiritual, ethical, and cultural values that the religious sphere engenders for the common good of society as a whole. As a result of this maturation of the state in terms of its own identity and nature, the government understands that the secular status of the state is not a religious definition or a defensive attitude toward its own sovereignty in light of the former union between the Crown and the cross. Nor does the definition apply to the nineteenth-century methods used to ensure the separation of church and state.[51] The state's secular status, subordinate to the principle of religious freedom, represents the new official modus operandi under a constitutional system of government—one that recognizes, promotes, and guarantees the social factor that originated in the heart of contemporary society as a result of the pluralistic religious accommodation—individual and collective, public and private—among the Mexican people. Along these lines, it should also be noted that, on the basis of the principle of religious freedom, the state defines itself as having no fundamental authority to act in matters of faith and religious practice, and neither is it the state's role to pressure or even to coincide with the religious faith of its citizens the way an individual would.

The fact that the state does not assume or profess any belief in a specific religion, and thus is nondenominational, does not mean, however, that the state should assume an agnostic, indifferent, or atheistic attitude. The absence of state authority in matters of religion allows it to assume religious beliefs as well as to negate those beliefs; either approach implies accepting the definition of these beliefs. Thus, an agnostic, atheist, or indifferent state is one that *professes* agnosticism, atheism, or indifference, and therefore would become a denominational state whose religious belief is agnosticism or atheism.

It is also important to bear in mind that religious freedom as a fundamental human right, above all, gives citizens immunity from pressure. As a result, no one can be prevented from living according to the dictates of his or her conscience and no one can be obliged to live by those same dictates.[52] Accordingly, this right to religious freedom, which could be called the freedom to profess fundamental convictions, affects both the believer and the nonbeliever—that is, an individual who professes a religion and one who does not. Thus, religious freedom provides legal recognition and safeguards to religious, agnostic, and atheistic attitudes alike. This is particularly important in order to create and maintain a platform for positive consensus on human standards and beliefs among Catholics, non-Catholic Christians, non-Christian believers, and nonbelievers.

Even though the right to religious freedom is single and autonomous, it is manifested in many ways, including, but not limited to, the following:[53]

- freedom of conscience;
- freedom of worship;
- freedom to propagate religious beliefs, ideas, and opinion;
- the right of church or religious community members to receive religious training;
- the right to meet and to demonstrate;
- the right of association; and
- the right to conscientious objection.

In light of the discussion of the secular status of the state and religious freedom—with its double axis of a human right and an informing principle of the state—it is necessary to mention that the distinguishing mark of the modern secular state is the requirement that it not only recognize but also guarantee, foster, and promote the right to religious freedom. In other words, the nineteenth-century liberal state has been transformed into today's pluralistic democracy under the rule of law or, as one may prefer to call it, the state of religious freedom.[54] In addition, the phenomenon of the internationalization of human rights is intertwined with this transformation. This feature involves international monitoring of human rights—and thus, the right to religious freedom—which also affects the concept of sovereignty that the liberal state held aloft as an absolute principle and paradoxically was a notion that was identified with a collectivist state.

FINAL CONSIDERATIONS

The democratic system that is evolving in Mexico is ineluctably conditioned on the consolidation of a new culture of human rights, especially the right to religious freedom, the cornerstone of all other human rights and one that should be promoted by public authorities as well as religious institutions. Religious freedom is a fundamental human right that is based on the recognition of the dignity of human nature as the supreme principle that informs the modern secular state. This human right to religious freedom constitutes the irreplaceable condition for transcending Mexico's divisive past.

Notes

[1] In the view of the illustrious agnostic jurist Emilio Rabasa, "religious unity in New Spain had been an unhampered, somewhat spontaneous, reality; thus it was that intolerance was not merely an institution as provided under law, but a necessity for the peace of mind of the people. Whereas religious unity is absurd and against the nature of any social group, at the dawn of Mexican independence, it constituted a natural and typical element; and, without it, that political communion could not have come into being as an organized people" (see Emilio Rabasa, *La Constitución y la Dictadura* [Constitution and Dictatorship], 4th ed. [Mexico City: Editorial Miguel Angel Porrúa, 1968], 16).

[2] See Oscar Celador Angón, *Estatuto Jurídico de las Confesiones Religiosas en el Ordenamiento Jurídico Estadounidense* [Legal Status of Religious Faiths in the U.S. Legal Framework] (Madrid: Editorial Dyckinson, 1998), 10.

[3] Emilio O. Rabasa, *El Pensamiento Político del Constituyente de 1824* [The Political Thought of the 1824 Constitutional Assembly] (Mexico City: Instituto de Investigaciones Jurídicas, Universidad Nacional Autónoma de México, 1986), 16.

[4] By the time the war ended, there were approximately 3,000 congregations of different faiths in the United States: 98 percent were Protestants (Congregationalists, Presbyterians, Anglicans, Baptists, Reformists, Society of Friends); and 2 percent were Catholics (with 50 congregations) and Jews (with 5 congregations).

[5] The first amendment to the U.S. Constitution sets forth that "Congress shall make no law respecting an establishment of religion [that is, separation

of church and state], or prohibiting the free exercise thereof [that is, religious freedom]..." and proceeds to specify the freedoms of speech, press, and assembly. In order to resolve the complex and conflictive relationship between the "establishment clause" and the "free exercise clause," the courts have traditionally applied a "balancing test" (see, for example, Celador Angón, *Estatuto Jurídico de las Confesiones Religiosas,* 26–60).

[6] Miguel Hidalgo y Costilla, known in Mexico as the "Padre de la Patria," was a priest who led Mexico's independence movement against Spain, beginning with a famous call to arms on September 16, 1810. Father Hidalgo was executed the following year. José María Morelos, also a priest, succeeded Hidalgo as a leader in the fight for independence. Morelos was executed on December 22, 1815.

[7] According to one historian, the Jesuits "strove to reconcile the different fields of knowledge with religious revelation, while avoiding the anti-Christian excesses and critiques of the most radical philosophers of the enlightenment" (see Elías Trabulse, "Francisco Javier Clavijero," in *La Ilustración Mexicana 1731–1787* [The Mexican Enlightenment, 1731–1787], ed. Alfonso Martínez Rosales [Mexico City: El Colegio de México, 1987], 50–51).

[8] Jean Meyer, *Hidalgo* (Mexico City: Clío, 1996), 36.

[9] Ibid., 37.

[10] Altamirano's quotation was taken from a book by the British historian, David A. Brading, *The Virgin of Guadalupe: Image and Tradition,* published in Spanish as *La Virgen de Guadalupe: Imagen y Tradición,* trans. Aura Levy and Aurelio Major (Mexico City: Taurus, 2002), 9. In another book, Brading states that the enduring strength of the Virgin of Guadalupe in Mexico is a cult that has outlived many of its European equivalents (see the Spanish edition of David A. Brading, *Mito y Profecía en la Historia de México* [Myth and Prophecy in the History of Mexico], [Mexico City: Editorial Vuelta, 1988], 69).

[11] "Juarista" refers to Benito Juárez, the nineteenth-century Mexican president who restored national sovereignty after the French imposition of "Emperor" Maximillian. Joel Ortega adds: "I think that this issue of a dispute among liberals, or between people from the center left and the church, has long since been left behind" (see Manuel Durán, "'Cristo es de izquierda,'" *Reforma* (Mexico City), July 20, 2002, sec. A).

[12] Alejandra Bordon, interview with Alejandro Encinas, as published in *Reforma* (Mexico City), July 22, 2002. In the same interview, Encinas stated: "We are redefining the terms of the relationship between the left and the churches, whereby this idea of an anticlerical, atheist, priest-devouring left is becoming a thing of the past, given one basic recognition: the majority of left-wing militants in our country are loyal Catholics, which is among the substantial changes in the life of our nation."

[13] The liberal 1857 Constitution was passed under oath by unanimous vote of the Congress members and then the president in front of a crucifix placed between two burning candles. According to Jean Meyer, "The 1857 Constitutional Congress appeared to be a council of priests and presided over by a pontificate who issued dogmatic declarations: the Constitution was sacred and could not be amended, and was ridden with political terminology redolent with religious content, such as the 'sacrament of the fatherland.' Ocampo drafted an epistolary to married couples that is still read today in the civil marriage ceremony, and attempts were made to create rites and civic liturgies" (see Jean Meyer, *La Cristiada* [The Cristeros Rebellion], 2nd ed., 3 vols. [Mexico City: Siglo XXI Editores, 1994], 26–27).

[14] The climate of the debates during the Constitutional Congress that issued the 1917 Constitution exhibited unanimity and absolute anticlerical sentiment; the attitude was, to a great extent, antireligious. One of the most moderate voices in the Constitutional Congress began a speech with these words: "If there are no ropes to strangle tyrants, a friar's belt shall be woven through my hand." The credo—at times explicit, at times not—was designed to punish the church for its "historic sins," especially because the church stood accused of having sided with Vitoriano Huerta in his overthrow of Francisco Madero. See Juan de Dios Bojórquez, *Crónica del Constituyente* (Mexico City: Botas, 1938; Federal Government, 1985).

[15] The best work on the Cristero War is a classic of Mexican historiography, Jean Meyer's *La Cristiada* (note 13).

[16] The first papal nuncio in Mexican history was Monsignor Francisco Meglia, who served in his post from December 1864 until May 1865. In 1992, when relations were reestablished, the Holy See designated Monsignor Girolamo Prigione as its papal nuncio and apostolic delegate to Mexico; Mexico sent Enrique Olivares Santana as its emissary to the Holy See.

[17] See Raúl González Schmal, *Derecho Eclesiástico Mexicano* [Mexican Ecclesiastical Law] (Mexico City: Editorial Miguel Angel Porrúa, 1997).

[18] For the 2000 census, see www.inegi.gob.mx. The three Mexican states with the highest Catholic population are Guanajuato with 96.41 percent, Aguascalientes with 95.63 percent, and Jalisco with 95.38 percent. The three states with the lowest Catholic population are Chiapas with 63.82 percent, Tabasco with 70.45 percent, and Campeche with 71.27 percent. Catholics make up 90.45 percent of the Federal District's population.

[19] The Law on Religious Associations and Public Worship contains 36 articles and 7 transitory provisions. The Ministry of Government is empowered as the executing authority and given 28 enforcement powers, several of which are discretionary and place under the ministry's authority a broad range of

control over the external life of the religious organizations, thereby affecting their autonomy in some cases and to some degree.

[20] Article 25 of the Law on Religious Associations and Public Worship establishes that "it is the responsibility of the federal executive branch, through the action of the Ministry of Government, to enforce this law. State and municipal authorities, as well as those of the Federal District [Mexico City], will assist the nation in the terms set forth in this legislation." Published in the *Diario Oficial de la Federación* [Official Daily Record], Ministry of Government (SEGOB), June 15, 1992. http://www.gobernacion.gob.mx/dof/pop.php. [Note: online files cover only 2001–2005.]

[21] Up until 1997 the Ministry of Government also had the entire electoral process under its purview, thereby enabling it to engineer electoral fraud.

[22] On September 11, 1999, Vicente Fox officially launched his campaign for the presidency, holding in his hand the banner of the Virgin of Guadalupe. In response, the PRI (until that time the government's official political party) lodged a complaint with the Federal Electoral Institute, which then fined Fox's National Action Party 17,000 pesos for using religious symbols for the purpose of proselytizing.

[23] For census data, see www.inegi.gob.mx. Worshippers who have left the Catholic Church have not joined traditional Protestant denominations; rather, they have gone to Pentecostal and evangelical movements (see Enrique Luengo González, "La Religión en el México de Hoy" [Religion in Mexico Today], in *La Iglesia Católica y la Política en el México de Hoy* [The Catholic Church and Politics in Mexico Today], ed. José de Jesús Legorreta Zepeda [Mexico City: Universidad Iberoamericana, 2000]).

[24] Guillermo H. Cantú referred to Labastida's modus operandi as "emulating Nicodemus, 'he came at night' and spoke to his friends in the church, bringing them an offering of seven points that comprised his proposal on religion…. As ever, the offer was tempting, but it had one defect, it wasn't made public. Afterward, nobody would be able to remind the president of his promises" (see Guillermo H. Cantú, *Asalto a Palacio* [Assault on the Palace] [Mexico City: Grijalvo, 2001], 239). It should be recalled that Labastida, moreover, had declared in different interviews that he was a Catholic believer and a "Guadalupan." On September 14, 1999, the PRI's future candidate visited the city of Puebla, where he prayed to "God for his victory" during a public meeting of the Alliance of Leaders. In response, the PAN lodged a complaint with the Federal Electoral Institute.

[25] During the campaign, on May 6, 2000, Vicente Fox presented his "platform for the nation on religious freedom and church-state relations" in a small book (see Guillermo Cantú, *Vicente Fox propone* [Vicente Fox Proposes]

(Mexico City: Ediciones 2000, 2000), 102–104. The 10 points he proposed are preceded by two texts, the first concerning freedom of religion and the second dealing with relations between church and state. Curiously, the book bears a publication date of February 2000. The 10 points also appear in Cantú, *Asalto a Palacio*, 239–241. The points enumerated and discussed on the pages that follow are from Fox's booklet.

[26] In January 2002, the Supreme Court of Justice, in an extraordinary move, issued an interpretive statement of Mexico's fundamental law in the following terms: "The Constitution protects the product of conception as a manifestation of human life, regardless of the biological stage at which it is found." This statement was issued in a case that the Court heard in which it recognized the constitutionality of two provisions of the penal code of the Federal District (Mexico City) that dealt with the authority of the Prosecutor's Office (Ministerio Público) to authorize the interruption of a pregnancy in the event of rape, as well as with the decriminalization, under certain circumstances, of so-called eugenic abortion.

[27] Article 14, Paragraph 2 of the Constitution, states: "No one may be deprived of life, liberty, properties, possessions, or rights, except through trial before previously established courts, where the essential particulars of due process are observed in accordance with laws established prior to the deed."

[28] Article 3, Paragraph 1 of the Constitution, provides as follows: "Freedom of beliefs being guaranteed under Article 24, said education shall be secular and, accordingly, shall be kept entirely free from religious doctrine."

[29] For some time now, as a matter of general practice, government employees have respected and guaranteed this right. Under the Fox administration, the Office of the Deputy Secretary for Population, Migration, and Religious Affairs has broadened its scope in hospitals and prisons, with the specific understanding that the office is required to do so because of its responsibility to ensure the right to religious freedom, as provided under Article 24 of the Constitution.

[30] This is the case with the distinguished jurists Ramón Sánchez Medal and Alberto Pacheco. The former believes that the prohibition against holding public office and positions does not affect human rights; rather, "it concerns true incompatibilities and not necessarily damage to or failure to recognize human rights, because here too the clergy or religious individuals should dedicate themselves to working entirely 'for the kingdom of heaven' and dedicate themselves 'with greater freedom to the service of God and of men'" (see Ramón Sánchez Medal, *La Nueva Legislación Sobre Libertad Religiosa* [The New Legislation on Religious Freedom] [Mexico City: Editorial Miguel Angel Porrúa, 1993], 48–49). Along these same lines, Alberto Pacheco emphasizes that this prohibition is not a problem for the ministers of the Catholic faith,

"given that their internal law finds greater incompatibility than the Constitution itself." Canon 285, Paragraph 3 of the Code of Canon Law holds that "the clergy are prohibited from accepting public positions that require the exercise of civil authority" (see Alberto Pacheco, *Temas de Derecho Eclesiástico Mexicano* [Issues of Mexican Ecclesiastical Law] [Mexico City: Ediciones Centenario, 1993], 126).

[31] Cámara de Diputados del Congreso de los Estados Unidos Mexicanos, *Diario de los Debates* [Daily Congressional Record of the Chamber of Deputies of the United Mexican States] 1, no. 22, Mexico City, December 7, 1991.

[32] *Enfoque* (Sunday supplement), *Reforma* (Mexico City), May 12, 2002.

[33] Antonio García Orozco, comp., "Legislación Electoral Mexicana 1812–1997" [Mexican Electoral Law, 1812–1997] in *Gaceta Informativa de la Comisión Federal Electoral* [Federal Electoral Commission Gazette] (Mexico City, 1978), 180–181.

[34] This was as a result of the controversial initiative to enact constitutional reforms in connection with indigenous peoples' rights and culture, presented by President Fox to the committee for constitutional review, which gave its approval with certain modifications. The reform was publicly decreed in the *Diario Oficial de la Federación* [Official Daily Record] on August 14, 2001; a third paragraph was added to Article 1 of the Constitution, which reads as follows: "All forms of discrimination are forbidden that are based on reasons of ethnic or national origin, gender, age, differences in abilities, social status, health status, *religion*, opinions, preferences, marriage status, or any other grounds that may violate human dignity and whose objective is to revoke or undermine a person's rights or freedoms." [Emphasis added] Available at http://www.gobernacion.gob.mx/dof/pop.php. [Note: online files cover only 2001–2005.]

[35] Article 16, Paragraph 2 of the Law on Religious Associations and Public Worship provides as follows: "Religious associations and religious officials may not own or manage, either by themselves or through intermediaries, franchises for radio or television stations or any type of telecommunications, nor may they acquire, own, or manage any of the media for public communications. Excluded from this prohibition are printed publications of a religious nature." Article 21 of the same law holds: "Religious associations may only, on an exceptional basis, transmit or broadcast religious ceremonies or rites through nonprint mass media with the prior authorization of the Ministry of Government."

[36] In December 1991, shortly before the initiative on constitutional reforms in religious matters was presented, Porfirio Muñoz Ledo, then a PRD senator, called upon the Senate of the Republic to "raise its authorized voice as the guarantor of the federal pact, to announce that the Constitution was in

force, that its articles were not the fruit either of whimsy or of chance, but of the history lived out by the Mexican people, and that they cannot be transgressed with impunity nor are they subject to de facto reforms." Cámara de Senadores del Congreso de los Estados Unidos Mexicanos, *Diario de los Debates*, December 3, 1991.

[37] All of the interventions and studies presented before the commission were published by the National Autonomous University of Mexico (UNAM) and are available in their entirety on CD-Rom, *Comisión de Estudios para la Reforma del Estado* (Mexico: UNAM, 2001).

[38] This panel was coordinated by Dr. Fernando Estrada Sámano, who also served as one of the general deputy coordinators of the commission. He is currently the Mexican ambassador to the Holy See.

[39] The Ministry of Government is the authority responsible for enforcing the legal provisions concerning religious matters. The responsibility is carried out through the Office of the Deputy Secretary for Population, Migration, and Religious Affairs, headed initially by Dr. Javier Moctezuma Barragán (December 2000–December 2003) and subsequently by Armando Salinas Torre (December 2003–present); under the office is the Directorate for Religious Associations, headed by Dr. Alvaro Castro Estrada. Both officials are renowned jurists and competent public officials. In fairness, acknowledgment should be given to the outstanding performance of their predecessors, Humberto Lira Mora, deputy secretary for population and migration (the Office of Population and Migration had not yet merged with the Directorate of Religious Affairs) and Jaime Almazán Delgado, director general for religious affairs (which has now changed the word "affairs" to "associations" in its current title).

[40] Far from suffering conflictive relations with the nineteenth-century liberal governments of Mexico, the Protestant churches were favored by the governments. Benito Juárez, Melchor Ocampo, and Sebastian Lerdo de Tejada sponsored the entry of U.S. missionaries representing Protestant denominations. According to the historian and sociologist Alberto Hernández, in the years following the Mexican Revolution, "the Protestant churches that cooperated with the state were unaffected by antireligious excesses and were given authorization to open temples, or they were tolerated and were not punished for any infraction of the religious code" (see Alberto Hernández, "Las Iglesias Evangélicas y la Ley de Asociaciones Religiosas y Culto Público" (Evangelical Churches and the Law on Religious Associations and Public Worship) in *Relaciones Estado-Iglesia: Encuentros y Desencuentros* [State-Church Relations: Encounters and Missed Encounters], ed. Patricia Galeana [Mexico City: General Archive and Ministry of Government, 1999], 240). It is a well-known fact that President Plutarco Elías Calles attempted to create a

Mexican church, independent of Rome, at whose head he placed the "Patriarch" Pérez and to which he gave the temples of La Soledad and Corpus Christi in Mexico City. Benito Juárez attempted to do the same, and in 1933, José Maria Luis Mora intended to create a schismatic Mexican church.

[41] See González Schmal, *Derecho Eclesiástico Mexicano* (note 17).

[42] The Law of Religious Associations and Public Worship, which regulates Articles 24, 27.II, and 130 (governing religious matters) of the Constitution, was passed by the federal Congress and went into effect on July 15, 1992, upon being published in the *Diario Oficial de la Federación*. Various provisions, such as the one pertaining to the institutional body responsible for sanctioning violations committed by religious associations, could not have been imposed because they required that the president of Mexico (with the technical support of the Ministry of Government) first issue an administrative regulatory framework. Said regulatory framework was issued 11 years later under the heading "Regulation of Religious Associations and Public Worship" and was published in the *Diario Oficial de la Federación* on November 6, 2003.

[43] Printed materials distributed by the Conference of Catholic Bishops on April 8, 2002, and partially reproduced in *Reforma* (Mexico City) on April 9, 2002.

[44] Ibid.

[45] Ibid.

[46] This is based on information reported by Sara Ruiz and published in *Reforma,* April 11, 2002, sec. A.

[47] "Religious Freedom in Democratic Mexico: A Message from the Mexican Bishops Ten Years After the Constitutional Reforms" (closing remarks, LXXIII Conference of Catholic Bishops, Cuautitlán Izcalli, Mexico, 2002).

[48] The opinions of Methodist Bishop Ramos are taken from an interview with the journalist Fernando del Collado, published in the *Enfoque* section of *Reforma* (Mexico City), May 12, 2002.

[49] In the United States, religious issues are largely governed by common law, but the courts must frequently weigh in on the effect of religious matters within the legal sphere of the country. Thus, the United States also has ecclesiastical law, which is approved by the U.S. courts.

[50] See Pedro Juan Viladrich and Javier Ferrer Ortiz, "Prinicipios Informadores del Derecho Español" [Principles Informing Spanish Law] in *Derecho Eclesiástico del Estado Español* [Ecclesiastical Law of the Spanish State] 3rd ed. (Pamplona, Spain: Ediciones Universidad de Navarra, 1993).

[51] Ibid., 201.

[52] See Raúl González Schmal, "El Derecho de Libertad Religiosa como Derecho Humano" [The Right to Religious Freedom as a Human Right], in *Las Libertades Religiosas* [Religious Freedoms], ed. Antonio Molina (Mexico City: Universidad Pontificia de México, 1997), 173.

[53] Iván C. Ibán and Luis Prieto Sanchiz, "El Derecho Fundamental de Libertad Religiosa" [The Fundamental Right of Religious Freedom], in *Lecciones de Derecho Eclesiástico* [Lessons from Ecclesiastical Law], 2nd ed. (Madrid: Editorial Tecnos, 1990), 146.

[54] See Raúl González Schmal, "Estado Laico y Libertad Religiosa" [Secular State and Religious Freedom], in *Revista del Senado de la República* [Review of the Senate of the Republic], Mexico City, no. 8 (July–September 1997): 152.

SEVEN

THE ROLE OF THE MEDIA IN MEXICO'S POLITICAL TRANSITION

Sergio Sarmiento

For several decades, the media were one of the main pillars of the Mexican political system that Mario Vargas Llosa called "the perfect dictatorship." Unlike the media in Communist regimes, Mexico's media were rarely subject to formal censorship. Journalists were usually not sent to prison for questioning the regime or for publishing information that might embarrass government authorities. The regime operated within a system that included veiled threats along with incentives to journalists and privileges for the owners of media outlets.

In the late 1970s, Octavio Paz, the poet and essayist, described the hegemonic Institutional Revolutionary Party (PRI) government as Mexico's "philanthropic ogre."[1] As such, the state could adopt a position that allowed violent repression of dissidence but could also exhibit extreme generosity to those willing to play by the party's rules. Criticism was acceptable, but within certain limits. According to journalists of the 1960s and 1970s, everything in Mexico could be questioned, with the exception of the president, the military, and the Virgin of Guadalupe. Reality, however, was much more complex.

By their very nature, many journalists tended to seek a critical and independent voice, constantly pushing the limits of what the regime deemed acceptable. In this way the horizons of free speech were expanded constantly. Perhaps the most important characteristic of the system was the absence of a clear definition of where the boundaries lay.

To exert its control over the media, the state used a series of informal contacts—generally by telephone—between communications directors of government agencies and the owners or general managers of the various media outlets. Information or commentary that would generate a reprisal at one moment would produce no reaction at another. The lack of clear rules created a chilling effect whereby the media would exercise self-censorship beyond what government functionaries might demand. This situation generated an internal conflict in the media between owners, who would use their editorial directors as censors rather than as generators of ideas, and journalists, who were always seeking to go one step beyond their colleagues and competitors in other media sources.

The multiplicity of newspapers and magazines in different regions of the country, particularly in Mexico City, reflected the efforts of different government agencies and individual politicians to have the means at their disposal with which to defend their positions and to promote their own political careers. In addition, government expenditures allocated for communication frequently became open subsidies geared toward the purchase of journalists' consciences. New publications proliferated when an election was approaching, with candidates and political parties investing money in exchange for positive endorsements that would increase their political visibility. Many magazines and some newspapers considered their basic objective to attack government officials and political candidates, whether provoked by other political personalities or as a way to sell protection. This extortion took place openly.

Broadcast media, which hold enormous importance in a country such as Mexico where few people read the newspaper, maintained an even closer relationship with the PRI government. For several decades, Televisa, the giant of Mexican television and radio broadcasting companies, adapted perfectly to its role as a source of information that supported the government and the PRI. In fact, Televisa's president from 1973 to 1996, Emilio Azcárraga Milmo, once declared that he was a "soldier of the PRI." Televisa's open support for the party in power was important, given the company's control of more than 90 percent of the television market.[2]

One reason for this virtual monopoly was that proprietary limits on television stations did not exist in Mexico as they do in the United States and other countries that have private television networks. Even though the government initially granted television concessions to different companies in an effort to create a competitive market, over time the system permitted a single corporation to absorb several broadcast operators. In fact, this concentration was not only permitted but also promoted. The government seemed to prefer to deal with a single large corporation rather than with several firms in competition with one another.

By law, concessions were granted at no cost to individuals and companies that had close ties to the government. Once television matured as a commercial market, the concessions essentially became licenses to profit. Thus, media company owners had a personal interest in defending the stability of a regime that facilitated their personal enrichment.

The first three television concessions in the Mexico City metropolitan area were granted to three different companies during Miguel Alemán Valdez's presidency. In 1949, the rights to channel 4, XHTV, were awarded to Televisión de México, S.A., owned by Rómulo O'Farrill Sr., who also owned the newspaper *Novedades*. In 1950, channel 5, XHGC, was granted to Guillermo González Camarena, a reputable technician who had independently developed a color television system. González Camarena owned a technology company called González Laboratories, but from the very beginning he had the support of his capitalist partner, Emilio Azcárraga Vidaurreta, who owned XEW and XEQ, the most popular radio stations at the time. The third concession, channel 2, XEWTV, was granted to Azcárraga Vidaurreta himself, who began television operations in 1951. Other concessions were gradually awarded in other regions of the country, but most were given to the owners of Mexico City's first three television stations.

The Mexican market at the time was rather small—not large enough to support all three television companies. Because very few people could afford a television set, businesses preferred to advertise their products on the radio. As a result, during those early years, owners of television stations lost enormous sums of money.

In an effort to alleviate the financial difficulties faced by television companies, the government authorized owners to seek alliances among themselves as a way to benefit from economies of scale. To avoid legal problems, the original companies continued to maintain the individual television concessions, but they all became part of a single corporation known as Telesistema Mexicano, S.A., thus creating an absolute monopoly. Emilio Azcárraga Vidaurreta—who, in addition to owning channel 2, had acquired channel 5 because of González Camarena's financial losses—was named president and general manager of the corporation; Rómulo O'Farrill Sr., the owner of channel 4, was named vice president. Both partners placed their sons, Emilio Azcárraga Milmo and Rómulo O'Farrill Jr., in important positions with the corporation, indicating from the outset that a family succession was in the works.

According to title deeds dated May 8, 1955, which created Telesistema Mexicano, the Azcárraga family owned 50 percent of the corporation: Azcárraga Vidaurreta held 40 percent of the company's shares; his son Emilio held 5 percent; and a nephew, Fernando Díez Barroso, held another 5 percent. Rómulo O'Farrill Sr. owned 40 percent of the company, and his son owned 5 percent. Ernesto Barriento Reyes, who also apparently represented the interests of the O'Farrill family, owned the remaining 5 percent. Despite the share distribution between the two families, Azcárraga clearly had total operating control, whereas O'Farrill was in charge of the corporation's finances.[3]

Mexico's television business gained strength vigorously in the years that followed. Transmission from Mexico City's channels was becoming interconnected, as technology permitted, with local broadcasters throughout the states of the republic. By the mid-1960s, Mexico had a national television system and an excellent business enterprise—a monopoly—controlled by Telesistema Mexicano. Only one station in Mexico City, channel 11, for which a permit had been granted to the National Polytechnic Institute, was beyond the monopoly's reach. However, channel 11's signal was not strong enough to reach most households, and the station's cultural programming appealed to a rather limited audience. In addition, because of its permit status, as opposed to a concessionary one, the station could not sell commercial time; as a result, channel 11 constantly faced financial shortages.

In 1967, the government of President Gustavo Díaz Ordaz (1964–1970) tried to open up the television market to competition, granting two new concessions to Mexican companies. Channel 8, XHTIM, was given to Fomento de Televisión, S.A., which was associated with Televisión Independiente de México, owned by the Grupo VISA de Monterrey (which later split into Grupo Alfa and Femsa). Channel 13, XHDF, was awarded to Corporación Mexicana de Radio y Televisión, S.A. de C.V., which was owned by Francisco Aguirre, a broadcaster and owner of nightclubs. Aguirre had to resort to a constitutional challenge (*amparo*) in order to obtain the concession that he had requested 18 years previously, as the government attempted to award the concession to another group that had just submitted its application.

The subsequent competition that developed was nothing short of ferocious. Telesistema Mexicano, which had been able to price its services at will because it was a monopoly, had to reduce its advertising fees. The new stations were competing for the scarce talent available and thus significantly increasing their costs. After Emilio Azcárraga Vidaurreta died in 1972, his son, Emilio Azcárraga Milmo, assumed control of Telesistema Mexicano. Azcárraga Milmo joined forces with the Garza Sada family, the principal investors in Televisión Independiente de México, and was able to convince them that it was preferable to merge the entities rather than have both parties engage in devastating competition. The outcome of this agreement was the creation of Televisión Vía Satélite S. A. (known as Televisa) in early 1973, which then controlled Mexico City's channels 2, 4, 5, and 8 as well as the channels' relay stations throughout the country. Thus, a near monopoly was established with Emilio Azcárraga Milmo as the new corporation's president. The Garza Sada family got 25 percent of the corporation's shares, but the O'Farrill family maintained its significant presence in the company. A surprising shareholder of the new group was Miguel Alemán Velasco, the son of former president Miguel Alemán Valdez, who had granted the original concessions for channels 2, 4, and 5.

President Luis Echevarría could not, or would not, stand in the way of Televisa's merger. However, he pressured Francisco Aguirre—who had already sold the government 10 percent of his shares in channel 13 and 40 percent to businessman Alejo Peralta—to sell the remaining shares of the television network to the government.[4] Thus, in 1973, a television company, Imevisión, was created as a new government-owned enterprise. The new company strengthened channel 13 by linking it with a series of relay stations throughout the country and also established channel 7 in the capital city and provided it with relay stations as well. Despite its control over two national networks, Imevisión was unable to weaken the dominant position held by Televisa, which kept more than 90 percent of both the audience and the advertising market.

One of the reasons for the open subordination of radio and television concessionaires to the PRI political system was a law that gave the federal government discretionary powers to grant or withdraw such concessions. The threat of an abrupt cancellation of the concession—although never exercised—offered a powerful incentive for concessionaires to continue to show their loyalty to the political system.

THE ROAD TO INDEPENDENCE

The Written Press

Over the decades there were sporadic outbursts of criticism from the press. These attempts at rebellion were generally fostered by the written press. Perhaps the press's first attempt to achieve and maintain an independent voice was made by a Mexico City newspaper, *Excelsior*, in 1968, after the government had violently suppressed a student protest movement. Julio Scherer García, an experienced journalist, had recently been appointed editor in chief of *Excelsior*, which was owned by a workers' cooperative. Scherer's left-leaning ideology caused him to identify with the student movement on a personal level.

Initially, *Excelsior*'s coverage of the 1968 student movement did not differ to any great extent from that of the rest of the country's newspapers. Nevertheless, *Excelsior* did not join the other publications' open criticism of the student movement or their fervent defense of President Díaz Ordaz's hard line. When the movement was coming to an end, and as Scherer became more confident and secure in his management role at the paper, he began to promote a more critical position in *Excelsior*'s stories and editorials.

In 1976, during the last few months of Luis Echevarría's presidency, a dissident movement arose within *Excelsior*'s workers' cooperative. The group took control of the newspaper and dismissed Scherer, appointing Regino Díaz Redondo as new editor in chief. Scherer and his closest collaborators openly accused President Echevarría of having orchestrated a "coup" against *Excelsior* in response to the paper's criticisms. There is no specific proof to substantiate this version of events, although there is no doubt that, after Scherer's departure, the newspaper assumed a clear policy of rapprochement with the government.[5]

Many contributors, writers, and executives left *Excelsior* along with Scherer, and over time they created two new and influential publications, which assumed clearly independent lines that were closer to those held by the country's left-leaning intellectuals. In 1977, Scherer himself created the weekly *Proceso* with the support of colleagues such as Vicente Leñero and Froylan López Narváez. At the same time, Manuel Becerra Acosta, general manager of *Excelsior* until Scherer's departure, founded the newspaper *Unomásuno*.

Before the *Excelsior* coup, Scherer had invited Octavio Paz, perhaps the most respected writer in Mexico at the time, to produce a cultural supplement to the newspaper entitled *Plural*. On the heels of the turnover in *Excelsior's* leadership, Paz also left, abandoning the supplement and founding a montly called *Vuelta*, which subsequently became the organ of a new liberal and democratic intellectual movement.

Other newspapers appeared in the years that followed. In 1981, Rogelio Cárdenas Pereznieto, who had been an *Excelsior* columnist during the 1950s, created *El Financiero*, the country's first newspaper devoted to economic issues. In 1982, Carlos Payán and others involved in *Unomásuno* became disturbed by what they called the hijacking of that paper by Becerra Acosta and founded *La Jornada*, a more openly leftist newspaper. All these publications had a common trait: they were critical of the PRI regime, even though they were occasionally obliged to survive by means of financial handouts doled out by the government itself.

Several newspapers in areas outside Mexico City also assumed independent stances during the 1970s and 1980s. One of these, the openly conservative *El Diario de Yucatán*, had ties to the National Action Party (PAN) at a time when the PRI was in absolute control of the country's political life. In Guanajuato, during the 1980s, the León newspaper *AM* emerged as an independent voice with great influence throughout the Bajío region. Beginning in the 1970s, in the Laguna region (which encompasses parts of the states of Coahuila and Durango), an old established newspaper, *El Siglo de Torreón*, became a vigorous voice unwilling to be intimidated by the government. In Hermosillo and in the rest of the state of Sonora, *El Imparcial* assumed the same role. In Guadalajara, *El Informador* skillfully evolved from a traditional and conservative newspaper into one that was able to take and maintain an independent position. Also in the same city, under the editorial direction of Jorge Zepeda Patterson, *Siglo XXI* broke from the mold of traditional journalism and published clever and independent articles. After a dispute with the owner of the publication, Zepeda's staff left

Siglo XXI and founded the newspaper *Público*, which continued on the same path and later would be acquired by the Multimedios de Oro group headquartered in Monterrey.

Some publications had to deal with attempts by the government to block their path to independence. In Monterrey, for example, the newspaper *El Norte*, managed by Alejandro Junco since the 1970s, was strongly pressured by Presidents Luis Echevarría and José López Portillo to abandon its critical position. At one point, López Portillo's government—taking advantage of the newsprint monopoly held by the government-owned Pipsa company—went so far as to limit the newspaper's paper supply. *El Norte* withstood the pressure and continued to publish smaller issues until the government authorized the restoration of newsprint. During the 1990s, the government decided to dissolve its monopoly over the distribution of newsprint. Publishers with close links to the PRI opposed this measure, because, even though it gave them greater freedom, it also meant elimination of the subsidies they had received to help pay for newsprint.

In 1993, during what had become a more benign climate marked by a lower level of hostility on the part of the government, Junco founded *Reforma*, a daily based in Mexico City, which initially was boycotted by the Union of Newspaper Vendors. For several decades this group of distributors, affiliated with the PRI, had maintained a total monopoly over the distribution of magazines and newspapers in the metropolitan area of Mexico City. The boycott contributed to giving greater publicity to *Reforma*, which very quickly became the most influential daily newspaper in the country. Other newspapers that were subsequently established in Mexico City also assumed independent positions. These included *La Crónica de Hoy*, managed by Pablo Hiriart, and *Milenio*, edited by Federico Arreola, a former *El Norte* columnist, who became adviser to Luis Donaldo Colosio, the PRI's presidential candidate assassinated in 1994.

At the end of the 1990s, newspaper publishers realized that increasing their readership and achieving commercial success in a more competitive market required them to be critical of the government in power. In fact, newspapers that were publicly perceived as more pro-government—such as *Excelsior, El Sol de México, Novedades, El Heraldo de México*, and *Unomasuno*, among others—suffered a marked decrease in circulation as well as influence. By the early twenty-first century, *Novedades* and *El Heraldo de México* had disappeared, while *Unomasuno* had become a mere sensationalist rag.

Radio

The broadcast media underwent a similar process—albeit a somewhat slower one—on their path to greater independence from the government. For a number of years, radio, which had reached the height of its popularity in the 1940s and 1950s—prior to the invasion of television—focused on music and entertainment and practically ignored informational programming. It was not until the 1970s that radio began to air news broadcasts, but the newscasts were limited to simply reproducing information that had already appeared in the written press. Broadcasters were well aware that their prosperity was tied to the concessions that the government had granted in a discretionary manner; therefore, radio abstained from broadcasting news or commentaries that might offend the government or the political party in charge.

The birth of independent radio journalism was in great measure attributable to the efforts of José Gutierrez Vivó, whose program, entitled "Monitor," has been aired by a station called Radio Red since 1974 and attracted a wide audience with a message that gradually became more critical of the government. Even though "Monitor" was later aired in several cities throughout Mexico, for the most part its influence was limited to Mexico City.

In view of the success of "Monitor," competitors soon emerged who offered the same formula of at least some degree of criticism and editorializing of the news. Pedro Ferriz de Con, the most successful competitor, joined with the music broadcaster Estéreo Rey to create "Para Empezar," a program that adopted a light and openly superficial approach to news. This broadcast formed the basis of the first national radio information network, later known as MVS Noticias.

The 1985 earthquake and its aftershocks, which destroyed an important section of downtown Mexico City and knocked Televisa off the air for several hours, forced millions of residents to depend on the radio as their main source of information. Coverage of the earthquakes became the litmus test for Mexican information radio. Criticisms of the Miguel de la Madrid government, which gave the impression that the disaster had paralyzed the country, increased to a level that was unprecedented in Mexico's electronic media.

Nevertheless, restrictions on journalistic freedom were imposed on radio networks from time to time. During the 1988 presidential campaign, which took place during Miguel de la Madrid's six-year term, Núcleo Radio Mil, a group with a presence mainly in Mexico City, was a target of government threats to revoke the radio concession for one of its stations—operating at 590Khz and known then as Radio VIP—for the "crime" of airing English-language broadcasts without having renewed the station's authorization to do so. Concessionaires, however, were made aware that the real problem was that journalist Miguel Angel Granados Chapa, who directed the morning informational programming at a different station owned by the group, had conducted an interview with Cuauhtémoc Cárdenas, the National Democratic Front's candidate for the presidency. Núcleo Radio Mil decided to fire Granados Chapa in order to gain the renewal of its concession.[6]

With time, however, the situation began to change. The government of President Carlos Salinas de Gortari preferred to use persuasion rather than pressure to achieve its objectives in the communications area. The gradual change in political rules, on the other hand, was creating spaces for the opposition. Radio networks realized that their medium represented an important political tool and that the political class was losing its power to control the networks. Concessionaires gradually lost their fear of airing the opposition's voices and sought to influence the national political process, which at the time was becoming more transparent and open.

Three groups began to devote a sizable portion of their broadcasts to news items and political and economic commentaries: Radio Fórmula, Acir, and Televisa-owned Radiópolis. Radio Red, with its influential program "Monitor," was sold by Radio Programas de México to the Grupo Radio Centro, which had previously focused almost exclusively on musical programming. Strong competition forced broadcasters to do what they could to eliminate restrictions on their freedom of expression. It was important for the companies to attract wide audiences in order to increase their commercial market and their profits; critical viewpoints were an easy way to increase ratings. The danger that the government might intervene and rescind a concession because of an unfavorable commentary or news report gradually subsided to the point of ceasing to be an effective deterrent.

Television

During the 1950s, when television first appeared in Mexico, concessionaires decided to leave the informational programming to members of the print media, because they had more experience in news operations. Thus, in Mexico City, Emilio Azcárraga's channel 2 yielded its news slot to the staff of the daily *Excelsior*, and Rómulo O'Farril's channel 4 did likewise with the journalists writing for his paper, *Novedades*. In 1968, however, when the student movement shook the foundation of Gustavo Díaz Ordaz's government, television broadcasters, apparently under government pressure, decided to take control of their own informational programming.

In 1973, Televisa created a virtual monopoly when it merged channels 2, 4, 5, and 8 (the latter subsequently converted to channel 9) in the Federal District and its relay stations in the rest of the country. The only independent station that remained was channel 13, owned by Francisco Aguirre. But the government took it over to establish a state-owned enterprise, Imevisión, the main purpose of which was to counterbalance the political power Televisa had acquired. As a result of the constant turnover of general managers and its bureaucratic structure, Imevisión was unable to become a real competitor of Televisa, which maintained more than 90 percent of the viewing public and television advertising market.

In 1993, Imevisión, whose name had been changed to TV Azteca, was sold for $649 million to a group of private entrepreneurs headed by Ricardo Salinas, a man who had no television experience. The following year, Carlos Salinas de Gortari's government granted Televisa 60 additional relay stations, a measure that permitted the company to finish creating three national networks and a "regional" network (with presence only in some cities) to compete with TV Azteca's two networks. In spite of the government's support for Televisa, TV Azteca grew rapidly and by 1997 had already garnered 30 percent of the viewing public and advertising market.

In 1995, channel 40, an ultrahigh frequency (UHF) station owned by Javier Moreno Valle, entered the television broadcasting market. Although

its ratings were not high, channel 40 aired informational and analytical programs—many produced and anchored by an independent and
articulate journalist, Ciro Gómez Leyva—that were openly critical of
the government. Channel 40 managed to increase its influence among
political groups and opinion leaders in the country, although its impact on the general public was limited.

THE MEDIA'S ROLE IN ELECTORAL DEMOCRACY

Competition among television broadcasters helped to make politics
considerably more transparent. In 1988, more than 90 percent of all
news coverage by television stations concentrated on the PRI's presidential candidate, Carlos Salinas de Gortari; the information aired
about other candidates was not only very limited but frequently negative. During the 1994 presidential campaign, after the privatization of
TV Azteca, the first debates among presidential candidates from different parties were televised. Even though the coverage continued to be
slanted in favor of the PRI candidate, Ernesto Zedillo, it was not as
overwhelmingly partial as it had been in the past. On election day, August 2, 1994, for the first time in a presidential campaign, television
stations reported the results of exit polls and early balloting results,
making electoral fraud more difficult.

Electoral reforms were enacted in 1996. The new law established
rules that gave a greater balance to the amount of time the electronic
media devoted to the various candidates. The legislation also limited
campaign expenditures, thereby restricting the advertising time political parties—notably the PRI—were able to purchase. Indications of
broadcasters' preferences for one candidate or party did not disappear,
but the new regulations laid the groundwork for the PRI's loss of the
overwhelming dominance it had previously enjoyed when it came to
media coverage of politics and advertising time. Consequently, in the
midterm elections of 1997, the PRI lost its long-standing absolute majority in the Chamber of Deputies, and in 2000, the party had to face
an open and competitive presidential campaign.

Some media adopted political positions during the 2000 campaign.
Dailies such as *El Sol de México, Excelsior, El Heraldo de México,* and
Unomásuno openly supported the PRI candidate, Francisco Labastida.
PRI members accused *Reforma,* a publication of antigovernment slant,

of supporting Vicente Fox, the candidate of the Alliance for Change, a coalition formed by the PAN and the Green Party of Mexico, even though *Reforma* published articles that were highly critical of all the candidates, including Fox. *El Universal* maintained a good balance both in its coverage and in the positions taken in its editorials and opinion pieces. *La Jornada* confirmed its traditional leftist stance by backing three-time candidate Cuauhtémoc Cárdenas from the Alliance for Mexico, a coalition whose main pillar was the Democratic Revolutionary Party (PRD).

For the most part, television stations and the leading radio broadcasters, especially those with headquarters in the Federal District, kept to their informal commitment to offer reasonably equal time to the three main presidential candidates. Very strict monitoring of the campaign, which was requested by the Federal Electoral Institute (IFE) and conducted by Berumen and Associates, a professional market research and polling firm, revealed the amount of time television and radio stations allotted to each of the candidates or their parties as well as the tone of the coverage—positive, negative, or neutral.

Local radio broadcasts in southeastern Mexico deviated the most from what can be considered adequate journalistic balance. IFE's monitoring revealed that Mexican society considers power more important than ideology. Thus, in states where deviations occurred, the coverage invariably favored the party in power, which was not necessarily the PRI. On national television, however, the opposition candidate, Vicente Fox, received more coverage, especially during the last weeks of the campaign. This phenomenon was not attributable to political backing but rather the result of candidate Fox's tremendous ability to attract broadcasters' attention with controversial statements and unconventional behavior. During the final weeks of the campaign, some leaders in the broadcast industry editorialized about Fox's "populism" or "intolerance" in the face of questions from the media, but Fox's popularity continued to grow nonetheless.

The strongest test for broadcasters and other media in the 2000 campaign took place on May 23, 2000, a day that journalists came to christen Fox's "Black Tuesday." On that date, a second debate had been scheduled to take place among the three candidates who were leading in public opinion polls. Negotiations to define the rules for the debate had broken off the previous weekend, leading the PRI and PRD candidates—Francisco Labastida and Cuauhtémoc Cárdenas, respectively—to suggest suspending or postponing the debate.

There were very good tactical reasons for these two candidates to postpone the debate or to avoid it altogether. Fox, a great polemicist, had emerged as the winner in the first debate, which had been held on April 25 and had included the six candidates who were in contention. In spite of their intellectual stature, neither Labastida nor Cárdenas were able to contend with the vehemence with which Fox expressed himself during debates. On the other hand, Fox desperately needed the May 23 debate in order to climb up in the opinion polls, in which a few points separated him from Labastida, who was leading the polls.

On the morning of May 23, in the presence of reporters covering his campaign, Fox telephoned Labastida and Cárdenas and invited them to meet with him that very afternoon to resolve their differences about the debate. Labastida and Cárdenas did not want to refuse and agreed to meet with Fox in Cárdenas's campaign headquarters in Mexico City at five o'clock. Fox insisted that the meeting itself should take place in front of the journalists covering the three campaigns. Televisa and TV Azteca started to transmit the discussion among the three candidates from the beginning, and for almost two hours the broadcasters aired the meeting live and without interruption so that the country could see first-hand the incisive "debate about the debate."

Prior to the meeting among the three candidates, Labastida and Cárdenas had apparently reached an agreement to propose postponing the debate for three days—to Friday, May 26. Fox rejected the proposal and kept reiterating: "Today, today, today." The first two candidates argued that the television stations were not prepared to telecast the debate that same day, an opinion that was corroborated by Joaquín Vargas, president of the Chamber of Industry of Radio and Television, who was also present during the discussion. However, first TV Azteca, then Televisa sent messages to the candidates' campaign headquarters stating that, in fact, they were prepared to air the debate that same evening, that is, May 23. The meeting among the three candidates ended without an agreement. TV Azteca offered part of the television time that had originally been scheduled for the debate to any of the candidates who would be present in its studios that night.

That evening, several high-level television executives, and suppos-edly representatives from other outlets, were subjected to pressure from the PRI and the federal government—a practice that was un-common by that time—to present in their newscasts the party's ver-sion of what had taken place at the meeting: that Fox had been defeated in the discussion about the debate and had shown himself to be pigheaded and intolerant. TV Azteca was asked not to grant Fox time for an interview during the time that had been scheduled for the debate, because he was the only candidate who had accepted the broadcaster's invitation to appear on the air that evening. TV Azteca refused to cave in to the pressure: it televised a half-hour interview with Fox that night that did not reflect the government's viewpoint. Almost all the other media outlets, both electronic and print, present-ed the government's version of the facts. For example, Manuel Mejido, a columnist for *El Sol de México*, offered a summary of the govern-ment's position, writing that "in two hours, Vicente Fox lost three years of campaigning."

The outcome of the debate over the debate—and its coverage by the media—was not the one that the government and the PRI had hoped for, however. Fox's popularity not only did not deteriorate as a result of the incident but gained strength in the days that followed. Both in the discussion in Cárdenas's headquarters and in the TV Azteca interview, Fox projected the image of a man confronting the old political system. His insistence that the debate be held "today, today, today"—far from being seen as a symbol of pigheadedness and immaturity—became a slogan chanted by the multitudes of supporters during the candidate's public campaign appearances. On July 2, 2000, the PAN's Vicente Fox became the first opposition candidate in the country's history to gain an official victory in a presidential election.[7]

THE COMPOSITION OF THE MEXICAN MEDIA

The media experienced a period of substantial expansion in the 1990s, culminating with Vicente Fox's electoral victory in the 2000 presiden-tial election. On the one hand, owners of media outlets wanted to gain political influence after greater freedom of expression had opened up new opportunities. On the other hand, media operators wanted to benefit from the subsidies and special privileges the government had traditionally afforded them.

Nevertheless, from the outset of Ernesto Zedillo's government (1994–2000), the chances to obtain special treatment from the government began to dwindle. The expansion of the media, which had to share a small private and government advertising pie, especially after the 1995–1996 economic recession, sparked competition that became increasingly more ferocious. Some media outlets began to operate under decidedly precarious conditions. As the 1997–2000 economic recovery took hold, several new publications appeared. But during the recession in 2001–2002, which began at a time when government subsidies to the media were already severely limited, the market began an important cleansing process.

The study of Mexico's communications market has been hampered by the tradition of many media operators to keep their circulation and audience figures, as well as their financial results, hidden. Even a newspaper as important as *Reforma*, which had clearly become the country's most influential daily by the second half of the 1990s, kept its daily circulation a well-guarded secret for some time.[8] In radio, discrepancies in ratings figures made it possible for different networks to assert that each was the highest rated among its audience, when the fact is that all of them presented biased versions of the same rating information. The fact that the two major broadcasting companies are quoted on the stock exchange—both in New York and in Mexico—compels them to provide more transparent information, although remarkable cases of manipulation of numbers have been reported.

A fundamental characteristic of the communications market in Mexico is its enormous concentration. Approximately 80 percent of Mexicans get information from television, whereas 20 percent receive it from radio and 18 percent get information from the print media.[9] Moreover, the television market operates as a virtual "duopoly": Televisa and TV Azteca capture more than 95 percent of the viewing audience and are the only two companies with a real presence in the national television market. These companies not only provide programming by means of five national networks and one regional one (Televisa's four and TV Azteca's two), but, contrary to what happens in the United States and other developed countries, Mexico's major television companies own their local stations.

Compared with other countries, even those in Latin America, cable systems and other pay-per-view television outlets that offer a greater variety of channels have a minimal presence in Mexico. Argentina for example, has a pay-per-view television penetration of more than 50 percent. Almost all of the 25 million households in Mexico have at least one television set, but only 3.6 million households have access to pay-per-view stations: 2.4 million on cable, 843,000 via satellite, and 330,000 via modified microwave.[10] On the other hand, many television viewers with pay-per-view systems, which offer a great number of options, use them primarily to watch basic television stations.

By contrast, in Mexico City alone there are more than 60 radio broadcasters,[11] which transmit 30-plus newscasts exclusively in the morning and more than 50 throughout the rest of the day. There are also more than 20 dailies in the Mexico City metropolitan area, although the daily circulation of all of them combined is less than 1 million copies. In the entire country, it is assumed that newspapers have a total daily circulation of about 2 million, including Mexico City.

Televisa continues to dominate the television market to an overwhelming degree. The Federal District's channel 2 network is the main reason for this predominance; the network has the largest audience by far in the country. During the first half of 2002, a popular nightly news segment anchored by Joaquín López Dóriga on channel 2 received an average rating of 15 points,[12] equivalent to a 35 percent share of the audience.[13] By contrast, the main TV Azteca news program, "Hechos," hosted by Javier Alatorre, averaged 7 rating points and a 15 percent audience share.

Competition among radio broadcasters is much greater. In Mexico City's metropolitan area, José Gutierrez Vivó's "Monitor" has a clear advantage over its competitors during the morning hours. But the Radio Fórmula network, which devotes several of its local broadcasts to local and regional news programming, reaches a larger total national audience with all its news programs. Other major networks include Acir, Televisa Radio (formerly Radiópolis), MVS, Imagen, and Multimedios Oro (the latter with a strong presence in northern Mexico). Many individual radio stations, however, have clearly defined market niches and exert a powerful political influence at the local or national level. As in other countries, the program host's personality is one of the features that play a major role in attracting public attention.

The dailies that have enjoyed greater financial success are those that have shown greater independence of thought vis-à-vis the government. Mexico City's *Reforma* appears to have become the country's most influential newspaper, but its daily circulation—audited at 140,000 copies in 2003—is not the widest in the country. It is estimated that the sensationalist tabloid *La Prensa* has a daily circulation of 150,000 copies, whereas *El Universal* might also reach a readership figure of 140,000. *La Jornada*, a left-leaning tabloid, has a daily circulation of about 60,000 copies.

The major difference among these newspapers is the market segment at which they are aimed. Eighty percent of *Reforma* readers, as opposed to 51 percent of *El Universal* readers, come from socioeconomic levels marked by greater purchasing power—a market that is avidly sought by advertisers.[14] However, many readers of *El Universal* buy it to check classified ads and show no interest in the sections that cover economics or politics. Other dailies occupy a well-defined market niche that provides them with an advertising income that allows them to survive. Examples of these targeted papers include *El Financiero*, with a daily circulation of about 40,000 copies printed in several plants throughout the country, and *Esto*, a newspaper specializing in sports that has a daily circulation of 100,000, except on Mondays, when it reaches 150,000 readers because of its printed summaries of national soccer matches.

Many newspapers in Mexico City have small readerships or survive on economically precarious terms. Some have been supported by their owners for many years or decades in their attempt to maintain political influence. Others have been supported by several government entities or by political groups seeking to promote their particular projects or ideas. The list of newspapers surviving by subsidies, either because they are politically important or are able to exploit a small market niche, is rather large: *Ovaciones, Excelsior, El Economista, El Sol de México, Record, Milenio, Diario Monitor, La Crónica, El Día,* and several others in Mexico City's metropolitan area alone. (Table 7.1 presents a list of Mexico City's newspapers and estimates of their circulation.) Not many of these publications seem able to operate at a profit. A number of newspapers, like *Novedades, The News, México Hoy,* and *El Heraldo de México* have disappeared over the past few years.

Table 7.1
Approximate Circulation of Newspapers in Mexico City (2003)

Morning Newspapers	Circulation
La Prensa	150,000
El Universal	140,000
Reforma	140,000
Esto	100,000
La Jornada	60,000
Ovaciones (morning edition)	40,000
El Financiero	40,000
Metro	40,000
Excelsior	40,000
Novedades	20,000
Milenio	15,000
El Economista	10,000
El Heraldo de México	10,000
El Sol de México	10,000
Unomasuno	7,000
La Crónica	7,000
México Hoy	5,000
Diario de México	1,000
El Día	1,000

Evening Newspapers	Circulation
Ovaciones (evening edition)	50,000
El Sol de Mediodía	10,000
Últimas Noticias	7,000
Cuestión	2,000
La Tarde	2,000

Note: The figures are the author's own estimates, based on information compiled from *Etcétera, Expansion* (results of survey conducted by Bimsa in Mexico City), and *México en Cifras* (number of copies as reported by publishers in Medios Publicitarios Mexicanos).

The situation outside the capital city is different: diversity has been replaced by virtual local monopolies. In Monterrey, the predominance of the Reforma Group's *El Norte* is almost total, although the paper faces some competition from *Milenio* (formerly *El Diario de Monterrey*, owned by Multimedios de Oro) and from *El Porvenir*, which until several decades ago was the principal newspaper in the city. Other cities in which a single newspaper has almost total dominance include Hermosillo with *El Imparcial*; Torreón and the Laguna region with *El Siglo de Torreón*; Culiacán with *El Debate* (although *El Noroeste* has grown substantially in the last few years); León with *AM*; Morelia with *La Voz de Michoacán*; Xalapa with *El Diario de Xalapa*; Veracrúz with *El Dictamen*; and Mérida with *El Diario de Yucatán*. New newspapers are beginning to generate competition in some of these cities, such as *Provincia* in Morelia and *Por Esto* in Mérida.

In Guadalajara, Mexico's second largest city in terms of population, the competition among newspapers is much stiffer. The greatest share of the market belongs to *El Informador*, followed by *Público* (owned by Multimedios de Oro), and *Mural* (owned by the Reforma Group).

In reality, Mexico has no national newspapers. A few copies of *Reforma*, *El Universal*, and *La Jornada*, among others, are sold in several cities in some states. *El Financiero* is printed in several plants around the country, which gives it good penetration in several markets, although it continues to be a relatively small newspaper that has minimal influence. *El País*, a prestigious Spanish daily, maintains its presence in Mexico by means of a local edition with a modest circulation.

Weekly magazines enjoy a greater national presence. *Proceso*, the publication created by Julio Scherer after his departure from *Excelsior* in 1976, clearly has the highest circulation—80,000 copies a week—as well as a truly national influence. Far behind are *Milenio*; *Vértigo*, produced by TV Azteca; *Siempre!* founded in 1953 by José Pagés Llergo; and several others. Some U.S. magazines have tried to enter the Mexican market but have met with little success. *Newsweek* and *Time* both distributed Spanish versions but later withdrew from the market.

CURRENT CHALLENGES

During the long predominance of the PRI in Mexico's political system, the great challenge faced by the Mexican media was to gain independence from an interfering government, which sometimes behaved as a censor. Given fewer government controls, the nature of the challenge has changed. Today, it no longer makes sense for a publication to demonstrate unnecessary courage as a way to distinguish itself from others. The great challenge today is professionalism, although members of Mexico's media still have a long way to go on this score.

Arguably, Mexico enjoys greater freedom of the press than do other countries, such as the United States, Canada, and the United Kingdom. One reason for this is that laws prohibiting libel, slander, and defamation of character place limits on the press in those countries, whereas these laws are not usually enforced in Mexico.

Mexico has laws that make those accused of libel, defamation of character, and slander subject to criminal or civil procedures. But litigants face enormous difficulties in bringing these charges to court and prosecuting them. To win such a case in Mexican civil courts, plaintiffs must be willing to spend more on legal fees than they would receive in compensation if the case were to be decided in their favor. On the other hand, in criminal cases involving defamation, libel, and slander, judges rarely hand out harsh sentences; sentences are usually so light that they seldom serve as effective deterrents.

A few recent well-known cases demonstrate that this situation is beginning to change. In 2001, Sasha Montenegro—a former movie actress and dancer and, at the time, the wife of former Mexican president José López Portillo—won a significant judgment against journalist Isabel Arvide, who had described the complainant in a derogatory way. Similarly, Ricardo Salinas Pliego, president of TV Azteca, won a judgment against La Jornada after a front-page article in the newspaper falsely accused the entrepreneur of having planned the assassination of journalist Ricardo Rocha. The fact is, however, that in the majority of Mexican media outlets, allegations are made lightly, leaving the offended party in the unfortunate position of having to defend against such claims.

Very few Mexican publications have fact-checking departments that can verify whether journalists' information is correct. Moreover, Mexican reporters rarely have substantial knowledge of the topics they cover, and journalists generally make little effort to include more than one viewpoint on the topic at hand. Refutations of defamatory or slanderous charges are usually published the day after the original article appeared, giving the accusers ample opportunity to undermine the reputation of the person or institution involved in the claim.

Even though Mexico's media have gained independence, they find it difficult to abandon some of the vices practiced in times of total dependence on the government. For example, simple statements made by politicians are considered news and placed on the newspaper's front page or in the news segments of radio and television broadcasts without further research or any attempt to match the words with the facts.

The media in Mexico adhere to clear political positions, which to some extent are a good reflection of the attitudes of their companies' owners. Although the media have achieved their independence from government interference, the owners continue to establish the journalistic line and often use their publications or radio and television stations as a way to gain political favor, defend their economic interests, or promote their ideology. The media's support for certain politicians, parties, and causes is not limited to editorials or opinion pieces but includes news coverage as well. Editorializing news pieces is a constant practice; unlike their counterparts in developed countries, Mexico's information professionals have not taken control of the media's editorial position.

In the printed media, and to a certain extent in radio, ferocious competition guarantees that different viewpoints are aired; as a result, the population has access to a large variety of opinions. In the case of television, market concentration within two large companies that are firmly controlled by their principal shareholders dramatically reduces the potential for diversity.

Examples of the use of the media to promote political or business interests are legion. *La Jornada* and *Proceso* invariably support the PRD, particularly the faction of the PRD loyal to former presidential candidate Cuauhtémoc Cárdenas. The influence exercised by *El Sol de México*, despite its low circulation in Mexico City, is based on its significant chain of newspapers, which are produced in several cities throughout the country and have consistently backed the PRI. *El Universal*, having supported Carlos Salinas de Gortari when he was president from 1988 to 1994, with no "ifs," "ands," or "buts," turned against him when he left the presidency. In fact, in 1995 the paper published a series of articles very critical of Salinas, including one bearing the headline "Salinas: Author of the Colosio Assassination." One had to read the main body of the article to find out that this affirmation was based on a public opinion poll and not on any credible evidence. *El Diario de Yucatán*, which has been particularly critical of PRI governments in its state, took up an almost fanatical defense of a man accused and convicted of murdering his wife because he tried to make the case that the accusation was part of a PRI conspiracy against him.

Television is subject to attempts to use it for political or business purposes as well. In 1999, when a TV Azteca personality was assassinated in broad daylight as he was leaving a local restaurant, the company launched an intense campaign accusing the mayor of the Federal District—the future presidential candidate Cuauhtémoc Cárdenas—of being responsible for the crime. The charge gave rise to open warfare between the Mexico City government and the PRD, on the one hand, and TV Azteca on the other. Another example of this occurred in 2001: when the Federal Commission on Competition issued an opinion opposing the merger of radio networks owned by the Acir Group and Radiópolis, the company that would be primarily affected by the decision, Televisa, began a nasty campaign of personal attacks against Fernando Sánchez Ugarte, the commission's president.

This type of abuse is controversial and is often questioned, however, even by the companies that are responsible for the abuses. The major newspapers are undergoing a clear process designed to increase the professionalism of print media. Even though *Reforma* was accused of backing the candidacy of Vicente Fox, the paper's coverage of his presidency once he assumed office has been extremely critical. *El Universal* has abandoned any pro-government stance and is now a clearly professional newspaper. Radio stations are forced to accept the discipline of an extremely competitive market, and television organizations, which are quoted on the stock market, have created boards with outside directors and have taken steps to make their news segments more professional.

The challenges the media face continue to be daunting, however. The quality of journalistic work in Mexico remains noticeably inferior compared with journalism in developed countries, or even in countries whose level of development is similar to Mexico's. The problem does not lie in the scarcity of financial resources or lack of knowledge of basic journalistic principles, but in owners' unwillingness to establish and follow universally accepted ethical criteria and to promote journalistic professionalism.

CONCLUSIONS

The media played a very important role in supporting the PRI regime. However, they were also crucial players in the difficult transition process toward a genuine democracy. The history of the media in twentieth-century Mexico is a saga of a profession that has taken critical steps to shape a necessarily independent course for itself. With the electoral victory of Vicente Fox, courage in the face of censorship or seduction by the state ceased to be the defining element of journalism in Mexico. Increasing and maintaining professionalism has become the media's paramount challenge today.

Several factors allow room for optimism when it comes to the future role of the media in Mexico. Mexican journalists, who for decades were rather poorly trained or underprepared and whose salaries buried them in misery or forced them into corrupt practices, today usually have completed university studies and, at least in major media outlets in principal cities, are able to earn a decent living. The emergence of journalistic personalities who are known throughout the country, competition among organizations to attract and retain talented writers and editorial staff, and the syndication of columns and opinion pieces—all these developments have led to the creation of a journalistic aristocracy that earns a high income. These journalists have no fear of losing their jobs, and they can easily reject political pressure. Many journalists now enter the profession with a desire to break with the vice and corrupt practices of the past.

Nevertheless, the quality of journalism in Mexico is still relatively low. Several factors contribute to this poor quality.

- There is no tradition of journalistic rigor in a country where being a good journalist was tantamount to having the courage to express opinions that were critical of the government.

- Many publications are still being used as vehicles to gain influence or for political propaganda, and they are no longer concerned about disseminating objective information.

- The lack of transparent information about the circulation of printed media can lead to corruption.

- Because radio and television concessions are still granted and renewed arbitrarily, concessionaires have a powerful incentive to support the group or party holding power.

- Concentration of ownership among television organizations— the principal source of information for most of the Mexican population—is excessive.

Any change in this situation requires legal reforms. For example, a more transparent system for granting and renewing radio and television concessions is critical. Television markets must be diversified, even though it may be a bit late to do so, because Televisa and, to a lesser extent, TV Azteca, currently have more power than the Mexican state itself has, and these two companies would block any attempt to break them up. Introduction of new television technologies and the Internet, both of which provide access to programming produced in other countries, could become the catalyst for a gradual transformation, however.

Other changes would not require legal reforms. The fact that Mexico's television broadcasting companies are quoted on the stock market—and must therefore answer to many investors—is gradually introducing professionalism into media corporations' internal decisionmaking processes. Furthermore, the Mexican public is learning to distinguish between information and propaganda. The competition, although limited on television, is imposing a market discipline that forces companies to operate more professionally.

In the print media, market forces appear to be initiating a gradual consolidation process that will allow the survival of only the best publications. Some newspapers and magazines are closing their doors or drastically reducing their operations. Professional journalists and those who are better educated are slowly assuming managerial positions, which were previously held by the owners and their sons. This process has begun in the radio industry as well. Given the medium's saturation by discordant voices, combined with the impossibility of exerting influence when the audience is limited, many broadcasters that do not have the capacity to produce quality news programs prefer to return to the cheaper—and therefore more profitable—musical format. This process is leaving many journalists without jobs, but it is also elevating the quality and the market penetration of those newscasts and informational programs that have survived.[15]

Mexico seems to be going through a process similar to Spain's experience at the end of the 1970s and in the early 1980s—that is, after the death of the dictator Francisco Franco. In the beginning, Spain witnessed a tremendous media explosion and an extreme level of sensationalism. Over time, however, the situation began to return to a more sustainable level, and today the quality of the Spanish media is similar to that in other European countries.

It is true that Mexico suffers from an economic and educational underdevelopment far greater than Spain's condition at the time of Franco's death. Even though the evolution of the independent media in Mexico has been more prolonged than in Spain, the process might be similar. The quality of journalism in Mexico is on the rise. It is only a question of time before it reaches a level of independence and professionalism similar to that found in developed nations.

Notes

[1] Octavio Paz, "El Ogro Filantrópico," *Vuelta*, August 1978. The essay was later included in a collection of political essays, Octavio Paz, *El ogro filantrópico: historia y política 1971–1978* (Barcelona: Editorial Seix Barral, 1979 and Mexico City: Joaquín Mortiz, 1979).

[2] See Claudia Fernández and Andrew Paxman, *El Tigre: Emilio Azcárraga y su imperio Televisa* (Mexico City: Grijalbo, 2000).

[3] Fernando Mejía Barquera, "Del Canal 4 a Televisa," in *Apuntes para una historia de la televisión mexicana*, comp. Miguel Angel Sánchez de Armas (Mexico City: RMC Communication, 1998).

[4] This version of the facts is based on the author's conversations with some of the sons of Francisco Aguirre.

[5] The classical narrative of the coup against the management of *Excelsior* can be found in Vicente Leñero's novel *Los Periodistas* (Mexico City: Joaquin Mortiz, 1978).

[6] Information about what really happened was related by Miguel Angel Granados Chapa and by a former concessionaire in private conversations with the author.

[7] For a partial, but interesting, history of what happened after "Black Tuesday" and lasted until the end of the campaign, see Francisco Ortiz Pinchetti and Francisco Ortiz Pardo, *El Fenómeno Fox: La Historia que Proceso Censuró* (Mexico City: Planeta Mexicana, 2001).

[8] *Reforma* executives explained that they are reluctant to publish circulation numbers because they claim that the simple addition of printed copies does not give a true idea of the influence of a publication, especially in the case of a daily that has such a strong focus on a market that has high purchasing power.

[9] "National Survey of Political Culture and Citizen Practices, Secretaría de Gobernación (SEGOB) and the Instituto Nacional de Estadística Geografía e

Informática (INEGI), 2001." The results were published in *El Universal* (Mexico City), July 29, 2002. The survey allowed multiple answers to a single question; hence the total is higher than 100 percent.

[10] Cámara Nacional de la Industria de Radio y Televisión (CIRT), 2001.

[11] Secretaría de Comunicaciones y Transportes, Dirección General de Sistemas de Radio y Televisión, "Estaciones de radio y televisión concesionadas y permisionadas por entidad federativa," 2002.

[12] One rating point is equivalent to 1 percent of the number of television sets in the country, whether they are turned on or off.

[13] A share indicates the number of television sets that are turned on and tuned into a given channel or program.

[14] Market study by Bimsa, as cited in the business magazine *Expansion*, July 10, 2002.

[15] In July 2002, MVS Noticias, previously one of the leaders in the information broadcasting market, announced the cancellation of its evening and nightly news broadcasts. Other information broadcasting outlets cut expenditures.

INDEX

Page numbers followed by the letters f and t refer to figures and tables, respectively.
Page numbers followed by the letter n refer to end-of-chapter notes.

Constitution *(continued)*
on reelection of legislators, 82; on
religion, 234, 240; on right to life,
266*n*.27; on state of the union
address, 67
Constitutional controversies, problem
with judgments involving, 124–25
Constitutional reforms: of 1992, 235–
36, 248–49; of 1994, 109–15; presidential veto power and, 52
Consultative Group on Religious
Affairs, 245–46
Corruption: drug trafficking and,
209, 213, 214, 216; in military,
vulnerability to, 216, 217
Council of the Federal Judiciary: 1999
reforms and, 115–16, 117, 118–19,
138*n*.16; characteristics of, 127–28;
creation of, 114, 135*n*.4; rationale
for reform of, 118; reinforcement
of, need for, 133; responsibilities of,
128; on selection of district judges,
120–21, 141*n*.28, 142*n*.29; Supreme
Court and, 118–19, 127
Counternarcotics operations: containment and "visible effort" as
goals of, 211–12; "kingpin" strategy
in, 212–13; military's role in, 194,
209–10, 215–16; new interdiction
initiative in, 213–15; U.S.-Mexican
cooperation on, 214, 223, 224–25;
war against terrorism and, 215
Courts. *See* Judiciary; Supreme Court;
specific types of courts
Credit, private-sector, 148, 153, 164
Credit bureaus, regulation of, 163
Creel, Santiago, 29, 225, 253–54
Cristera Rebellion *(La Cristiada)*, 234
La Crónica de Hoy (newspaper), 278

de la Madrid, Miguel, 218, 238, 280
Debt: domestic, growth of, 167 *(See
also* Budget deficit); foreign *(See
Foreign debt)*

Defense, military's responsibility for,
219–20
Defense Ministry, 200; absence of
civilians in, 207, 208; on armed
forces' nonmilitary role, 220; and
drug interdiction operations, 215;
Fox's selection of minister, 202–4;
and Ministry of the Navy, 206,
229*n*.9
Deficit. *See* Budget deficit
Democracy: divided government and,
2; media's role in, 282–85, 293–94;
minimum requirement for change
in, 20; transition to, 152, 249. *See
also* Divided government
Democratic Revolutionary Party
(PRD): on budget reform, 77, 92,
93, 98; on Chamber of Deputies
elections, 35, 36–38, 40; on congressional balance of power, 75;
electricity reform proposals and,
170, 175; on executive branch,
reform proposals for, 55; first minority system and, 42–44, 102*n*.17;
Fox's use of veto power and, 53;
growth of, 8; legislation introduced
under unified government, 6*t*, 7;
media support for, 292; on parliamentary government, 63–64; on
presidential appointment powers,
57, 60, 61; on presidential travel,
congressional authorization of, 74;
on presidential veto power, 53;
proportionality in Congress and,
31; on reelection of legislators, 86;
on religious education, 253; on
Senate elections, 42, 44–45; on
spring term of Congress, 80; on
state legislature elections, 47–48;
on state of the union address, 71
Deregulation, under Salinas, 147, 153
Development banks, laws governing,
163
DFS. *See* Federal Security Directorate

Payán, Carlos, 277
Paz, Octavio, 247, 271, 277
Peacekeeping operations, international: army's opposition to, 229n.9; attempt to involve Mexico in, 192–93, 228n.5
Pensions and social security, Fox's reform agenda for, 156
Peralta, Alejo, 275
Permanent Committee of Congress, 78, 79, 82; election of members of, 79, 105n.46
Perry, William, 224
Peso, appreciation of (1999-2002), 179
Peso crisis of 1995, 148; financial intermediation as precursor to, 150; impact of, 152; lessons learned from, 163–64; new credit flows and, 151; privatization and, 153
Peyrot, Marco Antonio, 204, 205
PFP. See Federal Preventive Police
PGR. See Attorney General's Office
PND. See National Development Plan
PNR. See National Revolutionary Party
Pocket veto, 51, 103n.25
Police force: Mexico's unwillingness to invest in, 218; perceived U.S. conspiracy to turn military forces into, 219–20. See also Law enforcement
Political parties: lack of cooperation among, implications for democracy, 2; transformation between 1988-1997, 8. See also specific parties
Popular Revolutionary Army (EPR), 222
Portes Gil, Emilio, 234
El Porvenir (newspaper), 289
PR. See Proportional representation
PRD. See Democratic Revolutionary Party
Preciado, Felipe de Jesús, 35

Presidency/presidents: appointment powers of, 56–62, 58t–59t; and budget proposal, 5, 89; on budget reform, 92; constitutional checks and balances on, process leading to, 1–2; constitutional powers of, 4; under divided government, 9; end of dominance of, 8–13; former, proposed limits on activities of, 74, 104n.38; as guardian of stability, 21; legislation introduced under divided government, 10–11, 10t, 19; legislation introduced under unified government, 5–8, 6t; meta-constitutional powers of, 3; and military, reliance on, 194; military's loyalty to, 199–200, 205; and National Development Plan, 74, 75; old model of, 3–8; partisan powers of, 4; PRI hegemony and, 1, 3, 62; in proponent-elector model, 15–16, 15f; religious convictions of, 237–38; today, 3; travel by, congressional authorization of, 72–74, 73t; veto power of (See Presidential veto power). See also Executive-legislative relations; specific presidents
Presidential elections: of 1988, 146; of 1994, media coverage of, 282; of 2000, 2, 9, 282–85; Constitution on, 49; reform proposals for, 49–50, 50t; runoffs in, controversy over, 49
Presidential system, reform proposals for, 62
Presidential veto power: over budget, 51, 52, 53, 74, 90, 91, 98–99; Constitution on, 51–52; Fox's use of, 9, 18, 52, 53, 90, 107n.67; and legislative process, 3, 4; in median party theory, 17–18; problems with, 51–52; in proponent-elector model, 15f, 16; reform proposals for, 52–56, 54t–55t; and status quo, maintenance of, 21

ABOUT THE AUTHORS AND EDITORS

José Ramón Cossío is a justice of the Supreme Court in Mexico. Previously, he was dean of the Department of Law and professor of constitutional law at the Instituto Tecnológico Autónomo de México (ITAM). The author of 15 books and several articles, he is also a member of the National System of Researchers and the Mexican Academy of Sciences, from which he received the National Prize of Research in the Social Sciences in 1998. Cossío received his doctorate from the School of Law at the Universidad Complutense of Madrid.

Raúl González Schmal is a professor in the Department of Law at the Universidad Iberoamericana in Mexico, where he teaches constitutional and ecclesiastic law. He is the author of *Derecho Eclesiástico del Estado Mexicano* [Ecclesiastic Law of the Mexican Federation] (Editorial Porrúa, 1997), *Programa de Derecho Constitucional* [Program of Constitutional Law] (Noriega Editores, 2003), and *La Libertad Religiosa en el Convenio Europeo de Derechos Humanos* [Religious Freedom in the European Human Rights Convention] (Editorial Porrúa, 2004), among other works. He graduated in law from the Universidad Nacional Autónoma de México (UNAM) and has a graduate degree in law from the Universidad Iberoamericana.

Jonathan Heath is head of research and chief economist for HSBC Mexico. He also teaches at the Universidad Panamericana in Mexico City and has written a weekly column for *Reforma* in Mexico City since 1993. He has taught at the Universidad Anáhuac, Universidad Iberoamericano, Instituto Tecnológico y de Estudios Superiores de Monterrey

(ITESM), and Universidad de las Américas. He graduated with a degree in economics from the Universidad Anahuac and has a graduate degree in economics from the University of Pennsylvania. He is an adjunct fellow of the CSIS Mexico Project.

Benito Nacif is a research professor and chair of the Division of Political Studies at the Centro de Investigación y Docencia Económica (CIDE) in Mexico City. His current research deals with the changing role of the Mexican Congress and the politics of executive-legislative relations in Mexico. Nacif is coeditor of *Legislative Politics in Latin America* (Cambridge University Press, 2002). His academic distinctions include a residential fellowship at the Helen Kellogg Institute for International Studies, University of Notre Dame (2000) and the British Foreign Office and Commonwealth Scholarship (1990–1992). He holds a doctorate in political science from Oxford University.

Armand B. Peschard-Sverdrup is director of the CSIS Mexico Project and has written extensively on Mexico. Among his recent publications, as a contributor or as author, are *U.S.-Mexico Border Security and the Evolving Security Relationship* (CSIS, 2004); *Managing Mexican Migration to the United States* (CSIS, 2004); *Forecasting Mexico's Democratic Transition: Scenarios for Policymakers* (CSIS, 2003); *July 6, 2003 Midterm Elections: Preelection Analysis* (CSIS, 2003); *The Impact of the War in Iraq on Mexico* (CSIS, 2003); and *U.S.-Mexico Transboundary Water Management: Recommendations for Policymakers for the Medium and Long Term* (CSIS, 2003). He holds a B.A. with honors in political science and economics from Carleton University and did graduate work in government at Georgetown University's School of Foreign Service Center for Latin American Studies.

Sara R. Rioff is research associate for the CSIS Mexico Project and co-author of *U.S.-Mexico Border Security and the Evolving Security Relationship* (CSIS, 2004). She is an institutional cosponsor of the U.S.-Mexico Binational Council, cosponsored by CSIS and the Mexico City–based Instituto Tecnológico Autónomo de México (ITAM). Rioff graduated Phi Beta Kappa and magna cum laude with a B.A. in international studies and a certificate in Latin American studies from Dickinson College.

Oscar Rocha is president of the Joaquin Amaro Foundation for Strategic Studies in Mexico City. Previously, he was minister for political-military affairs at the Embassy of Mexico in Washington, D.C. Prior to serving at the embassy, Rocha was adviser for national security and law enforcement affairs to Mexico's secretary of finance and budget. He also served as deputy press secretary for international affairs to the president of Mexico. Rocha is a member of the International Institute for Strategic Studies in London and the Mexican Council on Foreign Relations. He has lectured on national security affairs at numerous Mexican universities and centers. He holds a B.A. from El Colegio de México and an M.A. from both the Colegio de Defensa Nacional and Princeton University.

Sergio Sarmiento is a syndicated newspaper columnist whose articles are published in 22 Mexican newspapers, including *Reforma* in Mexico City and *El Norte* in Monterrey. He is also the host of a daily political talk show. Between July 1995 and August 1998, Sarmiento was vice president for news operations of TV Azteca, and he currently serves as the vice president of its editorial committee. Sarmiento is a recipient of the Juan Pablos Award for Editorial Merit given by Mexico's National Chamber of Publishers. He has also been made *chevalier* of the order of arts and letters by the government of France. He holds a B.A. with honors in philosophy and linguistics from York University in Toronto, Canada. He is an adjunct fellow of the CSIS Mexico Project.

Jeffrey A. Weldon is a professor of political science at the Instituto Tecnológico Autónomo de México (ITAM). Weldon has written numerous articles and chapters on the legislative branch and electoral system in Mexico. Weldon was a visiting research fellow at the Center for U.S.-Mexican Studies at the University of California, San Diego, in 2003–2004. He is the author of the CSIS Congressional Report Series, a quarterly report that analyzes the qualitative and quantitative productivity of each session of the Mexican Congress. He received a B.A. with honors in political science from the University of Washington and holds an M.A. in political science from the University of California at San Diego. Weldon is an adjunct fellow of the CSIS Mexico Project.